STATISTICAL CON

A Program for Self-instruction

STATISTICAL CONCEPTS

A Program for Self-instruction

CELESTE McCOLLOUGH and LOCHE VAN ATTA
Oberlin College

McGRAW-HILL BOOK COMPANY, INC.
New York   San Francisco   Toronto   London

Preface

This text presents the elements of statistical reasoning in a form suitable for self-instruction. The beginner in statistics may use it as an introduction and guide, although further reading or instruction will be needed if he has much occasion to perform statistical computations. For the person whose work requires considerable competence in statistics, the text may serve as an introduction preceding a formal statistics course, an aid to accompany the work in such a course, or a review to aid in the consolidation of material learned in a formal course.

Whole sections of the text may be studied without knowledge of other sections. The introduction to each lesson indicates which other lessons, if any, need to be studied before beginning that lesson.

The text was written originally for our own students of introductory psychology. To them, and to the more than 300 other students who participated in field tryouts, belongs much of the credit for the improvements that grew out of the suggestions they made. We are grateful to Blair Stewart for welcoming our experimentation with new educational techniques. For advice and criticism we thank John Barlow, Dalbir Bindra, Robert DeHaan, George A. Ferguson, Sister Mary Ferrer, Phil C. Lange, George F. Mair, Margaret Modlish, J. William Moore, Derek Nunney, Edward Ostrander, Edward Pohlman, Jack D. Rains, M. Daniel Smith, Paul A. Smith, Judith Ann Williams, and in particular, Samuel Goldberg. We are happy to acknowledge our debt to the Ford Foundation Fund for the Advancement of Education for a generous grant of financial support in the initial development of these programmed lessons.

We are indebted to Sir Ronald A. Fisher, F.R.S., Cambridge, and to Dr. Frank Yates, F.R.S., Rothamsted, and to Oliver & Boyd Ltd., Edinburgh, for permission to reprint Table III and IV from "Statistical Tables for Biological, Agricultural and Medical Research."

Celeste McCollough
Loche Van Atta

Instructions to the Student

Follow two rules to obtain the best learning and the greatest satisfaction from this text:

1. Conceal the answers to each item until you have written down your own answers.

2. Make your study periods *short;* 15 to 30 minutes at a time will be sufficient.

Here are the reasons for giving such advice.

What Is Meant by a "Programmed" Text

A textbook is written to provide the reader with a good pathway from start to finish in his study of a new subject. A *programmed* text is simply *more explicit* about the steps in the pathway. Each step is a *numbered unit* called a *frame,* and great care is taken to make sure that each step *follows logically* from the steps that have gone before.

Furthermore, some part of each frame is purposely left incomplete so that the reader who is following the pathway closely can supply the missing words from the knowledge he has recently acquired. These missing words are the "answers" which you are asked, according to rule 1, to write down *for yourself.*

Why and How to Use the Mask

Rule 1 says, "Conceal the answers." But since the answers are printed just to the right of each question, why not read the answers along with the questions? Why bother to write them down for yourself?

Writing down your own answers is the only way to find out *at once* whether you are getting the essential points or not. How many times have you read placidly for an hour only to find out later that you have missed something essential without realizing it? If you look too soon at the answers in this text, that sort of thing can happen easily. You may give yourself the *illusion* of having understood, as you have sometimes done in reading a textbook, only to find out later that you have "got lost" because something was not clear to you.

To help you conceal the answers conveniently, you will need a mask properly shaped to cover the answers for a frame until you have written down your own answers. You may make such a mask by cutting heavy paper or light cardboard to the following shape and dimensions:

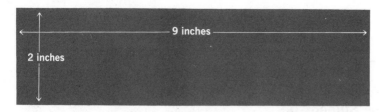

Place the mask lengthwise over the gray column at the right-hand side of the page. Slide the mask down the column frame by frame as you complete the items. Always write down your best idea of the missing words for the *entire* frame before you slide the mask down to look at the printed answers.

If you follow this procedure carefully, you will find that the material you are studying continues to make sense to you all the time. You will not necessarily recall all the logical steps you have taken. But when you have once followed the logic of the subject step by step, you will have a sense of statistical reasoning that would not arise merely from memorizing formulas and their definitions. This sense of statistics will be sufficient to carry you through most of the general reading you are likely to want to do. If your interests are more specialized, then you will find that this introduction to statistics has put you in a good position to grasp the content of courses in statistical techniques.

Make Your Study Periods Short!

Rule 2 suggests that you spend only 15 to 30 minutes at a time on this book. Such a study period is long enough to enable you to complete one or more of the sections in a lesson. It is long enough, therefore, to give you a sense of having learned something new. It is also short enough to make this a text which can be picked up at odd moments—before meal-times, between classes, or while you are waiting for someone. Each time you return to the text after an interval, look at the review frames at the end of the last section you studied. These frames will remind you of what you have just learned, and you can then pick up where you left off. At the end of each lesson, there are a few problems to help you pull the lesson together and check your understanding.

Students who have most enjoyed this kind of text are, in general, those students who have employed such brief study periods. You can spend longer times on it, of course, but the point is that this is the sort of text which *permits* you to turn to it in odd moments for a few minutes at a time. You are likely to be very pleased when you discover that you can learn a difficult subject by this method in the bits and pieces of time that you sometimes regret wasting.

Besides the review frames at the end of most sections and the problems at the end of each lesson, this book contains two other features which will help you in reviewing what you have learned. The Contents lists the descriptive titles of all the sections. Important words and phrases will be found alphabetically arranged in the Index, with the sections and frames in which these terms appear.

Symbols Used within Frames

The numbered units in a programmed textbook are called frames. A blank line within a frame indicates that a single word or number is to be supplied.

Example A textbook which asks the reader to supply answers within each of its numbered units is called a _____ textbook.

programmed

If the blank requires two or more words to be supplied, the blank will be a double line.

Example To use such a textbook most effectively, a student always conceals the printed answers until he has _____.

written his own answers

As these examples have illustrated, the answer to a blank appears on the same line of print with the blank to which it belongs. When two blanks appear on the same line, the two answers are separated by a dash.

Example Another suggested rule for using a programmed textbook is that a _____ period should be _____.

study — short

Occasionally, the answers which belong to two successive blanks may be interchangeable; that is, they would be correct in either order. In such cases, the dash is replaced by a double headed arrow, and such an arrow is included even when the two blanks do not fall in the same line of print.

Example When a coin is tossed, it will turn up either _____ or _____.

heads ↔ tails

Contents

Lesson 1. Introduction to Statistical Inference

Most decisions about practical matters have to be taken on the basis of incomplete evidence. It is rarely possible to know everything one would like to know before making up one's mind. The ability to draw conclusions which will continue to appear correct as further evidence accumulates may indeed be the key quality which makes successful business and political administrators.

In scientific investigation, it is also necessary to draw conclusions from a limited amount of evidence. The collection of evidence is a costly and time-consuming procedure; the investigator needs to know when he has sufficient evidence to permit his drawing a conclusion with a certain degree of confidence.

The special branch of mathematics called statistics provides a logical analysis of this problem of drawing conclusions on incomplete evidence. From the study of statistics, one learns that inferences can be made most easily when the evidence is collected and summarized according to certain clear-cut rules.

Lesson 1 will introduce some of the basic concepts upon which the rules of statistical inference depend. To begin with, the difference between a sample and a population will be pointed out in order to show more clearly the reason why statistical methods must be used for certain inferences.

A.   Samples and Populations

If you wished to make an investigation concerning the intelligence level of college students in the United States, you might undertake to obtain the IQ score of every individual enrolled in a college in the country. This set of scores would be a complete or exhaustive set of observations relevant to your investigation. With such a complete set of observations, you could make certain statements about college student IQs with perfect confidence. For example, you could make an exact statement about the range of variation or about the average of all U.S. college student IQs in that particular year (or moment) of investigation.

However, it is very rare to have the entire set of relevant observations available in a practical investigation. Usually it is not convenient to collect more than a small part of the relevant observations. The entire set of relevant observations is called a POPULATION; *that part of the set which is available is called a* SAMPLE. As soon as you have to deal with a sample instead of with the entire population of observations, you must begin to use the methods of statistics.

1-1   In ordinary usage, such as the phrase "population of the United States" or even "vital statistics on the U.S. population," the word "population" refers to an aggregate whose individual members are _____. In technical usage, however, a population is an aggregate of OBSERVATIONS.

persons (people)

1-2   In some cases, these observations are characteristics of persons, such as heights, incomes, number of children, and the like, but even in such cases, the population under consideration in statistics does not consist of the actual persons themselves but only of the _____ about some particular characteristic of these persons.

observations

1-3   Students of government and economics talk about "population statistics," meaning the description of characteristics of a population of _____ living in a particular geographical area. But the special concept of population *in* statistics—as a branch of applied mathematics—never refers to actual people but to observations. These observations are usually stated in the form of numbers, and the members of a *statistical population* are these numbers.

persons

1-4   The IQs of all college students would constitute a _____ of numerical observations. Such an aggregate can be spoken of even though not all students have taken IQ tests. A set of observations drawn from a population is called a SAMPLE. A limited number of college student IQs would be a _____ of these numerical observations.

population

sample

1-5   There are 27 persons living in a particular apartment house. A social psychologist chooses every third person in the house for a study of attitudes, and he obtains a questionnaire score from each person chosen. In this example, the members of the statistical population are not persons but _____.

scores

1-6 The number of (potential) members of the population is
_____, even though not all of them are actually obtained.
The concept of a population of observations applies to all the observations of a particular sort which *might* be obtained. It is not necessary
that all the scores *actually* be obtained in order to talk about the
population.

1-7 The number of members in the *sample* of questionnaire scores
is _____ .

1-8 Suppose that a new drug treatment for schizophrenia is being
tried. The population of relevant observations consists of the scores
indicating the effect of this new drug on _____ schizophrenics (not just on the ones included in the trial). Scores obtained
from those schizophrenics on whom the drug is actually tried would
constitute a _____ drawn from this population.

1-9 A limited number of observations made on the same individual
still constitutes a *sample* of all the observations of that kind which
might be made on that individual. A series of responses to tasks and
questions on an intelligence test is a _____ of the individual's intelligence-test-taking behavior.

1-10 Additional observations would only increase the _____
of the sample obtained; they could never be exhaustive enough to
include the entire population of observations relevant to the measurement of his _____ .

1-11 In emotion-provoking situations, a laboratory rat usually does
some squealing. One way to measure the rat's general nervousness
or emotionality is to count the number of squeals. Since the rat cannot be observed all the time, the entire _____ of observations of squealing cannot be available; only a sample can be obtained.

1-12 If a student of French is expected to learn 1,000 vocabulary
words during a semester and the final examination tests him on 75
words, the number of members in the population of relevant observations is _____ ; the number of members actually sampled,
in measuring his vocabulary knowledge, is _____ .

1-13 *When the word "population" occurs in statistics, it refers to an aggregate of* _____ *and not to a group of persons. If only part of the population is actually available for study, we can learn about the population only from this* _____ *.*

1-14 *All the IQ scores of all the students enrolled in a particular college would make up a* _____ *with respect to questions about IQs in that college at that time. The same aggregate of scores would make up a* _____ *with respect to questions about IQs of all college students. Any one of these scores is the result of a series of observations which make up a* _____ *with respect to questions about the intelligence-test behavior of that person.*

B.   Kinds of Inferences Made from Samples

1-15 The selection of a sample is called "drawing a sample." When samples are used, the investigator's interest is not in the sample for its own sake but in the population from which it has been _____ .

1-16 The investigator may be interested in making inferences about the *characteristics* of the population. Statements about the characteristics of a population are called DESCRIPTIVE statements. For example, one may wish to make a _____ statement about the emotionality of a certain genetic strain of rats when he has observed only a few rats of that strain and when, in fact, he has observed only a *sample* of the squealing behavior even of these few.

1-17 One may wish to make a descriptive statement about a person's level of intelligence on the basis of only a sample of the person's behavior in taking _____ . Or one may wish to make a descriptive statement about the average IQ of U.S. college students when, in fact, he has the _____ of only a limited number of college students available to him.

1-18 Very frequently, however, the investigator primarily wants to know whether two populations are *different* from each other. If he has drawn samples of squealing behavior from two different strains of rats, he may want to know whether one strain is more emotional than the other. He must use his samples to determine whether the _____ of squealing behavior from which they are drawn are different.

1-19   In such a case, the inference made from the samples is an inference about the existence of differences. The investigator, for the moment, cares little about describing the degree of emotionality of each strain. What he does care about is the question "Does heredity make a *difference* in emotionality?" To answer this question, he must determine whether his samples indicate that a _____ exists between the two populations of squealing behavior.

1-20   In laboratory experiments, an investigator often begins by setting up different conditions for two groups of subjects. Then he must be able to determine whether the observations indicate that the two groups are actually _____ from each other.

1-21   Suppose, for example, that the experimenter wants to find out whether French vocabulary words can be learned with fewer repetitions in the morning shortly after the learner wakes up than in the evening just before he retires. He may arrange an experiment which gives him two sets of observations: one set collected in the morning, the other collected in the evening. If this time difference really affects the ease of learning, the two sets of observations should prove to be _____ from each other.

1-22   The investigator is really interested in differences between two populations: observations (that is, "number of trials to mastery") made in the morning and observations made in the late evening. What he has available is only a sample from each of these populations. He must decide whether the _____ are different merely on the basis of the available _____ .

Review

1-23   *When a statement is made about the intelligence of an individual, this is a* _____ *statement which depends upon* statistical inference *from a* _____ *of the person's behavior in taking an intelligence test.*

1-24   *Descriptive statements result from one of the two kinds of inference which can be made from samples. The other kind concerns the*

existence of a _____ *between the populations from which*
two samples have been drawn. This kind of inference is necessary when-
ever an investigator is seeking to find out whether a particular factor
(such as heredity, time of day, and the like) produces a _____
in the particular observation being studied.

C.   Why Statistical Inference Is Necessary

1-25   If the entire population of observations is available for study, statistical inference is not necessary, either for descriptive statements or for the assertion that a difference exists. The need for statistical methods of inference arises only when the available observations are limited to a _____ drawn from the entire population.

1-26   It is easy to show that a descriptive statement about a whole population could not be made from a sample without special methods of inference. Different samples from the same population are not apt to be exactly _____ ; it would not be wise to assume, therefore, that the population is exactly like any one of the samples.

1-27   Since the characteristics of the population are likely to differ from those of samples, two different words are used for "character- istics." It is customary to talk about the population characteristics as population PARAMETERS and to talk about the sample characteristics as sample STATISTICS. Special statistical techniques have been devel- oped to permit the inference of population _____ from
sample _____ .

1-28   Later in this book (Lesson 13), you will learn how to make _____ statements about population _____ ,
through a process of _____ from sample statistics. In Lessons 1 to 5, we shall focus attention on the problem of inferring *differences.*

1-29   Suppose you are interested in knowing whether there is a dif- ference in the heights of two *individuals.* You measure them both, and you find that one is ¼ inch taller than the other. You might check your observations by making the measurements a second time, but if you got the same result again, you would not hesitate to report that there is a genuine _____ between their heights, although a small one. — *difference*

1-30 However, if you found that the mean height of a sample of students from Alpha College was ¼ inch greater than the mean height of an Omega College sample, you might hesitate to conclude that Alpha College students tend to be taller than Omega students. Such a small amount of difference might tend to disappear (or even to reverse itself) if you were to draw a second _____ from each college population. — *sample*

1-31 The greater certainty of the comparison between heights of *individuals* arises because *all* the relevant observations are available. Doubt about the difference between populations emerges when only a _____ number of the relevant observations are available. — *limited (small)*

1-32 Within the population of height measurements at Alpha College, there will be a great deal of *variation* among individual students. In fact, there is likely to be more _____ within either one of these populations than there is *between* the two college populations. — *variation*

1-33 Under such circumstances, a great deal would depend on the particular sample you happen to draw. For example, heights of men and women differ and the difference is a dependable one, but it would be possible to get a pair of unusual samples of heights of men and heights of women, one including mostly very short men and the other mostly very tall women, so that the average for the men's sample could actually be _____ than the average for the women's sample. — *smaller (less)*

1-34 Since one never knows in advance whether the sample is unusual or not, the fact must be kept in mind that some variation will occur even among samples drawn from the same _____. — *population*
The difference between the samples from Alpha and Omega Colleges might actually be no _____ than the difference one might frequently obtain between two samples from Alpha College alone. — *larger*

Review

1-35 *Whenever an entire population of observations is not available for study, there will be a need for _____ methods in order to draw inferences about the population from any available sample. If* — *statistical* one wishes to make inferences about the population characteristics, the problem is one of inferring the population _____ from the sample _____.

1-36 When the entire population of observations is not available, one cannot be sure that a difference between samples *implies* a difference between the _____ from which the samples were drawn. It must be remembered that some amount of difference will occur even between samples drawn from the _____.

D.   Significant Differences

1-37 The variability between samples drawn from the same population is called SAMPLING VARIABILITY. This variability is due to the accidental factors which determine the selection of _____ included in the samples.

1-38 Small differences between sets of observations may be due only to *chance*, in other words, to the accidental factors which determine the _____ of observations included in the samples. These small differences may be due to _____ variability.

1-39 Differences between sets of observations, if they are due to sampling _____, do not signify that the samples were drawn from _____ populations.

1-40 If two samples do come from the same population, there will be only one source of differences between the samples. This source is _____.

1-41 But if two samples come from *different* populations, there will be *two* sources of differences between the samples. There will still be sampling variability, producing some of the small differences between the samples. But there will also be a second source of differences: the fact that the _____ from which the samples are drawn are themselves different from each other.

1-42 These two sources of difference are likely to produce a greater total amount of difference than the first source alone. When two samples have been drawn from *different* populations, the differences between these samples are likely to be _____ than the differences between samples from the *same* population.

greater

1-43   If the difference between the sets of observations is so large that differences of this size would rarely occur because of sampling variability, this signifies that the two sets probably are samples from _____ populations. Such a large difference is called a SIGNIFICANT DIFFERENCE, because it signifies that a difference exists between the two _____ from which the samples were drawn.

different

populations

1-44   Suppose that the difference between the Alpha and Omega College height samples is very small in comparison to sampling variability. One would infer, then, that the small difference is really due to _____ and that, *as far as height is concerned,* Alpha and Omega college students belong to the _____ population.

sampling variability
same

1-45   If, on the other hand, the difference between the samples is so large that it would rarely occur between two samples from a single population, one would regard the difference as a _____ difference, and one would probably conclude that somehow the students at Alpha College have been drawn from a _____ population (with regard to height) from the students at Omega College. One might then look for an explanation in the admissions policies of the two colleges.

significant

different

Review

1-46   *The average height of a sample of men is likely to be greater than the average height of a sample of women, and the difference is likely to be _____ enough that it would rarely occur because of _____ alone. This result is likely, because men and women belong to _____ with regard to height.*

large
sampling variability
different populations

1-47   *When two samples have been drawn from* different *populations, the differences between these samples are likely to be _____ than the differences between samples from the* same *population.*

larger

1-48   *When a difference is so large that it would rarely occur because of sampling variability alone, it permits the conclusion, "These samples come from different populations." Such a difference is called a _____ difference.*

significant

E. Applying the Term "Significant Difference"

1-49 An intelligence-test score for one individual is not like a height measurement, because the intelligence-test score represents a _____ of the intelligence-test-taking behavior of that person. If another comparable test were given to the same person, a somewhat different score might be obtained simply because of _____ variability.

sample

sampling

1-50 There is no question about the _____ of a difference in *heights* between two individuals, but such a question ought to be raised about an apparent difference in their IQs. Unless the difference in IQ is sufficiently _____, it may be due to _____ alone.

significance

large
sampling variability

1-51 When we compare two persons' IQ scores, we want to know whether the one score differs from the other *more* than two different IQ scores from the _____ person would be likely to differ from each other. We are, in fact, asking whether the population of intelligence-test-taking behavior of one of the two persons is distinguishably different from the population of intelligence-test-taking behavior of the other person.

same

1-52 Even if the _____ of such behavior for the two persons are quite similar, the IQ scores as obtained on particular occasions might be somewhat different. This result would appear, for example, if one of the persons had been very tired during the test.

populations

1-53 But the greater the difference in IQ score, the _____ likely it would be that the populations are very similar to each other.

less

1-54 The question about significance of differences arises whenever the observations under consideration make up only a _____ of the relevant observations instead of including the _____.

sample
entire population

1-55 It arises in the comparison of heights of *groups* of people, even though each height measurement is a single observation, unless the height of every member of each group is included in the _____.

sample

1-56 It arises in the comparison of IQ scores of two individuals, even though the IQ score is a single number, because the IQ score really arises from a _____ of observations drawn from a much larger _____ of relevant observations.

sample
population

1-57 Suppose that two baseball players are being compared. In a comparison of the *batting averages*, the question of significance of the difference _____ (does, does not) arise. In a comparison of the batting *ability* of the two players, the question of significance of the difference _____ (does, does not) arise.

1-58 Since the batting average is an exact quantity, there can be no question of significance of difference any more than there is such a question about height as long as only the batting average itself is the object of attention. But if the batting average is to be taken as an indicator of batting *ability*, the question of significance does arise, for each average is the result of a set of observations which make up a _____ of the entire _____ of possible batting behaviors of each player. Many chance factors entered into the drawing of each sample.

Review

1-59 *A "significant" difference signifies that two samples probably came from _____. When we ask, "Are these two persons' IQs really different?" we are in effect asking, "Did this sample of test-taking behavior come from the _____ as this other sample or from a different one?"*

1-60 *If two math classes were compared with each other on the basis of the classroom test scores of samples drawn from each class, the question of significance of difference would arise, because a _____ amount of difference between these sets of scores would be expected to appear simply as a result of sampling variability. If two students from these classes were compared with each other on the basis of their classroom test scores, the question of significance of difference would again arise, because each test score is based on a set of _____ of classroom test behavior and a _____ amount of difference could appear by sampling variability alone.*

Problems for Lesson 1

On March 21 of a particular year, a person stopped 20 students at random on a particular campus and asked each to tell how many hours he had slept during the past three 24-hour periods (March 18–20). Again on April 18, he asked the same students to answer the same question with regard to the three days, April 15–17.

Consider, one at a time, each of the following numbered questions which the investigator might have wished to answer from his observations. Each question requires a comparison of two "populations" of observations, a population occurring in March and one occurring in April. For each numbered question, tell:

(a) What set of observations would make up the complete "March" population relevant to that question.

(b) Whether that entire set of observations is included in the observations actually collected or whether the observations collected contain only a *sample* from the March population.

(c) Whether it would make sense to ask, for that particular numbered question, "Is the difference between the observations collected in March and those collected in April a *significant* difference?"

1-1 Did the first student questioned sleep more hours on March 18, 19, and 20 than on April 15, 16, and 17?

1-2 Was that particular student spending more time in sleep during the month of March than during the month of April?

1-3 Did these 20 students sleep more hours on March 18, 19, and 20 than on April 15, 16, and 17?

1-4 Were these 20 students spending more time in sleep during the month of March than during the month of April?

1-5 Did the students on that campus sleep more hours on March 18, 19, and 20 than on April 15, 16, and 17?

1-6 Were the students on that campus spending more time in sleep during the month of March than during the month of April?

Lesson 2. Random Sampling, Expected Frequency, and Probability

In order to tell whether an obtained difference is significant, it is necessary to know whether it is larger than the amount of difference which might arise from sampling variability. Sampling variability is due to accidental or chance factors which affect the selection of observations to be included in the sample. These chance factors obey certain mathematical rules called the laws of probability; from these rules, it is possible to calculate how much difference can be expected between two different samples drawn from the same population.

The laws of probability apply only to samples that can be shown to be random samples. This lesson begins by defining random samples and distinguishing them from nonrandom or biased samples. Section B presents an example which will be used during the next few lessons to illustrate the procedure for determining whether a difference is significant. Sections C and D introduce the concept of probability, which will be developed in detail in Lessons 3 and 4.

A. Random Samples

2-1 There are two conditions which must be met if a sample is to be regarded as a random sample. First, the sample must be selected in a way which gives every observation in the _____ which is being sampled an *equal chance* of being included in the sample.

population

2-2 If the IQ scores of all Omega College students were written on identical slips of paper and shaken up in a hat, and if 10 per cent of them were drawn out of the hat by a blindfolded person, the sample so drawn would be a _____ sample because each member of the population of scores would have an _____ of being included in the sample.

random
equal chance

2-3 A sample that is not random is a BIASED sample. If some of the IQ scores of Omega College students were omitted from the hat, the sample drawn from the hat would be a _____ sample because not all members of the population of _____ would have an equal chance of being drawn.

2-4 If some students' scores were written separately on *two* different slips of paper and both slips were included in the hat, a sample drawn from the hat would be a biased sample because those scores would have a _____ chance of being drawn than scores written only once. In fact, each of these scores would have _____ chance(s) of being drawn, and each of the other scores would have _____ chance(s).

2-5 A second condition must also be met if a sample is to be random: The selection of one observation must be *independent* of the selection of any other observation. If the selection of any one observation does not affect the chances for _____ of any other observation, the condition of *independence* has been met.

2-6 If several students' scores were written on the *same* slip of paper, no one of these scores could be selected without *all* of them being selected. The sample drawn would be a biased sample because the chance for selection of one of these scores would not be _____ of the selection of the others written with it.

2-7 Suppose that a sample of voters in a certain district were selected by choosing every hundredth man from the list of registered voters and including both him and his wife in the sample. Would this be a random sample? _____ .

2-8 The sample would be a biased sample because (1) the inclusion of a woman is not independent of the inclusion of her _____ and (2) not all _____ voters have an equal chance of being included in the sample since only _____ women can be included at all.

2-9 In 1936, the *Literary Digest* magazine conducted a poll of voters to predict the outcome of the presidential election. They selected their sample by choosing names randomly from the telephone directories and auto registration lists. This sample was a _____ sample because all voters _____ an equal chance of being included.

The sample could include only persons who owned telephones or automobiles.

2-10 As a result of this poll, the *Literary Digest* predicted that Roosevelt would be defeated; Roosevelt actually won the election. The *Literary Digest* sample included a _____ proportion of persons who voted against Roosevelt than were actually contained in the _____ of voters.

larger

population

2-11 *In order to be a random sample, a sample must meet two conditions: the condition of _____ and the condition of _____. A sample that is not random is a _____ sample.*

equal chance —
  independence
biased

2-12 *The* Literary Digest *sample was selected randomly from telephone directories and auto registration lists. The result was a _____ sample of the population of voters but a _____ sample of the population of telephone or auto owners.*

biased
random

B.   Sampling T-maze Behavior (An Example)

Probability rules and the method of determining significance can be explained best with the help of a few examples. We shall find the characteristics needed for our first example in the "alternation" behavior of rats in a T maze. This behavior also happens to be of interest because it provides evidence for the existence of a "curiosity motive" or "exploratory drive" in animals no more intellectual than white rats. For this reason, the matter is of some importance to psychology, although here we shall be concerned only with its numerical and statistical characteristics.

In studies of alternation behavior, an animal is placed in a T maze at a position corresponding to the base of the T and is allowed to run into either of the two end boxes located at the ends of the right and left arms of the T. Neither end box contains food or water. Once the animal has reached an end box, he is removed from the maze and placed for a second time in the starting position. If he runs to the side opposite that to which he ran on the first trial, he is said to exhibit ALTERNATION *behavior; if he runs to the same side to which he ran on the first trial, we shall call this behavior* REPETITION *behavior.*

The difference between alternation and repetition behavior can be stated

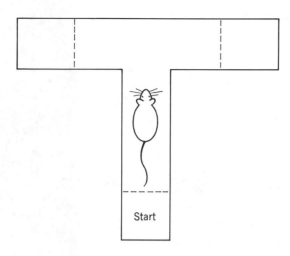

Start

in another way. A single observation requires a pair of runs. If, on the first run of the pair, the rat turns to the left side, then a turn to the right on the second run will be called alternation. A turn to the left on the second run will be called repetition. Let us designate the results of a pair of trials by a pair of letters, L for left and R for right; if the result is LR, it is a case of alternation, and if the result is LL, it is a case of repetition. Likewise, for the rat which turns to the right on the first run of the pair, the result RL is alternation and the result RR is repetition.

We shall confine our discussion to a sort of experiment in which each individual rat is allowed only one pair of runs. If it can be shown that rats most often show alternation behavior, it can be argued that the rats have a tendency to explore novel situations instead of returning to places where they have been before. An experimenter investigating exploratory behavior would wish to demonstrate beyond reasonable doubt that rats of a particular species tend to alternate under the conditions of this experiment. The next series of items will develop the logic needed for determining just how dubious or how convincing such a demonstration is.

In the items to come, we shall need to distinguish three kinds of conclusions which one might draw from the alternation experiment, depending on the results of the experiment. One might conclude that there is a definite tendency to ALTERNATE, provided the results show a sufficient preponderance of LR and RL pairs. On the other hand, one might conclude that there is instead a marked tendency to REPEAT if the results show a preponderance of LL and RR pairs. An intermediate case, however, would arise if there is no clear preponderance of either type of result. In such a case, one would have to conclude that what a rat does on the first run does not very much influence what he does on the second run, and we shall use the word "nonsystematic" for this conclusion, saying that the behavior of this group of rats in the alternation experiment is nonsystematic.

2-13 In the alternation experiment as we have just described it, the observer is interested in the choice made by a rat on the *second occasion* on which he is placed in the same T maze. Therefore, the number of observations that can be made on a single animal is only _____. In order to prove a tendency to alternate, he will have to observe many animals.

2-14 Although the observer is interested in the alternation tendency of a whole species, he will not be able to take observations from all the members of the species. He will have to take a limited number of observations only. Since he cannot observe the entire _____, he must select from it a _____ which he will study.

2-15 He must select his sample of observations in such a way that all the available members of the species have an _____ chance of being selected for observation. If he were to select, for example, those rats which come first to the cage door when the door is opened, he would have a _____ sample of observations which might well contain a preponderance of more than usually curious rats.

2-16 Furthermore, if his rat colony is housed in cages each of which contains two or three animals, he should not select his animals by whole cagefuls. If he were to select rats by cage groups, he would violate the requirement that selection of each observation must be _____ of the selection of any other observation.

2-17 Let us suppose that the investigator has met the requirements of equal chance and independence and that he now has a _____ sample of 100 observations about the first pair of choices made by each of 100 animals. Some of these choices he can designate as alternation behavior; the rest he can designate as _____ behavior.

2-18 The number of alternation choices observed is called the OBSERVED FREQUENCY of alternation choices. The number of repetition choices observed is called the _____ frequency of repetition choices.

2-19 If the rats have a marked tendency to alternate, the observed frequency of alternation choices should be _____ than the observed frequency of repetition choices.

2-20 If, on the other hand, the rats have a marked tendency to repeat their first-run choices on the second run, then the _____ of alternation choices should be smaller than that of repetition choices.

observed
frequency

2-21 Rats with no systematic tendency either to alternate or to repeat will show alternation behavior in some cases and repetition behavior in others. For such a group of rats, the observed frequencies of _____ and _____ should turn out to be about the same.

alternation ↔ repetition

2-22 There are two ways in which the population of observations could turn out to be systematic: There could be a preponderance of observations of alternation or a preponderance of observations of repetition. If there is no great preponderance of observations of *either* sort, then the behavior must be called _____ .

nonsystematic

Review

2-23 *The alternation example is concerned with the behavior of rats on the _____ run in a T maze. The critical observation is whether the rat runs back to the _____ side which he chose on the first run or to the _____ side.*

second
same
opposite

2-24 *In order to show that the rats have a tendency to alternate, the investigator must find that the _____ frequency of alternation behavior is _____ than the _____ frequency of repetition behavior. Just how much difference between these frequencies there must be will be shown in the following sections.*

observed
greater — observed

C. Determining Expected Frequency

2-25 In a nonsystematic population of observations, the frequencies of repetition and alternation behavior are expected to be about the same. The frequency that is logically expected on the basis of some definition (such as the definition of "nonsystematic") is called the EXPECTED FREQUENCY. If 100 rats are observed, and if their behavior is expected to be nonsystematic, the expected frequency of alternation behavior is _____ . The expected frequency of repetition behavior is _____ .

50
50

2-26 If 200 rats are observed, and if their behavior is expected to be nonsystematic, the expected frequency of alternation is _____ .

2-27 The expected frequency does not need to be a whole number. For example, if 75 rats are observed and their behavior is nonsystematic, the expected frequency of alternation is _____ . It cannot be literally true, therefore, that the expected frequency is expected to occur without fail. Something very *near* this expected frequency is expected to occur in nearly all experiments with 75 non-systematic rats.

2-28 Imagine that a large number of alternation experiments are carried out, each involving 75 rats. (Each of these experiments is a REPLICATION of the 75-rat experiment.) If the behavior of the rats is non-systematic, many of these replications will result in 37 alternations and 38 repetitions; many others will result in 38 alternations. Some experiments will produce 36 or 35 alternations, and a few may yield quite small or quite large numbers of alternations. But the *average* of all these different observed frequencies should equal the _____ frequency, which is _____ .

2-29 The reason for the variation of observed frequencies around the expected frequency is already known to you. When samples are drawn from a population, the samples will not all be exactly alike or exactly like the population as a whole because of _____ factors entering into the selection of observations. The variation of observed frequencies around expected frequency is due to _____ variability.

2-30 Let us return now to the investigator who wishes to provide evidence for alternation tendencies. *He* would like to show that the observations are systematic rather than nonsystematic. That is, he would like to show that there is a *significant difference* between the observations he has obtained and those observations one would *expect* from rats whose behavior is _____ .

2-31 He may find that the _____ frequencies from his experiment are different from the frequencies expected when rats show nonsystematic behavior. Instead of 50 alternations in 100 observations, he may find, for example, 52, or 55.

2-32 Will a difference between the observed frequencies and the expected frequencies always signify that his observations come from rats whose behavior is systematic? Remember that *some* variation around the expected frequency is expected in samples drawn from a nonsystematic population of observations because of _____ .

2-33   Before the investigator can tell whether his results are *significantly* different from those expected in a nonsystematic population, he must know how much of the observed difference can be attributed to sampling variability alone. If the observed difference is _____ than that amount, then it can be regarded as significant.

2-34   To find out whether the results indicate an alternation tendency, the investigator must first determine the _____ of alternation in a nonsystematic population (that is, in a population of observations from nonsystematic rats). Then he must calculate how much variation around this value is likely to occur merely because of _____ . Then he can determine whether his results differ from expected frequency by _____ than the expected amount.

Review

2-35   *The expected frequency is a number derived logically from a definition such as nonsystematic. The expected frequency is not expected to be matched exactly by the results from every sample drawn; the frequencies observed in particular samples will differ from the expected frequency because of* _____ .

2-36   *A difference between observed and expected frequencies is significant only if it is* _____ *than the difference which is expected to occur between different samples drawn from the same population.*

D.   Expected Frequency and Probability

2-37   In a nonsystematic population of observations, the expected frequency of alternation is 50 when a total of 100 observations have been made. The total number of observations is called the TOTAL FREQUENCY. The total frequency in this case is _____ , and the expected frequency of alternation is _____ .

2-38   The *ratio* of expected frequency to total frequency is obtained by dividing expected frequency by total frequency. This ratio in the present example is _____ . The ratio $\dfrac{\text{expected frequency}}{\text{total frequency}}$ defines the PROBABILITY of alternation behavior.

2-39   The _____ of alternation behavior in observations from nonsystematic rats is ½. This figure is obtained by dividing the _____ frequency of alternations by the _____ frequency of observations.

2-40   The probability of an event is always equal to the expected frequency of that event _____ by the total frequency of observations.

2-41   The probability of an event can be converted into a percentage through multiplying it by 100. Thus, the percentage of alternation choices which one expects to observe in a series of observations is ½ x 100 or _____ per cent. Some people like to think of probability in terms of an *expected percentage.*

2-42   What is the lowest value that the probability of an event can ever reach? If the expected frequency is 0, the probability itself will equal _____ .

2-43   The value of the probability can never be less than 0 because numbers less than 0 have a negative sign. It would not be meaningful to have a negative number for either the expected _____ or the total _____ of a particular event.

2-44   What is the highest value that the probability can ever reach? Of the two frequencies involved in the definition of probability, one— the _____ frequency—can never be larger than the other. The frequency of observations of alternation behavior can never be greater than the _____ of observations.

2-45   The expected frequency of an event *can* be as large as the total frequency, but it cannot be larger. When the two frequencies are equal, their ratio is equal to _____ . The highest value that the probability can ever reach is therefore _____ .

2-46   The probability of an event reaches its highest possible value whenever the event is expected to occur in _____ per cent of the cases observed.

2-47 *The probability of an event is defined as a ratio. It is equal to the* _____ *divided by the* _____ .

expected frequency —
total frequency

2-48 *The value of the probability can range between* _____ *and* _____ . *It reaches its lower limit when the event is* _____ *expected to occur in the series of observations. It reaches its upper limit when the event is* _____ *expected to occur.*

$0 \leftrightarrow$
1
never
always

E. Applying Probability Statements to Other Examples

2-49 The abbreviation generally used for probability is the small letter p. In the alternation experiment, we are interested in the p of alternation behavior; we shall represent this particular probability as p_A. For observations on nonsystematic rats, $p_A =$ _____ .

$\frac{1}{2}$

2-50 Instead of thinking about *pairs* of T-maze choices, let us now for a moment think about the choices on the *first* T-maze run. *Every* healthy rat, if left in a T maze long enough, will explore *both* alleys of the maze. In a healthy group of rats, the probability p_B of a rat's exploring both alleys is _____ .

1

2-51 If one alley of the T maze is dark and the other alley is lighted, more rats will turn to the dark side on the first run than to the lighted side. The expected frequency of turns to the dark is then more than 50 per cent. The probability p_D of a turn to the dark side must be greater than _____ , but it cannot be more than _____ .

$\frac{1}{2} - 1$

2-52 The concept of probability can be applied to many other situations. It can be applied to the behavior of a fair coin, that is, a coin which is expected to give, in a series of tosses, as many heads as tails when it is randomly flipped. For such a coin, the expected frequency of heads is _____ the expected frequency of tails.

equal to

2-53 For a fair coin, the expected frequency of heads is exactly _____ the total number of tosses of the coin. In 100 tosses, the expected frequency of heads is _____ .

half
50

2-54 The probability p_H of getting heads when a fair coin is tossed is equal to _____. For getting tails, the probability p_T is also equal to _____. In probability tables, the decimal form is often used for probabilities instead of writing the probabilities as fractions. In decimal form, $p_H = $ _____.

2-55 The coin example is parallel to the example of alternation behavior. When we assume that we may be dealing with rats whose behavior is *nonsystematic*, our assumption is like the assumption that we are dealing with a _____ coin, which will turn up heads just as often as it turns up tails.

2-56 There is one difference between the two examples as they have been stated so far. In the alternation example, each observation comes from a different rat, but in the coin example, the same coin is tossed repeatedly and each observation consists of a single _____ of the same coin. A single rat could be given a large number of *pairs* of runs, each pair on a different day. This modification (which is often followed in practice) makes the alternation example just like the coin example.

2-57 Consider another sort of example: the case of a six-sided die. If the die is a fair die, each one of its six sides ought to turn up equally often in a series of tosses. When the die is tossed 600 times, the expected frequency of the event ⚁ is _____.

2-58 The probability p_2 of getting the event ⚁ on a toss of the die is therefore _____ ÷ _____. Therefore, $p_2 = $ _____.

2-59 The example of the die is just like the coin example except that there are _____ kinds of events (instead of just two), all of which are expected to occur equally often if the die is a fair die.

Review

2-60 *A fair coin is a coin which gives heads and tails with _____ frequency in a long series of tosses. With a fair coin, the event heads has a $p_H = $ _____.*

2-61 *Imagine a wheel similar to a roulette wheel, which can stop its spin at any of 10 different regions around its circumference. Let it be a fair wheel, so that the frequency of stops at each of the 10 positions is the* same. The probability of its stopping at the position you are betting on, after a single spin, is _____ .

F.   Finite Populations and Random Sampling

A finite *population is a population whose members can be put into a sequential order so that there is both a* first member *and a* last member. *The rats living in a particular laboratory, the marbles contained in a bag, the students enrolled in a college, the books in a library—all these populations are finite populations. A population which is not finite is said to be* infinite. *"All the possible tosses of a coin" is an infinite population; although there may be a first member, there can never be a last.*

An investigator of exploratory behavior may think of his experiment as a study of the behavior of an entire species *of rats. His sampling of alternation behavior is then a sampling from an* infinite *population. If the investigator considers that he is merely determining the alternation tendencies among the rats in his laboratory, then he is sampling from a finite population, but he does not know in advance how the population is divided between alternation and repetition tendencies.*

The composition of certain finite populations may be known in advance; for example, it may be known to an investigator (but not to his subjects) that a set of 100 handwriting specimens contains 50 specimens contributed by men and 50 contributed by women. Let us examine the concept of probability in the case of such known finite populations, and we shall discover the fundamental reason for using random *samples.*

2-62   If a set of 100 handwriting specimens contains 50 male and 50 female specimens (each identified by a symbol on the back), the "expected frequency" of male specimens in the set is a *known* frequency and it is equal to _____ . The probability of drawing a male specimen at random is _____ .

2-63   In this case, the population is finite and its composition is known. In such a case, the probability of getting a particular kind of member, when one member is randomly chosen, is equal to the known frequency of that kind of member in the population divided by _____ .

2-64   If 50 specimens are randomly drawn from the set of handwriting specimens, the expected frequency of male specimens in the sample of 50 is _____. If only 25 specimens are drawn, the expected frequency of male specimens is _____.

25

12.5

2-65   There are many common examples of such finite populations. The standard deck of playing cards is a known, finite population: There are four suits (clubs, diamonds, hearts, spades), each of which has an equal number of cards (13), making a total of 52, The probability of drawing a heart at random from a well-shuffled deck is

_____.

¼

2-66   If 12 cards are drawn simultaneously and at random from a well-shuffled deck, the expected frequency of hearts drawn is

_____.

3

2-67   Likewise, this sample of 12 cards is "expected" to contain _____ spades, _____ clubs, and _____ diamonds. But in practice the sample rarely comes out exactly in the "expected" way. Variations from the expected frequencies are common, and slight variations are more common than large variations.

three — three — three

2-68   The proportions of different cards in a sample of 12 cards drawn randomly from a deck are expected to *approximate* the proportions present in the total population of 52. *The same is true for samples from any finite population.* If, for example, a population of 1,000 voters contains 800 Republicans and 200 Democrats, then a sample of 100 voters from this population is expected to contain approximately _____ Republicans and _____ Democrats.

80 — 20

2-69   This rule ought to hold just as well whether or not the composition of the population is known in advance. When the composition is not known, the rule may, indeed, be used to make *guesses* about the probable composition of the population. Thus, if 80 Republicans and 20 Democrats are found in a random sample, it is possible to infer that the larger population probably contains close to _____ per cent Republicans and _____ per cent Democrats. (The details of such inferences will be covered in Lesson 13.)

80

20

2-70   Thus, there is a close relationship among probability, expected frequency, and random sampling. When a population is *known* and *finite*, and when each member is equally likely to be drawn, the *probability* of a certain outcome can be defined in terms of the proportion of members of that sort contained in the _____. This probability can be used to determine the *expected frequency* of that outcome in a _____ of any size drawn from the population.

population

sample

2-71   When a population is *finite* but its composition is *unknown,* the *observed frequency* of an outcome in a randomly drawn sample can be used to infer the approximate frequency in the _____ of that sort of member.

population

2-72   For some populations (either finite or infinite), the expected frequency of a certain outcome is actually part of the definition of the population. Thus, in the case of a group of rats which are nonsystematic in the alternation experiment, the statement that $p_A = \frac{1}{2}$ is implied when we say that the behavior of these rats is _____ .

nonsystematic

2-73   Likewise, in the case of a hypothetical, infinite population of tosses of a fair coin, the statement that the coin is fair implies logically that $p_H =$ _____ .

½

Review

2-74   *Samples from either finite or infinite populations can be compared with hypothetical populations whose compositions are logically defined. If the observations in the T maze are drawn from a nonsystematic population, the observed frequency of alternation should approximate the _____ frequency of alternation in a nonsystematic population. If there is a significant difference, then we can conclude that the sample did* not *come from such a nonsystematic population.*

expected

2-75   *Thus, the frequency of an outcome of a particular sort may be arrived at in three ways: (1) by examining all the members of the population and counting the number of such members (this method is suitable only for _____ populations), (2) by examining a sample drawn randomly from the population and inferring the approximate frequency in the population from the _____ frequency in the sample, (3) by defining a population in such a way that the expected frequency is implied in the _____ itself. This method applies to assumed populations such as fair coins.*

finite

observed

definition

Problems for Lesson 2

2-1 When surveys are conducted on a campus, it is a common procedure to send out questionnaires by mail and ask for their return to a particular ballot box. It is unusual to have more than 70 or 80 per cent of the questionnaires actually returned. Assuming that an inquiry is sent out originally to a random sample of the student body, can the inquirer assume that the observations from the *returned* questionnaires are a random sample of the population of student responses to that question on that campus? If not, which condition for random sampling is violated—equal chance, independence, or both?

2-2 If, instead of mailing an inquiry, the investigator simply *asks* his question of all the students he happens to meet on a particular day, will the sample of observations obtained be a random sample of student responses on that campus? If not, which condition is violated—equal chance, independence, or both?

2-3 Ten rats were selected at random from a colony of 100. Each of the 10 was given two runs in a T maze, in which he had never been placed before. The results are given below. *L* means a left turn, *R* means a right turn, the first letter of each pair is the turn made on the first run by a particular animal, and the second letter is the turn made by the same animal on the second run.

$$
\begin{array}{cc}
LR & LR \\
RL & RR \\
RL & LR \\
LL & RR \\
RL & RL
\end{array}
$$

(a) How many of the 10 animals showed alternation? How many showed repetition?

(b) On the assumption that animals in this colony do *not* tend systematically either to alternate or to repeat on their first two runs in the T maze, what is the expected frequency of alternation in an experiment with 10 rats? Did the observed frequency of alternation correspond to expected frequency?

(c) Consider the question, "Did these 10 rats alternate more often than they repeated?" What population of observations is relevant to this question? Do the observations collected constitute a sample of this population or the entire population? Does the question of significance arise?

(d) Consider the question, "Do rats of this colony tend to alternate more often than they repeat on their first pair of runs in this T maze?" What population of observations is relevant to this question? Do the observations collected constitute a sample of this population or the entire population? Does the question of significance arise? When the observed frequency of alternation is found to be greater than the expected frequency, what *two* factors *may* have played a role in producing this difference?

2-4 A college contains 500 women students and 1,000 men students. If all 1,500 names are printed in alphabetical order in a 30-page directory, what is the probability of finding the name of a woman at the bottom of page 9? What is the probability that the name in that position will be the name of a man? If a random sample of 60 names is drawn from the directory, what is the expected frequency of men's names in the sample?

2-5 Suppose you do not know that the college has an enrollment of 500 women and 1,000 men. You observe 10 women and 20 men in a particular class of 30. *Consider carefully* what you could then say about the relative numbers of men and women in this college. Examine the list of statements below, and check those which you can accept on the basis of the evidence you have. Why are the remaining statements *not* acceptable?

(a) This class is a random sample of the students in the college.

(b) There may be something about this class which makes its members a biased sample of the students in the college.

(c) There are twice as many men as women in the college.

(d) The number of men in the college is greater than the number of women.

(e) There will be some sampling variability among even those classes which *do* constitute random samples of the students in the college.

Lesson 3. Computing Probabilities—I: The Expected Outcomes of Repeated Observations

Lessons 3 and 4 develop the probability rules which provide a basis for statistical inference. A student who omits these two lessons but who studies Lessons 1, 2, and 5 will understand the concept of probability as it is used in statistical inference, but he will not have been introduced to the way in which the applications of probability can be developed from simple situations involving chance.

A. Groups of Two Observations

In this section and the following three sections, imagine that an investigator who believes that rats tend to show alternation behavior is trying to convince a skeptic who believes that the same rats really show nonsystematic behavior. It may be well to take the skeptical view yourself and to consider what the investigator would have to present as evidence in order to convince you that he is right.

3-1 Begin with the simplest sort of experiment: The investigator has run one rat, and the rat on the second run turned to the opposite side, away from the side he chose on the first run. Obviously the skeptic will not yet be convinced. He will probably say, "Even nonsystematic rats have to turn in one direction or the other, and they would be expected to alternate in _____ per cent of the cases. You just happened to get such a case by chance, and the probability was _____ that you would get alternation from your one rat."

3-2 Suppose the investigator now runs a second rat, which also alternates. How likely is it that *two* rats from a nonsystematic population would *both* alternate? Notice that an observation with $p_A = \frac{1}{2}$ has now occurred _____ times in succession.

3-3 With two rats, the number of observations available will be *two*. There are more than two ways in which these two observations can turn out, however. The list below shows the possible combinations of two observations:

a. First rat alternates; second rat alternates.
b. First rat alternates; second rat repeats.
c. First rat repeats; second rat alternates.
d. First rat repeats; second rat repeats.

Logically, there are a total of _____ different combinations of observations which may occur in an experiment involving two rats.

four

3-4 In a one-rat experiment, the number of possible outcomes is only _____; in a two-rat experiment, there are _____ possible outcomes. Since we need to know the probability of combination *a* in the above list, we must determine the expected frequency of combination *a* in a large number of two-rat experiments. In other words, we want to know how often combination *a* would be expected to occur if one were to do many two-rat experiments on rats whose behavior is _____ .

two — four

nonsystematic

3-5 Consider the combinations *a* and *b* together; in both of these combinations, the first rat alternates. If 100 two-rat experiments were done, what would be the expected frequency of "first rat alternates"? Write the expected frequencies in the blanks below:

	Expected Frequency
Combination	
a. First alternates, second alternates	
b. First alternates, second repeats	_____
c. First repeats, second alternates	
d. First repeats, second repeats	_____

50

50

3-6 Out of the 50 experiments in which the first rat is expected to alternate, the expected frequency of "second rat alternates" is _____ . Write the expected frequencies in 100 experiments for all four combinations.

25

	Expected Frequency
Combination	
a. First alternates, second alternates	_____
b. First alternates, second repeats	_____
c. First repeats, second alternates	_____
d. First repeats, second repeats	_____

25
25
25
25

3-7   Thus each one of the four combinations should occur with equal frequency, and the *probability* of each one is _____ .

¼

3-8   Therefore, the probability that both rats will alternate in a two-rat experiment with nonsystematic rats is _____ . By adding a second rat and making two observations instead of one, the investigator has improved the possibility of demonstrating that the rats tend to alternate. If the rats' behavior is really nonsystematic, one would expect to obtain the result "both rats alternate" only one time in every _____ replications of the two-rat experiment.

¼

four

3-9   The skeptic, however, will still be inclined to say, "All right, this outcome would occur only once in four times with a nonsystematic population. But I still think it is possible that you were just lucky, and if you do the experiment again, you may get a different result." The skeptic would hold that the investigator could equally well have got the outcome "both rats repeat," which also has a probability of

_____ .

¼

3-10   The result "one rat repeats, one rat alternates" is more probable than the other two outcomes, however. In one out of four experiments, combination *b* should occur; in another one out of four, combination *c* should occur. Therefore, if the behavior is nonsystematic, one should expect to see one rat alternate and one repeat in _____ out of every four experiments.

two

3-11   From this point, we shall make a distinction between COMBINATION and KIND OF OUTCOME. We shall say that *AA, AR, RA,* and *RR* are *combinations* of two observations and that there are *three* different *kinds of outcomes* among them: "both rats alternate," "both rats repeat," and "one rat repeats, one alternates." The combinations _____ and _____ both represent the same kind of outcome, that is, the outcome _____ .

$AR \leftrightarrow RA$
*"one repeats, one
alternates"*

Review

3-12   *In a two-observation experiment, there are* _____ *combinations of observations which may occur. When p = ½ for an observation in a one-observation experiment, that observation has a p of* _____ *of occurring on* both *observations in a two-observation experiment.*

four

¼

3-13   *If there are two ways in which a single observation can turn out,* *then the probability of getting one observation of each sort in a two-observation experiment is _____ . This probability is greater than the probability of getting the same observation twice because, out of the four possible combinations of observations, there are _____ combinations producing an outcome of this kind.*

½

two

B.   The Summation Rule for Either–Or Cases

3-14   It will now be convenient to represent the event "alternation" by the letter A and the event "repetition" by the letter R. In talking about two-rat experiments, we shall use two letters. The first letter refers to the behavior of the first rat, the second to the behavior of the second rat. Thus, the letters AR represent the combination "first rat _____ and second rat _____ ."

alternates — repeats

3-15   Two events are mutually exclusive when both cannot occur in the same experiment. The event A and the event R are mutually exclusive events in a one-rat experiment. The event AR and the event AA are _____ events in a two-rat experiment. Any combination is an event; any event is a combination *unless* it is an outcome of a one-observation experiment.

mutually exclusive

3-16   The probability of "one rat alternates and one rat repeats" in a two-rat experiment is ½. The same outcome can be described as "either AR or RA"; therefore, the probability of "either AR or RA" is equal to _____ .

½

3-17   The outcome "either AR or RA" includes two of the four possible combinations from a two-rat experiment. If the expected frequency of AR is 25 in 100 experiments and the expected frequency of RA is 25, the expected frequency of "either AR or RA" is _____ .

50

3-18   When the expected frequency of *each* of two mutually exclusive events is known, then the expected frequency of occurrence for *either the one or the other of the two events* is equal to the _____ of the expected frequencies of each of the two events.

sum

3-19   Expected frequencies can be *added* in these either–or cases provided the events are mutually exclusive. Probabilities can also be added, since a probability is a ratio of expected to total frequency.

Thus, $^{25}/_{100} + {}^{25}/_{100} =$ _____. The probability of "either AR or RA" is therefore _____ because this is the sum of the two separate probabilities.

$^{50}/_{100}$

$\frac{1}{2}$ (or $^{50}/_{100}$)

3-20 In a similar way, the probability of getting either AA or RR can be determined. The probability of AA is _____; the probability of RR is _____. The sum of these two probabilities is _____, and this is the probability of either AA or RR.

$\frac{1}{4}$

$\frac{1}{4}$

$\frac{1}{2}$

3-21 This result corresponds to what we would obtain if we reflected that all the four possible combinations from the two-rat experiment have equal expected frequencies and the outcome "either AA or RR" includes _____ of these four possible combinations.

two

3-22 The summation rule can be applied to the one-rat experiment with interesting results. In a one-rat experiment, the probability of A is $\frac{1}{2}$ and the probability of R is $\frac{1}{2}$. As we have noted in frame 3-15, the events A and R are mutually exclusive in a one-rat experiment; therefore, the summation rule can be applied. The probability of "either A or R" is _____ plus _____, which equals _____.

$\frac{1}{2} - \frac{1}{2}$

1

3-23 A probability of 1 means that the event is *certain* to occur. When one rat only is observed in an alternation experiment, it is certain that one will get either A or R. A probability of 1 can arise only when the _____ frequency equals the _____ frequency.

expected ↔ *total*

Review

3-24 *In a two-rat experiment, $p_{AR} = \frac{1}{4}$ and $p_{RA} = \frac{1}{4}$ for choices made by rats whose behavior is nonsystematic. The probability of "either AR or RA" is equal to the* _____ *of these probabilities, or* _____.

sum

$\frac{1}{2}$

3-25 *Suppose we were to take our sample of observations from rats whose behavior tends to show three times as much alternation as repetition, so that $p_A = \frac{3}{4}$ and $p_R = \frac{1}{4}$ for each one-rat experiment. In a one-rat experiment, the probability of getting either A or R is equal to $\frac{3}{4}$* _____ *$\frac{1}{4}$, or* _____. *The* _____ *of p_A and p_R must always equal* _____, *since one or the other of these events is certain to occur.*

plus — 1 — sum

1

C. Applying the Summation Rule to Groups of Three Observations

3-26 Complete the following table of possible combinations in a *three*-rat experiment. Notice how the table is constructed.

Outcome	Rat 1	Rat 2	Rat 3
a	A	A	A
b	A	A	R
c	A	R	A
d	A	R	___
e	R	A	A
f	R	___	R
g	R	R	A
h	___	R	R

R

A

R

3-27 The table was constructed systematically. The first four combinations include all the cases in which rat 1 alternates; the last four, all the cases in which rat 1 repeats. Within the first four combinations, the first two are cases in which rat _____ alternates and the first one of these is a case in which rat _____ alternates.

2

3

3-28 To construct a table for a four-rat experiment, another column would have to be added before the column for rat 1 above and the entire table would have to include _____ combinations, because all the combinations of a three-rat experiment could occur together with *alternation* by rat 4 and all the same combinations could also occur together with *repetition* by rat 4.

16

3-29 In a three-rat experiment, the number of possible combinations is _____. Since the probability of alternation on a single observation is ½ for our nonsystematic rats, all these combinations should occur with equal frequency. (If this statement is not clear, review frames 3-5 and 3-6. The reasoning presented there for the two-rat case can be extended to the three-rat case.) The expected frequency of AAA in 100 such three-rat experiments is therefore

_____.

eight

12.5

3-30 The probability p_{AAA} of AAA is _____. And $p_{RRR} = $ _____, since RRR also occurs only once among the eight possible combinations.

⅛

⅛

3-31　Out of the eight combinations of a three-rat experiment, there are _____ combinations in which two rats alternate and one repeats. *Each* of these three combinations has a probability of _____ .

3-32　The rule for either–or cases can be applied here. Just as the probability of "either AR or RA" is the sum of p_{AR} and p_{RA} (see frames 3-16 and 3-17 above), so the probability of "either AAR or ARA or RAA" is the sum of _____ , _____ , and _____ , since the events AAR, ARA, and RAA are mutually exclusive.

3-33　Each of these three combinations has a probability of ⅛. The probability of "either AAR or ARA or RAA" is the _____ of the probabilities of these three outcomes, and the probability is therefore equal to _____ .

3-34　The probability of "either AAR or ARA or RAA" is the same as the probability of _____ rat(s) alternating and _____ rat(s) repeating.

3-35　The probability of one rat alternating and the other two repeating is the same as the probability of "either _____ or _____ or _____ ." Since each of these combinations has a probability of ⅛, and since they are mutually exclusive, the probability of getting one or another of these three combinations is _____ .

Review

3-36　*Now, putting these statements into a more general form, we can say that in any three-observation experiment there are _____ possible combinations which may result. An event with a $p = $ ½ in a one-observation experiment has a probability of _____ of occurring on* all *three observations in a three-observation experiment.*

3-37　*If there are two ways in which a single observation can turn out, then the probability of getting two observations of one kind and one observation of the other kind is _____ than the probability of getting all three observations alike. This difference in probability exists because there are only _____ combinations out of the eight in*

which all three observations are alike; the remaining _____ *six*
combinations all have two observations alike and one different.

<hr>

D. The Product Rule for Both–And Cases

3-38 To develop one more of the basic probability rules, let us return to two-rat experiments. Since the combination AR is one of the four possible combinations of two observations, we already know that $p_{AR} = \frac{1}{4}$ when the rats are nonsystematic. The event AR can also be considered as the outcome "both A from the first rat and R from the second rat." In order to obtain the combination AR, it is necessary to have _____ of these observations occur. *both*

3-39 The probability of the combination AR can also be determined from the probabilities of the separate events, getting A from the first rat and getting R from the second rat. Since $p_A =$ _____ *½*
for the first rat, the expected frequency of "A from the first rat" is _____ in 100 such experiments. *50*

3-40 Out of the 50 occasions on which A is expected from the first rat, the second rat is expected to give the response R a total of _____ times, since $p_R = \frac{1}{2}$. *25*

3-41 The expected frequency of AR has thus been determined by first multiplying the number of observations (100) by the probability of the first event and then multiplying the result by the probability of the second event. The same result will be obtained if the probabilities of the two separate events A and R are first multiplied together and the product is then multiplied by 100. Thus, ½ x ½ gives _____ , *¼*
which times 100 is _____ . *25*

3-42 From this example we can formulate a general rule: When *both* of two independent events must occur and the probability of each event alone is known, the probability of getting *both* is obtained by _____ the two probabilities. *multiplying*

3-43 Notice that the statement in frame 3-42 includes the word "independent." The events A and R are independent of each other, since the behavior of the first rat cannot affect the outcome of the observation made on the _____ rat. In order to apply the *second* rule, we must know that the two events are _____ of each other.

3-44 It is for this reason that the definition of a random sample specifies not only that the selection procedure must give all members of the population an *equal chance* of being selected but also that the selection of any one member must be _____ of the selection of any other member. If this condition is not met, the sample is not _____ and therefore the basic product rule in probability does not apply.

independent

random

3-45 This product rule for both–and cases can be extended to experiments with more than two observations. We know from Section C, on three-rat experiments, that the probability of the combination AAR is ⅛. To obtain this combination, the first and second rats must _____ and the third rat must _____ .

alternate — repeat

3-46 The probability p_A for rat 1 and rat 2 is ½; the probability p_R for rat 3 is also ½. If these three probabilities are multiplied, we obtain the product _____ . This is the probability of getting *all three* of these events in the same three-rat experiment.

⅛

3-47 The product rule is also applicable when the probabilities are not equal to ½. Take again the example of frame 3-25, in which $p_A = ¾$ and $p_R = ¼$ for a particular group of rats. For such a case, the probability p_{AR} in a two-rat experiment would be _____ x _____ , or _____ .

¾ ↔
¼ — ³⁄₁₆

3-48 In two-rat experiments with such a group of rats, the probability of the combination AA would be _____ whereas the probability of the combination RR would be _____ .

⁹⁄₁₆
¹⁄₁₆

3-49 In three-rat experiments with such a group, the probability of two alternations and one repetition would *not* equal the probability of one alternation and two repetitions. The probability p_{AAR} would be equal to _____ , while the probability p_{RRA} would be equal to _____ .

⁹⁄₆₄
³⁄₆₄

3-50 *When* all *of a set of independent events must occur jointly, the rule for both–and cases applies and the probabilities of the different events must be* _____ . *When* any one *of a set of mutually exclusive*

multiplied

The Product Rule for Both–And Cases   37

events will suffice, the rule for either–or cases applies and the probabilities of the separate events must be _____ .

added

3-51 When probabilities less than 1 are added, the resulting sum is _____ than any one of the components. When such probabilities are multiplied, the resulting product is _____ than any one of the components. Unless one of the separate events has a probability of 1, the probability of getting both of two events is always _____ than the probability of getting either the one or the other of the two.

greater
less

less

E. Applying These Rules to Coin, Dice, and Card Problems

3-52 The discussion of the alternation experiment can be applied directly to the consideration of coins, where p_H is the probability of obtaining heads on a single toss of the coin and p_T is the probability of obtaining tails. If $p_H = p_T = \frac{1}{2}$, the coin is a fair coin. On two tosses of such a coin, $p_{HH} =$ _____ , $p_{TT} =$ _____ , and $p_{HT} = p_{TH} =$ _____ .

$\frac{1}{4} - \frac{1}{4}$
$\frac{1}{4}$

3-53 The probability of getting one head and one tail is obtained by _____ p_{HT} and p_{TH}. It is equal to _____ .

adding — $\frac{1}{2}$

3-54 Since the probability of ⚀ on one toss of a fair die is ⅙ and the probability of ⚂ on one toss of the die is also ⅙, the probability of obtaining either ⚀ or ⚂ on one toss is equal to _____ .

$\frac{1}{3}$

3-55 On an experiment which includes two independent tosses of the die (or one toss of each of two dice), the probability of getting ⚀ *twice* is _____ .

$\frac{1}{36}$

3-56 On a two-toss experiment, the probability of getting ⚀ on the first toss followed by ⚂ on the second toss is _____ . Notice that a particular combination, ⚀ followed by ⚂, is required.

$\frac{1}{36}$

3-57 Besides this combination, there is another possible combination giving the same kind of outcome: The combination ⚂ followed by ⚀. In other words there are two different combinations which involve one ⚂ and one ⚀. The probability of getting either the one or the other of these two combinations is ⅟₃₆ + ⅟₃₆, or _____ .

$\frac{1}{18}$

3-58 Suppose two cards are drawn from a deck of 52 containing 13 cards of each of the four suits. Assume that the deck is well shuffled and that each card is replaced in the deck before the next card is drawn. (This is called "sampling with replacement.") The probability that the first card drawn is a spade is _____ . The probability that the second card is a spade is _____ . The probability that *both* cards will be spades is _____ .

$\frac{1}{4}$

$\frac{1}{4}$

$\frac{1}{16}$

3-59 What is the probability of getting one spade and one club when two cards are drawn at random and with replacement? There are _____ sequences in which one spade and one club can occur.

two

3-60 The probability of *each one* of these two sequences is _____ , just like the probability of getting two spades or of getting two clubs. The probability of getting either the one or the other is the _____ of the probabilities of the separate sequences. Therefore, the probability of one spade and one club in two random draws with replacement is _____ .

$\frac{1}{16}$

sum

$\frac{1}{8}$

3-61 Four of the cards in a deck of 52 are aces. The probability of getting an ace on a single random draw from the deck is _____ . The probability of getting *two* aces on *two* draws with replacement is _____ .

$\frac{4}{52}$ *(or* $\frac{1}{13}$*)*

$\frac{1}{169}$

3-62 Why is the condition "with replacement" an important condition? Suppose that one ace has been drawn and *not replaced.* Now, the total number of cards remaining in the deck is _____ . The total number of aces remaining is _____ . The probability of drawing an ace on the second draw *without replacement* would be _____ .

51

three

$\frac{3}{51}$ *(*$\frac{1}{17}$*)*

3-63 When the first card is not replaced, the probability of getting two aces in a row is _____ x _____ , or _____ . Compare this with the probability $\frac{1}{169}$ of two aces on two draws *with* replacement.

$\frac{1}{13} \leftrightarrow \frac{1}{17}$

$\frac{1}{221}$

3-64 Suppose a student is taking a four-choice multiple-choice examination. The examination consists of 100 items, each with four alternative answers only one of which is correct. If the student has no information and simply guesses at random, the probability that his answer to the first item is correct is _____ .

$\frac{1}{4}$

3-65 On such an examination, a student who is perfectly innocent of the material covered by the examination and who simply marks one of the four answers at random for every item can take comfort in knowing that the expected frequency of correct answers by chance alone is _____ out of the 100 items.

Problems for Lesson 3

3-1 A single card is drawn from a standard deck of 52 playing cards. What is the probability that the card drawn is a spade?

3-2 A second card is drawn from the same deck after the first card drawn was replaced in the deck and the deck was reshuffled. What is the probability that the new card drawn is a spade?

3-3 A spade has been drawn from the deck and laid aside. Now still another card is drawn from those cards remaining in the deck. What is the probability that the new card drawn is a spade? What is the probability that it is a club?

3-4 Twenty-six cards are drawn in turn, and each is replaced in the deck after its identity has been noted. The deck is reshuffled after each draw. A standard deck contains 12 face cards. What is the expected frequency of face cards in the 26 draws?

3-5 What is the probability of getting *either* a spade *or* a club on a single draw from a standard deck?

3-6 What is the probability of getting an ace on both of two successive draws from a standard deck when the first card is replaced before the second draw and the deck is reshuffled?

3-7 What is the probability of getting two red cards and one black card, in any order, on three successive draws from a standard deck (cards being replaced and reshuffled after each draw)? What is the probability that the first two cards drawn will be red? Write down all the combinations of red and black cards that might occur in three successive draws. How many combinations are there? How many different kinds of outcome are there?

3-8 A die is tossed three times, and each of the three times it turns up ⚀. What is the probability of obtaining this series of outcomes from an unloaded (unbiased) die?

3-9 A die is tossed three times. Two of the three times it turns up ⚁, and once it turns up ⚀. What is the probability of this result if the die is unbiased? What is the probability that the first two tosses will both give ⚁ (regardless of the third toss)?

3-10 Another die is tossed three times. It turns up one ⚀, one ⚁, and one ⚂. What is the probability of obtaining this outcome from an unbiased die? What is the probability that these events will occur in the orderly sequence ⚀ ⚁ ⚂?

3-11 A coin is biased toward tails, so that the probability of tails is 0.9 and the probability of heads is 0.1. What is the probability on two tosses of this coin of obtaining two heads? Of obtaining two tails? Of obtaining one head and one tail? Your three probabilities should add up to 1.00. Do they?

3-12 Suppose you are trying to predict the guesses which will be made by a newcomer on two tosses of a coin. From your viewpoint, the probability of his calling "heads" on the first toss can be considered to be ½; you have no reason to assign a different probability. But it would be incorrect to say, "The probability of his calling 'heads' on *both* tosses is ¼." Why?

Lesson 4.   Computing Probabilities— II: The Factorial Rule

In earlier lessons, we have considered the probability rules for experiments with up to three observations. In Lesson 4, we shall work out a short cut for figuring these probabilities, and with the aid of the Special Answer Sheet (back of book), we shall carry the procedure up to experiments having as many as 10 observations. Remove the Special Answer Sheet for Lesson 4 from the back of the book, and write your answers on it whenever the item indicates that you should do so. Other answers should be written on a regular answer sheet, as before.

You will find that the arithmetic for some items in this lesson takes a little time. Don't try to hurry through; allow yourself time enough to do these items correctly. You will understand the principles better if you actually see how they work out in these examples.

A.   Determining the Total Number of Combinations

4-1   In an alternation experiment with just one rat, there are only _____ events which could be the outcome (i.e., alternation and repetition). If the rat's behavior is nonsystematic, each event has a probability equal to _____ .

two

½

4-2   In an alternation experiment with two rats, there are _____ combinations of observations which are possible. The number of combinations is equal to 2 x _____ , or $(2)^2$. This term is read "2 squared" or "2 to the second power."

four

2

4-3   In such an experiment, each of the four combinations has a probability equal to _____ . The probability of each of the combinations is therefore $(½)^2$, that is, ½ x ½.

¼

4-4   In an experiment with three rats, there are _____ combinations of observations which are possible. The number of com-

eight

binations is equal to $(2)^3$, or 2 to the _____ . Each of the combinations has a probability of _____ , or $(\frac{1}{2})^3$, that is, $\frac{1}{2} \times \frac{1}{2} \times \frac{1}{2}$.

4-5 With one rat, there are $(2)^1 = 2$ events.
With two rats, there are $(2)^2 = 4$ combinations.
With three rats, there are $(2)^3 = 8$ combinations.
With four rats, there are _____ combinations.

4-6 From these statements, we can now establish a rule. When an experiment includes N number of observations, and when each observation can turn out in two possible ways, the total number of combinations of N observations is 2 to the _____ power.

4-7 On the Special Answer Sheet, the column at the extreme left (labeled N) gives various numbers of observations up to 10. The second column, labeled $(2)^N$, shows how many combinations of observations there will be for each of the numbers of _____ .

4-8 For example, when there is one observation (as in an experiment with one rat), there are two events. The number 2 goes in the second column opposite the number _____ in the first column.

4-9 Write the proper numbers in the second column as they appear from top to bottom.

4-10 The third column on the Special Answer Sheet is labeled $(\frac{1}{2})^N$. This column represents the *probability* of any one of the combinations, assuming that each single observation has $p = \frac{1}{2}$. Fill in this column.

Review

4-11 *In the statement "A coin is tossed N times," the letter N stands for the* _____ . *On N tosses of any coin, the number of combinations of the N observations is* _____ . *There will be* _____ *observations in each of these combinations.*

4-12 *On one toss of a coin, $p_H = p_T = \frac{1}{2}$ if the coin is a fair one. The probability of any one of the combinations of N observations is equal to* _____ .

B. Combinations Giving the Same Kind of Outcome

4-13   In a two-rat experiment, there are two combinations of observations which include one alternation and one repetition. These are the combinations _____ and _____ .

AR ↔ RA

4-14   In a three-rat experiment, there are *three* combinations in which all but one of the rats alternate. The one exceptional rat may be the _____ , the _____ , or the _____ rat of the three.

first — second — third

4-15   For the expression "all but one," one can write $N - 1$. When there are N observations, there are always N combinations in which $N - 1$ of the observations turn out in a particular way. Always recall that there are _____ positions in the set of N observations which the "odd" or exceptional event can occupy.

N

4-16   In a two-rat experiment, there is always only one combination in which both rats show alternation. There is also only one combination in which both show repetition. In a three-rat experiment, there is always only _____ combination in which all three rats alternate.

one

4-17   When there are N observations, there is always only one combination in which _____ observations can turn out in the same particular way.

all N

4-18   The triangular pattern on your Special Answer Sheet will help you to visualize and to work out the number of combinations in which particular kinds of outcomes can occur. Consider the second row in the table opposite $N = 2$. This row gives all the kinds of outcomes for experiments which contain _____ observations. There are _____ spaces in this row.

two

three

4-19   In the left-hand space, write the number of combinations in which the outcome "two repetitions" can occur in a two-rat experiment: _____ . In the right-hand space, write the number of combinations in which the outcome "two alternations" can occur: _____ .

one

one

4-20   In the middle space of the same second row, write the number of combinations in which the outcome "one alternation, one repetition," can occur: _____ . This is the same as getting alternation from all but one, or _____ , rats. The sum of

two

(N − 1) (or 1)

the numbers in the second row is _____, and this equals the total number of possible _____ of observations in a two-rat experiment.

4-21   The space at the extreme left of any row of the triangular table is for the number of combinations in which all N rats repeat. This number is always _____, no matter how many observations an experiment includes. Put this number in all the left-hand spaces. The same number must be put in all the right-hand spaces, since those spaces are for the number of combinations in which all N rats alternate.

4-22   The second space in each row is for the number of combinations in which $N - 1$ of the rats repeat. This number will be *different* for each row; it will always be equal to the value of _____ for that row. The same number goes in the next-to-last space in the row, since that space is for the number of combinations in which $N - 1$ of the rats alternate. Put in these numbers.

Review

4-23   *For a five-rat experiment, N =* _____. *Each combination of the N observations will include* _____ *observations. Write down all the possible combinations which would meet the requirement "all five rats alternate."* _____ *How many such combinations are there?* _____.

4-24   *Write down all the possible combinations of five observations which would meet the requirement "N − 1 rats alternate."* _____. *How many are there of this sort?* _____. *In an N-rat experiment, there are always* _____ *combinations in which N − 1 behave in the same particular way.*

C.   The Factorial Rule

4-25   In order to complete the triangular table, we need a further rule for working out numbers of combinations. The rule makes use of *factorial numbers*. A factorial number is written with ! following it, such as 2! or 4! The expression 2! is called "factorial two." It means the product of 2 and all the positive whole numbers less than 2, in other words, _____ x _____ .

2 — 1

4-26 4! means the product of 4 and all positive whole numbers less than 4. Therefore, 4! means the product of _____ and _____ and _____ and _____ . This product is _____ .

4
3 — 2 — 1
24

4-27 Since the definition of a factorial number applies only to positive whole numbers, and since zero is not a positive whole number, the definition does not apply to factorial zero (0!) However, it is convenient to define 0! in a special way, so that it is equal to 1. The product of 2! and 0! is _____ .

2

4-28 Factorial numbers make it possible to set up a rule for determining the number of combinations of N observations which give a particular kind of outcome. For example, the rule for the number of combinations of four observations which give two alternations and two repetitions is 4!/2!2! = _____ .

6

4-29 It can be verified that there are, indeed, six combinations in which two alternations and two repetitions can occur in a four-rat experiment. The two alternations can be made by rats 1 and _____ , 1 and _____ , 1 and _____ , 2 and _____ , 2 and _____ , or 3 and _____ .

2 — 3 — 4
3 — 4
4

4-30 The fraction 4!/2!2! tells in how many combinations it is possible to obtain two alternations and two repetitions in four observations. The fraction has as its *numerator* the factorial of the number of _____ . The *denominator* of the fraction contains the factorials of two numbers, the number of alternations and the number of _____ .

observations

repetitions

4-31 The same form can be applied, with different numbers, to calculate the number of combinations of four observations giving three alternations and one repetition. The fraction has 4! in the numerator and 3!1! in the denominator. The number of combinations is _____ . And we have already shown that with four observations there will be _____ combinations in which *all but one* of the observations come out in the same particular way because there are _____ positions which the "odd" event can occupy.

four
four

four

4-32   We can also determine the number of combinations of four observations which give four alternations and zero repetitions. The numerator of the factorial fraction will be factorial 4, and the denominator will be factorial _____ times factorial _____. The number of combinations is _____. You have already written this number in the right-hand space of the fourth row of the triangular table.

4-33   The rule can be applied to experiments with more than four observations. Suppose there are five rats in the experiment. The number of combinations of five observations which give three alternations and two repetitions can be calculated from the fraction in which 5! is the numerator and the denominator is _____. The number of combinations is _____.

3! 2!

10

4-34   In a 10-rat experiment, N is equal to 10. The number of combinations of 10 observations which give eight alternations and two repetitions can be calculated from the fraction _____. The number is _____.

$\dfrac{10!}{8!\,2!}$

45

Review

4-35   *The factorial rule can now be stated in general form. Let the letter k represent the number of alternations included in the kind of outcome we are interested in. Then if there are N observations, there must be N − _____ repetitions in this kind of outcome.*

k

4-36   *The numerator of the factorial fraction always contains only the factorial of the number of _____. The denominator always contains the factorial of the number of _____ times the factorial of the number of _____.*

observations

alternations

repetitions

4-37   *Therefore, the number of combinations of N observations which will give k alternations and N − k repetitions is calculated from the fraction _____.*

$\dfrac{N!}{k!\,(N-k)!}$

D.   Completing the Triangular Table

4-38   Rows 1 through 4 of the triangular table are now filled. In the fifth row there are still two spaces empty. The first of these from the left is for the number of combinations of _____ observa-

five

tions which give _____ alternations and _____ repetitions. The space next to it on the right (that is, the fourth space from the left) is for the number of combinations which give _____ alternations and _____ repetitions.

4-39 The number of combinations which give two alternations and three repetitions can be calculated from the factorial fraction $5!/2!3!$. The number is _____. The number of combinations which give three alternations and two repetitions can be calculated from the fraction _____, which is numerically equal to the fraction just worked out. Write these numbers in the table.

4-40 There is a simple way to locate any desired kind of outcome in the triangular table. Consider row 5, in which $N =$ _____. The *first* space on the left is for the number of combinations which give five repetitions and _____ alternations. The second space is for four repetitions and _____ alternations. The third space is for _____ repetitions and _____ alternations, and so on.

4-41 Think of the spaces in a row as numbered from the left. Then the position number of a space is always one number _____ than the number of alternations in the kind of outcome it concerns.

4-42 In the sixth row, how many alternations are in the kind of outcome with which the *second* space is concerned? _____. Which space in the sixth row is concerned with four alternations? _____.

4-43 Which space in the sixth row is concerned with four repetitions? (Here, you must first determine how many alternations occur when four repetitions appear in six observations.) The space is number _____ from the left. Which space in the seventh row is for the number of combinations having four repetitions? _____.

4-44 The fourth space in the sixth row is for the number of combinations which give _____ and _____ in a six-rat experiment. Determine the number for this space. The factorial fraction is _____, and the number is _____. Put this number in the correct space.

4-45 Figure the number of combinations which give six repetitions and two alternations in eight observations. The number is

two — three

three — two

10

$\dfrac{5!}{3!\,2!}$

5

zero
one
three — two

greater

One

The fifth

3
The fourth

three alternations
    ↔ three repetitions
$\dfrac{6!}{3!\,3!}$ *— 20*

_____, and it belongs in the _____ space from the left in the _____ row.

28 — third
eighth

4-46 Now notice the following regularity in the triangular table: Any number in the table is equal to the sum of the two numbers nearest to it in the row *directly above it*. Thus, in the third row and second space, the number 3 is the sum of the numbers _____ and _____ just above it. In the sixth row, the number in the fourth space is the sum of the numbers _____ and _____ just above it.

1 ↔
2
10
10

4-47 Using this simple rule of addition, fill in the remaining rows in the table. A correct completed triangular table appears on page 361.

Review

4-48 *The triangular table is an aid to easy calculation of the numbers of _____ which give particular numbers of alternations and repetitions. If you had to make up the table by yourself, you should first recall that it is a symmetrical (equilateral) triangle with its apex pointing in the _____ direction.*

combinations

upward

4-49 *The number of positions in the first row of the table, for N = 1, would have to be _____. Each successive row would contain _____ more position(s) than the row above it. To find the number to put in a particular position, you would add _____.*

two
one
the two numbers nearest to it in the row above it

4-50 *All the positions at the extreme right and extreme left of the table must contain the number _____. With these facts, you could reproduce the triangular table unaided at any time.*

1

E. Using the Triangular Table

4-51 From this table, you can now answer many questions about probability. Suppose 10 rats are run in the alternation experiment. The *total* number of combinations of 10 observations which can occur is _____, as you can tell from the second *column* in row _____.

1,024
10

4-52 If the rats' behavior is nonsystematic, the probability of *any one*

Using the Triangular Table   49

of these combinations is equal to _____, as you can tell from the _____ column in the same row.

4-53   In a 10-rat experiment, suppose you observe that nine rats alternate and one repeats. The number of combinations of 10 observations giving this kind of outcome is found in the _____ space in row 10 of the triangular part of the table. The number is _____. Therefore, the probability of getting nine alternations and one repetition from 10 rats whose behavior is nonsystematic is the *sum* of the probabilities of these _____ combinations. The probability is _____.

4-54   This table can be used for other kinds of observations as well. Recall the example of the fair coin. If a coin is tossed ten times and heads occurs eight times, the probability of this kind of outcome is the same as the probability of getting _____ alternations and _____ repetitions in the alternation experiment.

4-55   Since we are now interested in heads rather than in alternations, we must think of the first space in row 10 of the table as concerned with the outcome "zero heads," the second space with "one head," and so on. The number of combinations which give eight heads and two tails can be found in the _____ space in row 10. The number of combinations is _____.

4-56   Since there are 45 combinations of 10 observations which give eight heads and two tails, and since the probability of any *one* of these combinations alone is _____, the probability of getting eight heads and two tails is _____.

4-57   A probability of 45/1,024 means that, with perfectly fair coins or perfectly nonsystematic rats, the outcome "eight heads and two tails" would be expected to occur approximately _____ times in 1,024 replications of the whole 10-observation experiment.

4-58   If the coin had turned up heads only seven times and had turned up tails the other three times, there would be _____ combinations in which this outcome might occur. The probability of such an outcome would be _____.

4-59   The probability of the coin's turning up heads three times and tails the other seven times is equal to _____. It is exactly the same as the probability of seven heads and three tails in 10 tosses.

4-60   If a person draws a sample of 10 specimens of handwriting from the collection of 50 male and 50 female specimens, the probability that any particular specimen will be male is _____ . The expected frequency of male specimens in the sample of 10 is _____ .

4-61   If the person draws, instead, six male and four female specimens in his sample of 10, he has obtained an outcome which should occur by chance _____ times in 1,024 repetitions of this sort of situation, since there are _____ combinations in which six male and four female specimens could be drawn and the probability of any single combination is 1/1,024. This result, then, is almost as common as five male and five female specimens in 10; this combination ought to occur by chance _____ times in 1,024.

4-62   The number of combinations *of* 10 *observations* which give five alternations is _____ . The number of combinations *of* 8 *observations* which give five alternations is _____ . The number of combinations *of* 6 *observations* which give five alternations is _____ .

4-63   The probability of five alternations in a 6-observation experiment is _____ . The probability of five alternations in an 8-observation experiment is _____ , and in a 10-observation experiment is _____ .

Problems for Lesson 4

4-1 A coin is tossed nine times. How many different combinations can occur in the nine tosses? How many kinds of outcomes? Assuming that the coin is unbiased, what is the probability of getting any one particular combination? How many different combinations would give six heads and three tails? What is the probability of getting exactly six heads and three tails in nine tosses of an unbiased coin?

4-2 An experimenter does an experiment with 11 rats. He obtains eight alternations and three repetitions. How many different combinations can occur with 11 rats? What is the probability of any one of these combinations, assuming that the rats are nonsystematic? How many combinations would give eight alternations and three repetitions? What is the probability of getting exactly this outcome?

4-3 **(a)** An experimenter does a four-rat experiment, and he obtains three alternations and one repetition. What is the probability of this result if the rats are nonsystematic?

   (b) The experimenter now does a second four-rat experiment and gets two alternations and two repetitions. What is the probability of this result if the rats are nonsystematic?

   (c) Now what is the probability that an experimenter who does *two* four-rat experiments will get three alternations on the *first* and two alternations on the *second* experiment if the rats are nonsystematic? What is the probability that he will get three alternations from one of the two experiments (*either* one) and two alternations from the other experiment?

   (d) Suppose the experimenter considered *all eight* rats as if they had been in one eight-rat experiment, the outcome of which was five alternations and three repetitions. What is the probability of five alternations and three repetitions in an eight-rat experiment? The probability you obtain is *not* equal to the probability of getting three alternations from one and two alternations from the other of two four-rat experiments. Why not?

Lesson 5.   Testing the Null Hypothesis

The investigator whose alternation experiment was described in Lesson 2 must show that his results differ significantly from the results expected when behavior is nonsystematic. Otherwise he cannot claim that his rats show a distinct tendency to alternate. He will be able to make this claim only if it is sufficiently improbable *that he would have obtained his observed results from rats which are nonsystematic.*

In Lesson 3, we thought of the investigator as starting with just one rat and finding that a skeptic could say, "Getting alternation from just one rat means nothing; the probability is ½ that you would get alternation even if the rat's behavior is, as I prefer to think, nonsystematic." We then allowed the investigator to add a rat, making it a two-rat experiment, and we found that the outcome "both rats alternate" still is not very improbable with nonsystematic rats. One would expect this outcome, in fact, in one out of four such two-rat experiments even when behavior is nonsystematic. In other words, the probability is ¼ that a two-rat experiment would turn out this way.

We are now going on to consider the probability of certain kinds of outcomes when the number of observations (i.e., number of rats) is further increased. The student who has skipped Lessons 3 and 4 should notice carefully that the probabilities we shall be talking about are probabilities of getting a particular kind of outcome (*such as three out of three rats alternating*) in a large number of replications (*reduplications*) of the same experiment.

A.   Probable and Improbable Outcomes

5-1   Suppose now that the investigator has carried out a three-rat experiment and has found that all three rats alternated. This kind of outcome has a probability of ⅛ (see Lesson 3C for calculation of this probability). The expected frequency of this outcome in a series of eight complete replications of the three-rat experiment is

_____ .

5-2   The investigator has obtained a result which would be expected by chance only about _____ times in every hundred times his three-rat experiment is replicated. This result is evidently not the *most* common sort of thing which might occur when the behavior is nonsystematic, but it is not highly improbable.

12.5

5-3   Now suppose that the investigator repeats his experiment with another three rats and again obtains three alternations. The probability of getting three alternations twice in succession from a nonsystematic population is equal to ⅛ x ⅛ (see Lesson 3D), which equals _____ .

¹⁄₆₄

5-4   This result would be expected to occur by chance only _____ time(s) in every 64 replications of the experiment, where the experiment now refers to a *pair* of three-rat experiments.

one

5-5   If the behavior of the rats is truly nonsystematic, such a result would be relatively rare. After getting this result, one can choose between two conclusions: One can conclude that the rats' behavior is indeed nonsystematic but a relatively _____ event has occurred, or one can conclude that the rats' behavior is *not* _____ .

rare (improbable)

nonsystematic

5-6   Suppose that, for good measure, the investigator repeats his experiment one more time, with still another three rats, and that the outcome is again three alternations. The probability of getting this outcome is equal to ⅛ x ¹⁄₆₄, or _____ , when the rats' behavior is actually nonsystematic.

¹⁄₅₁₂

5-7   An event occurring by chance only once in 512 such experiments is quite a rare event. A person would now be very likely to prefer the conclusion that the rats' behavior is _____ .

not nonsystematic

5-8   He is likely to prefer the conclusion that the rats in this experiment are systematically biased in favor of alternation behavior. The probability of obtaining the observed result from such biased rats is _____ than the probability of obtaining the result from nonsystematic rats.

higher

5-9   In the same way, if the investigator were to obtain nine *repetition* choices out of nine observations of rats in this experiment, he would be likely to conclude that the rats were not nonsystematic. He would

probably conclude that the rats were biased toward _____
choices.

repetition

5-10 If only eight of the nine rats had alternated, the argument would proceed in exactly the same way. The probability of getting eight alternations in nine observations is, of course, somewhat larger than the probability of getting nine alternations. One would conclude that the rats' behavior is biased *only* if the probability of obtaining such a result from nonsystematic rats is sufficiently _____ .

small (low)

Review

5-11 *Although the investigator may have undertaken his experiment because he does* not *believe the rats' behavior is nonsystematic, he calculates the* _____ *of obtaining his observed results from a* _____ *population.*

probability
nonsystematic

5-12 *If this probability is low, he may draw either of two conclusions: that he has happened by chance to get a very* _____ *result from what is really a* _____ *population or that he has got a more common result from a population that is* _____ .

rare
nonsystematic
not nonsystematic
(biased)

B. The Null Hypothesis

5-13 The investigator of alternation behavior first had to treat his result *as if* it came from rats with nonsystematic behavior. In effect, he had to say to himself: "Suppose I am really wrong and the rats have no more of a tendency to alternate than to repeat. How _____ would my results be if this were true?"

probable (improbable)

5-14 He had thus to adopt a particular attitude toward his observations, a rather skeptical attitude. He had to look at them with the *assumption* in mind that they might perhaps have come from nonsystematic rats and to judge whether there was good reason to believe that the results were *too extreme* for this assumption to be _____ .

true (justified)

5-15 The assumption that the observations have come from a population that is *not different* from a nonsystematic population is a NULL

HYPOTHESIS. A null hypothesis is a hypothesis that no _____ *difference*
exists between two particular populations.

5-16   In this case, the two populations involved are the population of
observations from which the actual observations were drawn (i.e.,
observations on the same rats or the same kind of rats) and the population of observations which is logically defined as _____, *nonsystematic*
in which alternations and repetitions occur with equal frequency.

5-17   In other kinds of experiments, both populations may be populations from which samples have been drawn. We had such an example
in Lesson 1C, where we compared the heights of samples of students
from Alpha and Omega Colleges. In that example, the _____ *null*
hypothesis would be the hypothesis that the two samples really came
from the *same* population, in other words, that there is _____ *no*
difference between the populations from which the two samples were
drawn.

5-18   The investigator of alternation behavior is also comparing two
_____, although only one has been sampled, and his *populations*
_____ states that there is no difference between the two. *null hypothesis*

5-19   This example contains a trap unless you are wary. It would be
easy to think that the null hypothesis involves the assumption that
there is no difference between the probability of alternation and the
probability of repetition, because this happens to be true, in this particular case, for the nonsystematic population of observations with
which the _____ are being compared. *actual observations*
(observed results)

5-20   But such an interpretation of the null hypothesis would get you
into trouble if the experimental question were slightly different. Suppose that an opponent were willing to argue, "The probability of
alternation is ¼, and the probability of repetition is ¾." He would be
proposing a new *hypothetical population* to be compared with the
population actually sampled. In order to test his proposal, you would
have to assume the _____ that your results actually came *null hypothesis*
from a population which is _____ from a population in *not different*
which alternation occurs one-third as often as repetition and calculate
the probability of obtaining your results by chance from such a
population.

5-21   This hypothesis is still a null hypothesis, even though it does not involve assuming $p_A = p_B = \frac{1}{2}$. To test this null hypothesis, one must instead assume that $p_A =$ _____ .

5-22 The null hypothesis, therefore, must be firmly understood as a hypothesis stating that there is no difference between two specific _____ . It is *not* the hypothesis that there is no difference between two probabilities (such as the probability of alternation and the probability of repetition).

Review

5-23 *A null hypothesis is a hypothesis that* _____ *exists between* _____ .

5-24 *If the obtained results have a* high *probability when the null hypothesis is assumed, the investigator will probably conclude that the populations are actually* _____ .

5-25 *If the obtained results have a* low *probability when the null hypothesis is assumed, the investigator is likely to conclude that the populations are actually* _____ .

C. Null Hypotheses in Other Examples

Our first example in this section concerns the testing of a new drug for its ability to cure schizophrenia. Suppose that a group of eight patients is selected to receive this drug; another group, matched with the drug group for length and severity of illness, is selected as a control group *which will not receive the drug. Instead of the new drug, the control group receives a "placebo," a compound (usually sugar) which is not expected to affect recovery. After some weeks, the patients of both groups are studied and psychiatrists give each patient a rating, "improved" or "not improved." The results of the experiment are* frequencies: *the number (frequency) of patients "improved" and the number "not improved" in the drug group and the number of patients "improved" and "not improved" in the control group.*

5-26 The eight observations of drug group patients are a *sample* drawn from the population of possible observations on schizophrenics. We can think of the frequency of "improvement" as analogous to the frequency of alternation in our previous example, and the frequency of "no improvement" as analogous to that of _____ .

5-27   According to the null hypothesis, the population of observations from which the drug group sample was drawn is _____ from the population from which the control group sample was drawn. The true frequency of improvement in both populations should be _____ according to the null hypothesis, and any observed difference in frequency is due merely to sampling variability.

5-28   It is important to be clear about the identity of these two populations, which, according to the null hypothesis, are not different in frequency of improvement. One population is the entire population of possible observations of schizophrenics after receiving the new drug. The other population is that of possible observations of schizophrenics who have _____ and who have received no other specific treatment.

5-29   The null hypothesis amounts to the assumption that the drug has made *no difference* in a patient's chance of improvement. If the drug has made no difference, then both sets of observations should belong to the _____ ; the two populations are in reality not different from each other.

5-30   If a difference in frequency of "improved" ratings is found between the two samples, this difference may or may not be a _____ difference. A small difference in frequency could arise between samples which are drawn from the same population simply because of _____ .

5-31   If the difference in frequency is large enough, however, it will be necessary to conclude that the two samples probably did not come from the same population. In such a case, one can conclude that the _____ hypothesis is not the best hypothesis to fit the facts. The null hypothesis is then said to be REJECTED.

5-32   In Lesson 1B, we considered whether there might be differences in ease of French vocabulary learning at morning and evening hours, and we proposed that an investigator could have morning and evening groups study the same material. His observations would be "average number of repetitions for mastery." According to the null hypothesis, there should be _____ between the _____ from which the two sets of observations are drawn. Rates of learning in the morning and in the evening should be _____ if the null hypothesis is correct.

equal

5-33 If the observations do come from the same population, then there may be some differences between the two samples, but these differences will be _____ in size and can be attributed to _____ .

small
sampling variability

5-34 If the differences are very large, then the conclusion will be that the samples did not come from the same population and the null hypothesis can be _____ .

rejected

5-35 Again, be sure that you are clear about the two populations which are supposed equal according to the null hypothesis. Certainly these are not populations of *persons;* the morning and evening groups do not include the same _____ , learning the same material twice, so there could be no question as to whether the same individuals are in both groups.

persons

5-36 The populations are populations of possible _____ about number of repetitions for mastery of the material given. One population is the population of all possible such observations made when learning occurs _____ ; the other, the population of possible observations when learning occurs _____ .

observations

in the morning ↔
in the evening

Review

5-37 *A difference which is so large that it would rarely occur because of sampling variability alone is called a _____ difference. It signifies that the samples probably were drawn from _____ .*

significant
different populations

5-38 *The populations referred to in the null hypothesis are the populations which include _____ observations of the kind (or kinds) actually made.*

all possible

5-39 *When the difference between the samples is significant, we conclude that the populations _____ and that the null hypothesis can be _____ .*

are different (are
 not the same)
rejected

D. The Alternate Hypothesis

5-40   The procedure involved in deciding whether to reject a null hypothesis is called TESTING the null hypothesis. When someone sets up the hypothesis that his observations were drawn from a particular population and then calculates the probability of getting such results from that population, he is _____ the null hypothesis.

testing

5-41   However, an experimenter usually has in mind another hypothesis as well, the ALTERNATE HYPOTHESIS, which he intends to *accept* if the null hypothesis can be rejected. The investigator interested in alternation behavior holds the hypothesis "Rats will show alternation behavior more frequently than repetition" as his _____ hypothesis.

alternate

5-42   Another investigator might favor the hypothesis "Rats will make repetition choices more frequently than alternation." This hypothesis would also be an _____ , which could be accepted only if the _____ were rejected.

alternate hypothesis
null hypothesis

5-43   Some investigators would prefer a more cautious alternate hypothesis than either of these. They might take the hypothesis "Rats will make systematic choices that are either predominantly alternation or predominantly repetition; their behavior will *not* prove to be nonsystematic." This hypothesis is also an alternate hypothesis, to be accepted only if it is possible to reject the hypothesis "These observations are _____ from what would be expected if the rats' behavior is nonsystematic."

not different

5-44   In testing the null hypothesis, one counts on finding that his results are too *extreme* to occur frequently if the hypothesis is true. The further the results deviate from what is expected according to the null hypothesis, the more likely they are to be _____ .

significant

5-45   In making his claim, the experimenter reasons like this: "Small variations from what is expected will occur often because of sampling variability. But my results are *way out*. Results as extreme as these do not occur very _____ in populations like the one assumed under the null hypothesis. They would be _____ common in populations like the one assumed under the alternate hypothesis."

often
more

5-46   Notice the phrase "extreme as these" in frame 5-45. The experimenter is arguing his case on the basis of the *infrequency* of such extreme results, and he must not forget that *even more extreme results* are expected to occur once in a very great while. In order to say just how infrequently such an extreme result occurs, he must state the expected frequency of results at least as extreme as his own results *and* even _____ extreme.

5-47 This point will be clearer in the following example. Suppose that an experimenter has the alternate hypothesis "Rats will show more alternation behavior." He obtains eight alternations in nine observations. He must calculate the probability of getting eight alternations and one repetition from nonsystematic rats. But he must also consider the probability of getting a *more extreme result*, namely, _____ alternations.

5-48 All the possible cases of *at least as many* alternations must be included if he is to say, "Such extreme numbers of alternations are truly _____ in the sort of population assumed under the null hypothesis."

5-49 This experimenter, however, does *not* have to think about the equally rare outcomes, eight or nine repetitions. These outcomes would be even more unlikely under his _____ hypothesis than under the null hypothesis. He is interested only in the probability of extreme results in one direction—the direction stated in his ===============.

5-50 On the other hand, an investigator with the alternate hypothesis "Rats are systematic in one direction or the other (but I don't care which)" can reject the null hypothesis when the observed results involve either large numbers of _____ or large numbers of _____. He will be just as interested in knowing the expected frequency of "at least eight repetitions" as in knowing the expected frequency of "at least eight alternations," for either one would fit his _____.

5-51 Whether the experimenter will include the repetition extreme in his calculations depends, therefore, upon the nature of his *alternate hypothesis*. If extreme results *in either direction* would make his alternate hypothesis more plausible than the null hypothesis, then he will calculate the probability of getting results at least as _____ as his results in _____ direction.

5-52 Suppose that such an experimenter observes eight alternations in a nine-rat experiment. He must calculate the probability of getting eight or nine _____ or _____ in order to determine whether he may reject the null hypothesis. If the probability is sufficiently low, he may reject the null hypothesis and accept his _____ .

alternations —
repetitions

alternate hypothesis

5-53   But the experimenter with the alternate hypothesis "Rats will give more alternations" must consider only the probability of getting _____ . Results at the opposite extreme would not enable him to accept his _____ , and they are therefore irrelevant to his test of the _____ .

8 or 9 alternations
alternate hypothesis
null hypothesis

Review

5-54   *Testing the null hypothesis involves calculating the probability of getting a result at least as _____ as the obtained result if the null hypothesis is correct.*

extreme

5-55   *If the alternate hypothesis does not specify the direction in which difference is expected to occur, then the test of the null hypothesis requires consideration of extreme results in _____ direction.*

either

5-56   *If the alternate hypothesis does specify a direction in which difference is expected to occur, then the test of the null hypothesis requires consideration of extreme results in _____ direction.*

one (that)

E.   Levels of Significance

As yet, nothing has been said as to just how infrequent an event must be in order to be considered rare. Now we will take up the question, "How low a probability is required if one is to be justified in rejecting the null hypothesis?" In order to answer this question, we shall take a few probabilities as examples. Let us assume that the alternate hypothesis, *in each of the following cases, is the hypothesis "The behavior is not nonsystematic." Since this alternate hypothesis does not specify the direction in which systematic differences are expected to occur, we shall have to consider extreme results in* both *directions in testing the null hypothesis. That is, we shall examine the probability of obtaining either a large number of alternations or a large number of repetitions.*

5-57   If the behavior is nonsystematic, the probability of obtaining 10 alternations in 10 observations is 1/1,024. The probability of obtaining 10 repetitions is also 1/1,024. The probability of obtaining *either* 10 alternations or 10 repetitions is the *sum* of these two probabilities, or _____. Such an extreme result would occur with non-systematic rats about once in _____ replications of this 10-rat experiment.

5-58   The probability of a result as extreme as 9 alternations in a 10-rat experiment includes the four probabilities, the probabilities of getting _____ or _____ _____ or _____. The probability is 22/1,024. This result would occur with nonsystematic rats about _____ times in 100 such experiments. Such a result would generally be thought rare enough to permit rejection of the null hypothesis.

5-59   The probability of as extreme a result as eight alternations in a 10-rat experiment is 112/1,024, or about _____ times in 100 such experiments. This is not a very rare outcome, and it would generally *not* be thought rare enough to justify rejecting the null hypothesis.

5-60   It is conventional to reject the null hypothesis *only* if a result at least as extreme as the observed result would occur *no more than five times in 100 experiments as a result of sampling variability*. There-fore, the null hypothesis is generally _____ if the proba-bility of the observed result or a result just as extreme is 5/100 or less. The null hypothesis is not rejected if the probability of such an extreme result is _____ than 5/100.

5-61   The probability 5/100 can also be written 0.05, and it is often spoken of as the .05 LEVEL OF SIGNIFICANCE. The probability of getting a result as extreme as nine alternations in 10 observations is 22/1,024; this probability is _____ than 0.05.

5-62   Nine alternations in a 10-rat experiment is therefore a result which is *significant beyond the .05 level*. A result is significant _____ the .05 level when its probability, according to the null hypothesis, is less than 0.05, as it is in this case.

5-63   The probability of a result as extreme as eight alternations is 112/1,024. This probability is _____ than 0.05. Eight alternations is an event which is *not* significant at the .05 _____.

5-64 Higher levels of significance are also frequently mentioned. The level of significance is *higher* when the result is *more* significant. A *more* significant result has a _____ probability of occurring under the null hypothesis than a less significant one.

lower

5-65 Therefore, the .02 level of significance is a _____ level of significance than the .05 level. This manner of speaking will be confusing at first, because the number 0.02 is a lower number than the number 0.05.

higher

5-66 In speaking of levels of significance, a lower number means a _____ significance level because the lower number means that the event has a _____ probability of occurring under the null hypothesis. Events with a lower probability are significant at a _____ level of significance.

higher
lower

higher

5-67 The probability of a result as extreme as nine alternations in 10 observations is slightly less than 0.02. Nine alternations is _____ *at* the .02 level.

significant

5-68 The probability of a result as extreme as 10 alternations in a 10-rat experiment is about 0.002. Ten alternations is therefore a result which is significant *beyond* the .02 level. It is also significant _____ the .01 level. It is significant _____ about the .002 level.

beyond — at

5-69 The selection of the _____ level as the conventional level for rejecting the null hypothesis is purely arbitrary. Sometimes one is willing to accept lower levels of significance (for example, between .05 and .10), and sometimes one is not satisfied without still higher levels. This conventional level merely provides a kind of average standard to go by.

.05

5-70 A level of significance between .05 and .10 is a _____ level than the .05 level. On the basis of such a level, experimenters often conclude that there is some *likelihood* of significance but that more investigation is needed to make quite sure.

lower

5-71 If an experimenter obtains a result that is quite surprising, a higher level of significance is often demanded. Experimenters working with extrasensory perception, for example, seek to provide evidence that subjects can detect events in another place which they cannot possibly experience through normal sensory channels. They must demonstrate that the subjects' responses are *different* from responses drawn from a population of pure guesses. Because people are skeptical about the claim that extrasensory perception exists, a _____ level of significance is commonly required.

higher

Review

5-72 *The conventional definition of a "rare" event is "an event which has a probability not greater than _____." Such an event would occur by chance no more often than _____ times in 100 experiments, and such an event is said to be _____ at the _____.*

0.05
five
significant
.05 level

5-73 *When the probability of an event is* lower *than 0.05, the event is said to be significant _____ the .05 level. Such an event is _____ significant than an event which has a probability of 0.05. An event with a probability of 0.01 is significant at a _____ level of significance than an event with a probability of 0.05.*

beyond
more
higher

F. Type I and Type II Errors

5-74 An event with a probability of 0.05 is actually *expected* to occur, on the average, 5 times in every _____ times the same experiment is performed *even if the null hypothesis is correct.*

100

5-75 When an experimenter does only *one* such experiment, he has no way of knowing for sure whether his experiment may, indeed, be one of the _____ experiments in 100 which are expected to have such an extreme result.

5

5-76 Since there are only 5 such experiments in every 100 experiments of the same kind, the probability is only _____ that he has in fact stumbled upon one of these odd five cases. If the experimenter were to do 20 experiments of the same kind, he might expect to have _____ of the 20 turn out to be significant at the .05 level even if the null hypothesis is correct.

0.05

1

5-77 The probability 0.05 is therefore the probability that the experimenter will make a certain kind of error: *the error of rejecting the null hypothesis when it is actually true.* In rejecting at the .05 level, the experimenter is taking a certain risk. Every time he tests a null hypothesis which is actually *true,* the probability of his making a mistake and *rejecting* that hypothesis is _____ .

5-78　If an experimenter performs a great many experiments and *always* rejects the null hypothesis when results are significant at the .05 level, he can never be sure on statistical grounds that he is not making this kind of error in at least some decisions. Suppose that he tests 100 null hypotheses, all of which are *true;* the probability is that in _____ of the 100 cases, the obtained difference will be sufficiently large for him to reject the null hypothesis. He cannot be *sure* he is not making such an error unless he has independent grounds for believing that the null hypothesis is actually false.

> An experimenter's decision to reject the null hypothesis at the .05 level is seldom challenged in practice, unless the alternate hypothesis is thought to be less plausible than the null hypothesis. But in such doubtful cases, it *may* be challenged. A critic can argue that the case in question was indeed one of the five cases in 100 in which sampling variability alone can produce a large difference.

5-79　If the experimenter is anxious to avoid this kind of error, he may decide to be very cautious and to reject the null hypothesis *only* when he obtains a result that is significant at the .01 level. In this way, he will decrease the risk of making the error of _____ the null hypothesis when it is actually _____ . If he applies this new rule of action, then every time he tests a null hypothesis which is actually true the probability of his making a mistake and rejecting that hypothesis is only _____ .

5-80　But in doing this, the experimenter will *increase* another kind of risk: the risk of ACCEPTING *the null hypothesis when it is actually false!* Results which are significant at the .05 level may indeed arise under the null hypothesis but more rarely, perhaps, than under some alternate hypothesis. The alternate hypothesis may really be true when the experimenter obtains a result significant at the .05 level, but if he rejects *only* when the result is significant at the .01 level, he will _____ the null hypothesis in such a case. This is another kind of error.

5-81　An experimenter in testing a null hypothesis therefore always takes some risk. He runs the risk of possibly rejecting the null hypothesis when it is actually _____ and the risk of possibly accepting the null hypothesis when it is actually _____ .

5-82　These two kinds of error are important enough that they have been given different names. They are called, respectively, TYPE I and

TYPE II ERRORS. The key words in describing these errors are REJECTING and ACCEPTING. Try to associate the word "rejecting" with Type I and the word "accepting" with Type II. Make up for yourself a rule for remembering this association, such as "1 comes before 2, but R for rejecting comes *after* A for accepting." When you have your rule clearly in mind, fill in the blanks below:

Type I error: _____ the null hypothesis when it is
_____ .

Type II error: _____ the null hypothesis when it is
_____ .

rejecting
true
accepting
false

5-83 In order to decrease the risk of a Type I error, the experimenter may decide to reject the null hypothesis only at a _____ level of significance.

higher

5-84 When he decides to use a higher significance level, however, the experimenter increases his risk of a Type _____ error.

II

5-85 To decrease the risk of a Type II error, the experimenter would have to decide to reject the null hypothesis when the probability of his obtained result, under the null hypothesis, is _____ .

higher

Review

5-86 *In order to determine whether his experimental results are significant, an experimenter sets up two hypotheses: a _____ hypothesis, which states that there is _____ between his results and those expected or observed in some other population of observations, and an _____ hypothesis, representing what he believes may possibly be true.*

null
no difference

alternate

5-87 *His alternate hypothesis may or may not specify the _____ in which the difference is expected to occur.*

direction

5-88 *He must calculate the _____ of obtaining his results or some result at least as _____ on the assumption that the _____ hypothesis is correct.*

probability
extreme
null

5-89 *Whether he will include a consideration of extreme results in* both *directions or in only* one *depends upon the nature of his _____ hypothesis. He includes both directions only when that hypothesis _____ (specifies, does not specify) the direction in which the difference is expected to occur.*

alternate

does not specify

5-90 If the probability he calculates is as low as 5/100, he will reject the
_____ and accept his _____, provided he is using
the conventionally accepted level of _____ .

null hypothesis —
  alternate hypothesis
significance

5-91 In doing this, he knows that he may make errors of Type
_____ as many as 5 times in every 100 times he follows such
a rule.

I

5-92 In order to avoid making many errors of this type, he may decide to
use a _____ level of significance, that is, to require that the
probability be _____ than 0.05 before he will reject the null
hypothesis.

higher
less

5-93 Choosing a higher level of significance than .05 will, indeed, decrease the risk of making errors of Type _____, but unfor-
tunately it will at the same time increase the risk of making errors of
Type _____ .

I

II

Problems for Lesson 5

5-1   A college has 500 women students and 1,000 men students. The introductory zoology course has 90 students, of whom 50 are women. Suspecting that women tend to elect zoology more frequently than men do, you decide to test your hypothesis statistically with the observations from this class.

(a)   What is the null hypothesis you should use in making this test?

(b)   What is the expected number of women in a class of 90 on the basis of this null hypothesis?

(c)   If the null hypothesis is true, how would one account for the difference between the observed frequency and the expected frequency?

(d)   What is your alternate hypothesis?

(e)   What probability must you calculate in order to test the null hypothesis?

(f)   Under what circumstances can you accept your alternate hypothesis?

5-2   A friend of yours claims that he can tell the difference between instant coffee and "real" coffee. To test his claim, you arrange 10 samples, 5 of instant and 5 of "real" coffee, and ask him to tell which kind of coffee is in each of the 10 cups.

(a)   What is your null hypothesis?

(b)   What are the three possible alternate hypotheses? Do not overlook the possibility that your friend *can* tell a difference between the two kinds of coffee but thinks that the instant is the "real" coffee and therefore gives the samples the wrong names.

(c)   Suppose your friend is right eight out of ten times. What is the probability of getting a result *as extreme as this* on each of the three alternate hypotheses? (You must find three probabilities.) Can any one of the three alternate hypotheses be accepted at the .05 level?

(d)   When you use the conventional .05 level of significance, which of the alternate hypotheses will give you, in this case, the greatest amount of worry lest you commit a Type I error?

5-3   An experimenter tested for differences in attitudes toward smoking before and after a film on lung cancer was shown. He found a difference which was significant between the .05 and .02 levels.

(a)   What is the null hypothesis?

(b)   Which level of significance indicates the *greater* degree of significance—.05 or .02?

(c)   If he employs the .05 level in drawing his conclusion, will he reject the null hypothesis? Will he reject it if he employs the .02 level? In choosing the .02 level *instead of* the .05 level, he *increases* the risk of making one of the two types of error. Which type?

Lesson 6. Frequency Distributions

It is customary to begin the study of statistics with a discussion of frequency distributions. The very word "statistics" suggests to most of us a confusing mass of numbers; getting numbers into the form of a frequency distribution is the first step toward simplifying them into a manageable form. We have been able to get along until now without the use of frequency distributions because we have discussed the basic ideas of statistical inference in connection with very simple groups of numbers. However, from this point on we shall need better methods of description in order to handle larger groups of numbers conveniently.

Because some students may prefer to begin in the more usual way with frequency distributions before studying Lessons 1 through 5, this lesson has been written in such a way that it does not depend upon concepts covered in the earlier lessons. Occasional references may be made to terms or examples used in earlier lessons, but these references are included only to provide continuity for students who have studied those lessons first. Understanding of Lesson 6 does not depend upon any of the terms referred to in this way.

A. Kinds of Variables

6-1 Any characteristic of persons or things which can assume different values is called a VARIABLE. A person's driver's license states the particular values which several important _____ assume in his individual case: height, weight, eye color, sex, birth date, and the like.

variables

6-2 Some of these variables assume _____ which can be stated in *numbers*. This is true of three of the five variables given as examples: _____, _____, and _____.

values

height ↔ weight ↔ birth date

6-3 The _____ which the other _____ assume cannot be put into numbers. They are designated by *names*, such as "blue," "brown," or "hazel" and "male" or "female."

values — variables

6-4   When a variable assumes values that can be designated only by *names*, we shall call its values NOMINAL values. (The Latin word for "name" is *nomen*.) Eye color and sex are variables which assume _____ values.

6-5   The other variables given as examples all assume *numerical* values, and furthermore, all of them can be stated in the units of a measuring system or scale. In the case of height, these _____ are inches and they represent *equal intervals* along the scale of height or length.

6-6   Some kinds of numerical values do not possess such a scale of equal _____. Take, for example, the variable "rank in graduating class," a fact which colleges often require on admissions applications. This variable has values which are stated in numbers, and the values are therefore _____ rather than nominal values.

6-7   But the values for this variable do not possess an equal interval scale. It would not usually be correct to say that the difference in academic achievement between the students with ranks 1 and 11 is the same size as the difference between students with ranks 41 and 51. Although the numerical difference in rank is the same, these two intervals are not _____ to each other in most cases; they do not represent _____ differences in academic achievement.

6-8   Many variables in psychology and education are ranked variables, that is, variables whose values are numbered according to a serial or *ordinal position*. It will be convenient to give them the special name ORDINAL values. Variables with ordinal values occupy an intermediate position between variables with nonnumerical or _____ values on the one hand and variables with _____ values which have an equal interval scale on the other.

6-9   Variables of these three different sorts require different kinds of statistical treatment. It is therefore important to be able to tell which kind of variable one is dealing with. If we give the name INTERVAL values to values of the equal interval kind, the three sorts of variables are variables with _____, _____, and _____ values.

6-10   If a person arranges a series of colors in order of preference, from most preferred to least preferred, the "preference" value for each color can be expressed in numbers which are _____ values.

ordinal

6-11 IQ is commonly described in numbers on a scale which has equal intervals. Therefore, IQ is a variable with _____ values.

interval

6-12 Following a new drug treatment, schizophrenic patients might be classified as either "improved" or "not improved." The effect of the drug is a variable which assumes _____ values in such a case.

nominal

6-13 *Characteristics of persons or things which can assume different _____ are called _____.*

values — variables

6-14 *Certain variables assume only nonnumerical or _____ values. Variables with numerical values may be of two sorts: When the values can be arranged in an equal interval scale, they are _____ values, and when they can be arranged only according to serial position, they are _____ values.*

nominal

interval

ordinal

B. Classes of a Variable, Frequencies, and Frequency Distributions

6-15 Each value of a variable that is obtained in an investigation will be called an OBSERVATION. Suppose that the arithmetic test scores of 1,000 third-graders were obtained and that the scores were whole numbers between 60 and 100 on an equal interval scale. There would be a total of _____ observations, each of which is an _____ value of the variable "arithmetic score."

1,000
interval

6-16 Since there are 1,000 observations but only 41 whole numbers between 60 and 100, it is certain that some of the 1,000 observations are *identical*. Certain scores must have been made by more than _____ child.

one

6-17 All the scores which are identical can be grouped together into one category or CLASS. The score 61 would thus constitute one class, the score 62 another, and so on up to the score 100. There would be 41 such _____ in the example given.

classes

6-18 The number of scores in any particular _____ is the FREQUENCY of that _____. If there are 10 scores of 100, then the _____ of 100 would have a frequency of _____.

class
class
class
10

6-19 Suppose that there are 10 scores of 100, 12 scores of 99, 13 scores of 98, and so on. The class of 100 has a _____ of 10, the class of 99 has a _____ of _____, the class of 98 has a _____ of _____.

frequency
frequency — 12
frequency — 13

Table 6-1   **A Sequence of 80 Draws from an Urn, Recorded as *B* or *W* in the Order of Drawing**

B	W	B	B	B	W	W	B	W	B
W	W	W	W	W	W	B	W	B	B
B	W	B	W	W	B	B	B	W	W
B	B	W	B	B	B	B	B	B	W
W	W	B	W	B	W	W	B	B	B
B	W	W	W	B	W	B	B	B	B
B	W	W	B	B	B	W	B	B	W
B	B	W	B	B	B	W	W	W	B

6-20 Variables which do not have interval values can be treated in this same way. In the example shown in Table 6-1, 80 balls were placed in an urn. Some balls were white, and some were black. The balls were withdrawn one at a time from the urn until all 80 balls had been drawn, and as each ball was taken from the urn, it was recorded as *W* or *B* in the table. In this example, the variable is "color," and the two categories *W* and *B* are _____ values of the variable.

nominal

6-21 Each draw from the urn constitutes a single _____ of the variable. When the results are recorded in order, as in Table 6-1, it is difficult to tell at a glance which of the two _____ has the greatest _____.

observation

values
frequency

6-22 Determine the frequency of *W* in Table 6-1 by counting. The frequency of *W* is _____. Since there are 80 observations in all, the frequency of *B* is _____. These 80 observations are now in a more manageable form, since they are stated in just two numbers.

35
45

6-23   In this case, we can treat each of the two values as a *class*. Complete the following table:

Class	Frequency (*f*)
W	_____
B	_____

6-24   This table is called a FREQUENCY DISTRIBUTION. It shows the _____ of the 80 observations between the two _____ of the variable. Note that the sum of all the frequencies equals the total number of observations.

6-25   The total number of observations will be symbolized by the letter N (for number). The sum of the _____ of all the _____ of the variable will always equal _____ .

Review

6-26   *A frequency distribution is a table which shows all the _____ into which the values of a variable have been classified and shows the _____ for each of these _____ .*

6-27   *When we have enumerated the frequencies of all the classes of a variable, we have described a _____ for the observations we have made.*

C.   The Class Interval

6-28   Some variables are called DISCRETE variables because they can assume only certain clearly separated values. The "number of persons in a group" is a discrete variable; there may be 2, 3, 4, or more individuals, but never 3½ persons. The number of children in a family is also a _____ variable.

6-29   Scores on the arithmetic test in Section B were assumed to be whole numbers. Since no scores were fractions, "arithmetic score" was a _____ .

Margin answers:

35
45

distribution — classes

frequencies
classes — N

classes
frequency — classes

frequency distribution

discrete

discrete variable

Table 6-2 **Heights of 295 Adult American Males Measured to the Nearest Inch**

Class	Midpoints of Intervals	Frequencies (f)
79.5–80.49	80	1
78.5–79.49	79	2
77.5–78.49	78	1
76.5–77.49	77	3
75.5–76.49	76	6
74.5–75.49	75	12
73.5–74.49	74	21
72.5–73.49	73	25
71.5–72.49	72	30
70.5–71.49	71	44
69.5–70.49	70	55
68.5–69.49	69	33
67.5–68.49	68	26
66.5–67.49	67	15
65.5–66.49	66	11
64.5–65.49	65	5
63.5–64.49	64	1
62.5–63.49	63	2
61.5–62.49	62	1
60.5–61.49	61	1
		$N = 295$

6-30   Table 6-2 is a _____ of heights of 295 adult males, measured to the nearest inch. Height is *not* a discrete variable, for it can take on any value including fractions of an inch. Such a variable is called a CONTINUOUS variable. Weight can take on all values including fractions of pounds; weight is a _____ variable.

frequency distribution

continuous

6-31   Variables with *nominal* and *ordinal* values, such as sex and rank in an academic class, are always _____ variables because they can assume only certain clearly separated values. Such variables can never be _____ variables.

discrete

continuous

6-32   Notice, however, that Table 6-2 has treated the variable "height" *as if* it were a discrete variable by stating heights measured to the nearest _____ . A man who actually measured 70.3 inches would be classified in this table as if he measured _____

inch
70

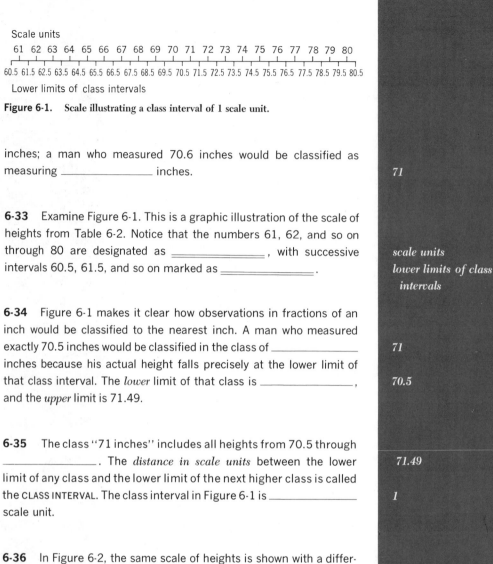

Scale units

```
61  62  63  64  65  66  67  68  69  70  71  72  73  74  75  76  77  78  79  80
```
60.5 61.5 62.5 63.5 64.5 65.5 66.5 67.5 68.5 69.5 70.5 71.5 72.5 73.5 74.5 75.5 76.5 77.5 78.5 79.5 80.5

Lower limits of class intervals

Figure 6-1.   Scale illustrating a class interval of 1 scale unit.

inches; a man who measured 70.6 inches would be classified as measuring _____ inches.

71

6-33   Examine Figure 6-1. This is a graphic illustration of the scale of heights from Table 6-2. Notice that the numbers 61, 62, and so on through 80 are designated as _____, with successive intervals 60.5, 61.5, and so on marked as _____ .

scale units
lower limits of class
intervals

6-34   Figure 6-1 makes it clear how observations in fractions of an inch would be classified to the nearest inch. A man who measured exactly 70.5 inches would be classified in the class of _____ inches because his actual height falls precisely at the lower limit of that class interval. The *lower* limit of that class is _____ , and the *upper* limit is 71.49.

71

70.5

6-35   The class "71 inches" includes all heights from 70.5 through _____ . The *distance in scale units* between the lower limit of any class and the lower limit of the next higher class is called the CLASS INTERVAL. The class interval in Figure 6-1 is _____ scale unit.

71.49

1

6-36   In Figure 6-2, the same scale of heights is shown with a different class interval. The class interval in Figure 6-2 is equal to _____ , and a man whose height is 70.5 inches will be classified together with all men whose heights are not less than _____ inches nor greater than _____ inches.

2

70.5 — 72.49

Scale units

```
61  62  63  64  65  66  67  68  69  70  71  72  73  74  75  76  77  78  79  80
```
60.5   62.5   64.5   66.5   68.5   70.5   72.5   74.5   76.5   78.5   80.5

Lower limits of class intervals

Figure 6-2.   Scale illustrating a class interval of 2 scale units.

Table 6-3   **Heights of 295 Adult American Males Measured to the Nearest Inch**

Exact Limits of Intervals	Midpoints of Intervals	Frequencies (f)
78.5–80.49	79.5	3
76.5–78.49	77.5	4
74.5–76.49	75.5	18
72.5–74.49	73.5	46
70.5–72.49	71.5	74
68.5–70.49	69.5	88
66.5–68.49	67.5	41
64.5–66.49	65.5	16
62.5–64.49	63.5	3
60.5–62.49	61.5	2
		$N = 295$

6-37   Table 6-3 is a frequency distribution for the height observations from Table 6-2, but with the new class interval of 2. Notice that the frequency of the class 60.5–62.49 is equal to the *sum* of the frequencies (in Table 6-2) of the classes 60.5–61.49 and 61.5–62.49. Instead of designating this class in Table 6-3 as "60.5–62.49" we could also designate it by the MIDPOINT of the interval 60.5 to 62.5, which is

_____ .   *61.5*

Scale units

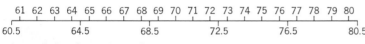

Lower limits of class intervals

Figure 6-3.   Scale illustrating a class interval of 4 scale units.

6-38   It is possible, of course, to use a class interval of any size we want. Figure 6-3 shows how the scale would appear if the class interval were increased to _____ units. In this case, any height falling   *4*
within the range 60.5 to 64.49 inches would be counted as a frequency in the class whose midpoint is _____ inches.   *62.5*

6-39   Whenever observations have been grouped into a frequency distribution, all the observations within a particular class are considered as *having the value of the midpoint of the class interval.* Thus, in Table 6-3, all the 46 observations in the class 72.5–74.49 have the value _____ , which is the value of the _____   *73.5 — midpoint*
of the class interval 72.5 to 74.5.

6-40 *Large numbers of observations can be simplified by constructing a frequency distribution and expressing the entire set of observations as _____ falling within separate _____ .*

frequencies — classes

6-41 *Nominal and ordinal observations always fall into discrete classes. But interval observations, such as heights, may involve variables which are _____ rather than discrete.*

continuous

6-42 *Observations of continuous variables can be simplified by defining precise _____ for the class and then treating all the observations which fall within these _____ as if they had the value of the _____ of the class _____ .*

limits
limits
midpoint — interval

D. Graphical Methods of Describing Frequency Distributions

6-43 Table 6-4 is a frequency distribution of test scores. This distribution has a class interval of _____ unit(s). Each score, 1 to 9, is the midpoint of a class interval, and the limits of the class intervals lie at 0.5, 1.5, and so on. The score of 5 is the midpoint of an interval whose lower limit is _____ and whose upper limit is _____ .

1

4.5
5.5

Table 6-4 **Frequency Distribution of Test Scores**

Score	f
9	1
8	2
7	4
6	8
5	10
4	8
3	4
2	2
1	1
	N = 40

6-44   Figure 6-4 is a graph of the frequency distribution in Table 6-4. Let us call the vertical axis the Y *axis* and the horizontal axis the X *axis*, according to conventional usage. The scores from Table 6-4 have been laid out along the _____ axis, and the frequencies are placed along the _____ axis.

X

Y

6-45   This kind of graph is called a HISTOGRAM, in which the frequencies are represented in the form of vertical bars. The width of each bar is equal to the size of the _____. The height of each bar is equal to the _____ of that class.

class interval

frequency

6-46   The width of a bar in a _____ will always equal one class interval, and the height of a bar will equal the frequency. Area equals width times height; therefore, the area of a bar equals one times the _____ of the class. Thus the area of a bar, as well as its height, represents the _____ of its _____.

histogram

frequency

frequency — class

6-47   In Figure 6-4, the tallest bar represents the frequency of the score _____. Its height is _____ units; therefore this score has a _____ equal to _____. Since the bar has a width of one class interval, its area is _____ units, and this area is also equal to the _____ of that score.

5 — 10

frequency — 10

10

frequency

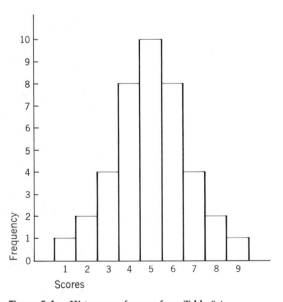

Figure 6-4.   Histogram of scores from Table 6-4.

6-48 In Figure 6-4, the score 6 occurs with a frequency of
_____, and the bar representing this frequency has an
area of _____ units (where the unit is a class interval
wide and 1 frequency unit high). Both the _____ and the
_____ of the bar can be considered to represent the frequency of the score 6.

6-49 The total frequency N for the distribution of Figure 6-4 and
Table 6-4 is _____. The total area of all the bars added
together is _____ units.

6-50 The total area in any histogram is equal to the sum of the
_____ of all the bars, and this total area is equal to the
quantity _____, or total _____.

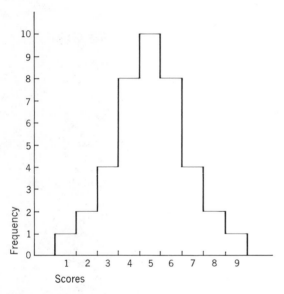

Figure 6-5. Histogram with vertical boundaries removed.

6-51 Figure 6-5 is the same histogram shown in Figure 6-4, but the
vertical boundary lines between the bars have been removed. What is
the total area of Figure 6-5? It is _____ units. Simply re-
moving the boundary lines between the bars has not changed the
total area in the histogram.

6-52 Figure 6-6 is a different kind of graph for the same distribution
shown in Figures 6-2 and 6-3. The X axis and the Y axis are unchanged,
but in Figure 6-6 the _____ of each _____ is shown

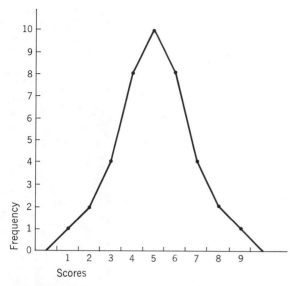

Figure 6-6. Frequency polygon of scores from Table 6-4.

by a *dot placed directly over the midpoint of the class interval.* Since the frequencies of scores 0 and 10 are equal to zero, points have also been included for these midpoints so that the graph reaches zero on each side.

6-53 Figure 6-6 is a FREQUENCY POLYGON. Straight lines have been drawn between the dots, making the set of frequencies clearly visible. Each dot has been placed directly over the _____ of its ════════════ .

midpoint
class interval

6-54 A polygon is a figure with many sides. The graph in Figure 6-6 is called a _____ polygon because its many sides (it has 8) give a picture of the _____ in a frequency distribution.

frequency
frequencies

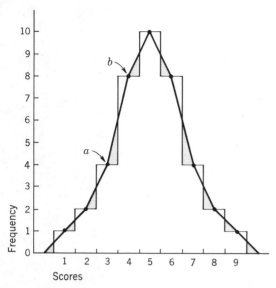

Figure 6-7. Frequency polygon superimposed on histogram.

6-55 Figure 6-7 is really a composite graph which contains both Figures 6-5 and 6-6. The frequency polygon has been superimposed on the histogram. The dots of the _____ appear exactly in the *middle* of the bar tops of the _____ because these points are the _____ of the _____ .

6-56 In Figure 6-7, as the lines of the polygon pass from midpoint to midpoint, they cut across the outer boundaries of the histogram, *forming pairs of identical triangles.* One such pair of triangles lies between the points marked *a* and *b* in Figure 6-7; one member of the pair is shaded, the other is unshaded. Since the two members of each pair are *identical triangles,* the area of the shaded triangle is _____ the area of the unshaded triangle.

6-57 Since, for each pair of triangles, the area of the shaded triangle is equal to the area of the unshaded triangle, the sum of the areas of all the *shaded* triangles is _____ the sum of the areas of all the *unshaded* triangles.

6-58 Now notice that, as the frequency polygon passes over the histogram, it cuts off the outer, unshaded triangle and leaves it outside. Each unshaded triangle is an area which falls *inside* the _____ but *outside* the _____ .

6-59 At the same time, however, the frequency polygon takes in the inner, shaded triangles. Each shaded triangle is an area which falls *inside* the _____ but outside the _____ .

6-60 Thus, the _____ triangles lie inside the polygon and outside the histogram, while the _____ triangles lie outside the polygon and inside the histogram. Since the total area of the shaded triangles is equal to the total area of the unshaded triangles, the total area under the polygon equals the total area in the

_____ .

6-61 In Figure 6-7, the areas in the histogram and under the frequency polygon are exactly equal. Since the area in the histogram is equal to _____ , the area under the polygon is also equal to _____ .

Review

6-62 *Two ways of graphing frequency distributions have been illustrated. In one kind of graph, bars are drawn whose width exactly corresponds to one _____ and whose height exactly corresponds to the _____ of that _____ . Such a graph is a _____ .*

6-63 *In the other kind of graph, a dot is placed directly over the _____ of each _____ at a height which corresponds to the _____ of that class. Such a graph is a _____ .*

6-64 *The total area in the histogram is equal to _____ , which is the symbol for _____ . The total area under the frequency polygon is also equal to _____ .*

Problems for Lesson 6

6-1 Classify the following variables according to the type of scale (nominal, ordinal, or interval) appropriate to the measurement of each:

(a) The numerals on the jerseys of a football team. (Be careful!)

(b) The diagnostic categories "schizophrenia," "mania-depression," "paranoia," and "senile dementia."

(c) IQ test scores.

(d) The outcome of a horse race, in which each horse is assigned a number indicating his finishing position: first, second, third, . . . , nth.

(e) The temperature of the surface of the planet Venus as measured by the Mariner II space probe.

6-2 Classify each of the following variables as either "discrete" or "continuous":

(a) Length, measured in centimeters.

(b) The number of members in the United States Senate.

(c) Life expectancy as computed from insurance companies' actuarial tables.

(d) A baseball player's daily batting average.

(e) The numerals on basketball players' jerseys.

6-3 Suppose there is a class in a distribution of children's weights, in pounds, designated "81–90". What is **(a)** the lowest weight that can be placed in this class, **(b)** the highest weight, and **(c)** the midpoint of the class? If you were classifying weights to the nearest pound, would you classify the observation 90.5 pounds in the class 81–90 or in the next higher class? Explain.

6-4 Plot a frequency polygon and a histogram for the data in the frequency table below. (You may, if you wish, plot both figures on the same set of coordinates.)

Scores	Frequencies
95–99	2
90–94	3
85–89	9
80–84	15
75–79	28
70–74	38
65–69	45
60–64	32
55–59	20
50–54	11
45–49	6
40–44	2
35–39	1
	$N = 212$

Lesson 7.   The Chi-square Test

The chi-square test is a simple and direct test of significance. It is suitable for most cases in which the observations can be classified into discrete categories and treated as frequencies. *The chi-square test can be studied at this point in the book because it does not require the more detailed methods of describing frequency distributions which will be introduced later.*

Lesson 7 gives examples of a number of cases in which the chi-square test can be used to test a null hypothesis. The understanding of Lesson 7 depends upon Lesson 6 (Frequency Distributions) and upon the principles of significance testing covered in Lessons 1, 2, and 5.

The chi-square test is named for a mathematical quantity which is designated by the symbol χ^2. The Greek letter chi, written χ, is pronounced "kye."

A.   Observed and Expected Frequencies

Example: A new drug treatment is being tested, to determine whether it produces improvement in schizophrenic patients. From the schizophrenics in a particular hospital, 53 are selected randomly to receive the drug; 55 are selected as a control group to receive a neutral agent (such as sugar) instead of the new drug. The two groups are similar in severity and duration of illness. Following the period of drug administration, psychiatrists give each of the 108 patients a designation, "improved" or "not improved." Thus, the observations can be classified into two discrete categories and set down as frequencies in a table (Table 7-1, page 86).

7-1   Table 7-1 shows the observations classified into four categories. The four numbers inside the heavy lines represent the _____ with which observations appeared in each of the four categories.

frequencies

7-2   The frequencies in the table are the OBSERVED FREQUENCIES. The question to be decided is whether these frequencies give evidence for a significant difference between the _____ group and the _____ group in frequency of improvement.

drug ⟷ control

Table 7-1   Observed Frequencies

	Number Improved	Number Not Improved	Totals
Drug Group	45	8	53
Control Group	18	37	55
Totals	63	45	108

7-3   The *null hypothesis* in this example is the hypothesis that these two groups could have been drawn by chance from the _____ and that there is really no difference between them which could not be accounted for by _____ .

7-4   If the null hypothesis is true, we ought to find the same *proportion* of each group in the "improved" category. At even a casual glance, this hypothesis does not appear to be true; in the drug group, _____ out of the 53 patients are in the category "improved," whereas only _____ of the _____ control group patients are in this category.

7-5   If the null hypothesis is true, then both groups of observations must come from the same population. In the whole group of 108 patients, there are _____ patients who were rated improved. The proportion ⁶³⁄₁₀₈ is 58.3 per cent.

7-6   If both groups come from the same population, the percentage of improved patients in *each* group should be approximately the same as the percentage improved in the entire group. Therefore, about _____ per cent of each group should appear in the category "improved."

7-7   If the drug group contains no more than its fair share of improved patients, then _____ of its 53 observations should appear in the column "improved." The remaining _____ observations should be in the column "not improved."

7-8   Similarly, the control group should have 58.3 per cent of its observations (or 32.1) in the column _____ and the other 41.7 per cent (22.9) in the column _____ . These frequencies based on the null hypothesis are called the EXPECTED FREQUENCIES.

7-9   Notice that the *marginal totals* are taken as the starting point in computing the expected frequencies. The null hypothesis in the chi-square test is, in fact, the hypothesis that the distribution of frequencies for each *row* of the table is not significantly different from the distribution of frequencies in the _____ .

7-10   The line of argument is this: If there is really no difference between the two groups in improvement rate, then the *proportion* of patients who improve should be the _____ in both groups. The proportion of patients improved in either group should be the _____ as the proportion improved in the whole sample consisting of both groups.

7-11   Since the actual number of patients in the drug group is slightly _____ than the number in the control group, the expected *frequency* of improved patients is a little higher for the _____ group than for the _____ group. It is the _____ of improved patients which is expected to be the same in both groups, not the *frequency*.

7-12   The null hypothesis in such an example, then, is the hypothesis that the _____ of observations falling into a particular category is really the same for all groups.

7-13   The actual observations appear in the table as the _____ frequencies. The frequencies determined on the basis of the null hypothesis are called the _____ frequencies.

7-14   To test the null hypothesis, it is necessary to calculate the probability of obtaining such a large amount of difference between the _____ if the two groups really are drawn from the same population.

Review

7-15   *The chi-square test can be used when the observations can be _____ into discrete _____ and written down in a table as a set of _____ frequencies.*

7-16   *The null hypothesis to be tested is the hypothesis that the _____ of observations appearing in a particular category is the same for all the groups being compared.*

7-17   *On the null hypothesis, the _____ frequencies are* calculated from the proportions observed for all groups combined, *as shown in the* _____ *totals.*

7-18 *Testing the null hypothesis involves testing whether the* _____ *frequencies are significantly different from the* _____ *frequencies.*

B. Degrees of Freedom

7-19 In the example of Section A, there were two different groups and observations from each group were classified into _____ different categories. The resulting table had four CELLS, arranged into two columns and two rows. (The marginal totals are not counted as columns or rows.)

7-20 Such a table is called a TWO-BY-TWO TABLE (or 2 x 2 table). Similarly, a table with three rows and three columns would be a _____ table, and it would contain _____ cells.

7-21 The expected frequencies for each _____ in a two-by-two table can be calculated by multiplication. Thus, the expected frequency for "drug group, improved" can be obtained through multiplying the percentage of patients which improved in the *whole* group (drug and control) by the number of patients in the _____ group.

7-22 However, it is not necessary to perform such a multiplication in order to determine *all* the expected frequencies. Once the frequency for "drug group, improved" is found to be 30.9, the frequency for "drug group, not improved" can be obtained by subtracting 30.9 from 53, the number of patients in the _____ group.

7-23 And since the total number of patients in the category "improved" is 63, the expected frequency for the _____ representing "control group, improved" can be determined by subtracting _____ from _____ .

7-24 The last cell is "control group, not improved," and it can be filled by subtracting 32.1 ("control group, improved") from 55 (number of patients in the _____ group).

7-25 Therefore, the calculation of expected frequency based on the null hypothesis of equal proportions actually has to be carried out for only _____ cell(s) in the two-by-two table. All the other cells can be filled in by _____ from the marginal totals.

one
subtraction

7-26 It is never necessary to calculate proportions for more than one expected frequency in a two-by-two table. After one expected frequency is determined, all the others are automatically fixed. Therefore there is said to be only one DEGREE OF FREEDOM in such a table. Only one _____ is independently determined through calculation based on the null hypothesis.

expected frequency

7-27 When only one expected frequency is determined by the "equal proportions" procedure, there is only one _____ .

degree of freedom

7-28 Other examples will help to make clear the meaning of degrees of freedom. Suppose the psychiatrists had made a more detailed classification of patients into "improved," "slightly improved," and "not improved." The table of observed frequencies (Table 7-2) would contain _____ horizontal rows as before, but it would now contain _____ vertical columns. The table is not 2 x 2, but is _____ instead.

two
three
2×3 *(or* 3×2*)*

7-29 In Table 7-2, spaces for the expected frequencies have been left below the slanted lines. Since $^{26}/_{108}$, or 24.07 per cent, of all patients are in the category "improved," there should be _____ per cent of 53, or 12.76, drug group patients in the category "improved." Make a copy of Table 7-2 for use in this and later frames. Write 12.76 in the proper cell.

24.07

7-30 Now determine as many of the other five expected frequencies as you can *without applying the equal proportions hypothesis* again. In short, write in as many more as you can determine *by subtraction alone.*

*Only one more
can be found by
subtraction
alone: the ex-
pected frequency
for "control
group, improved,"
which is 13.24
(by subtracting
12.76 from 26).*

Table 7-2 **Observed and Expected Frequencies**

	Number Improved	*Number Slightly Improved*	*Number Not Improved*	*Totals*
Drug Group	20	25	8	53
Control Group	6	12	37	55
Totals	26	37	45	108

7-31 Four cells still remain to be filled, so we shall determine another expected frequency by equal proportions. Since $37/108$ of all patients, or 34.26 per cent, are in the category "slightly improved," 34.26 per cent of _____ gives the expected frequency of "drug group, slightly improved." This expected frequency is 18.16.

53

7-32 Write 18.16 in the appropriate cell, and fill as many of the remaining three cells as you can *by subtraction alone.*

All three can be filled. See Table 7-3.

7-33 Table 7-3 could not be completed until _____ of its expected frequencies were calculated by multiplication according to the null hypothesis of equal proportions. This table has *more than one* degree of freedom. The null hypothesis was required for determining _____ expected frequencies, and therefore the table has _____ degrees of freedom.

two

two
two

Table 7-3   **Observed and Expected Frequencies**

	Number Improved		Number Slightly Improved		Number Not Improved		Totals
Drug Group	20	12.76	25	18.16	8	22.08	53
Control Group	6	13.24	12	18.84	37	22.92	55
Totals	26		37		45		108

7-34 Another example will show the result with a still larger table of observed frequencies. Suppose that a test designed to measure "awareness of social science principles" is administered to the students of a college, and the frequencies of high, middle, and low scores in the four college classes are those in the 3 x 4 table shown as Table 7-4. On the null hypothesis that attendance through four years at that college does *not* make a difference in scores on this test, the proportions of high, middle, and low scorers should be the _____ for all four classes.

same

Table 7-4   **Observed Frequencies**

	Freshmen	Sophomores	Juniors	Seniors	Totals
High Scorers	60	120	200	220	600
Middle Scorers	100	180	110	110	500
Low Scorers	240	90	50	20	400
Totals	400	390	360	350	1,500

7-35 You can determine the number of degrees of freedom in this table as follows: Imagine, without actually doing the computations, that you are proceeding to calculate the expected frequencies by multiplication according to the equal proportions hypothesis. Circle each observed frequency in Table 7-4 for which you would make such a calculation, *but* do not circle any observed frequency for which you could obtain the expected frequency simply *by subtraction,* using some of the expected frequencies whose cells you have already marked by a circle. How many numbers do you have to circle? _____ . *six*
How many cells can be filled, instead, by subtraction alone? _____ . *six*

7-36 In the 3 x 4 table, therefore, you have to use the null hypothesis to determine only _____ of the three expected frequencies *two*
in any of the *columns* and only _____ of the four expected *three*
frequencies in any of the *rows.*

7-37 This observation leads to a general rule for determining the number of degrees of freedom. It is customary to let the letter k stand for the number of *columns* (k = _____ in Table 7-4) and *4*
to let r stand for the number of *rows* (r = _____ in Table *3*
7-4).

7-38 The number of expected frequencies which must be determined directly by the null hypothesis is $(k - 1) \times (r - 1)$. This quantity for Table 7-4 is _____ x _____ , which equals *3 — 2*
_____ . *6*

7-39 This rule is a general one for all tables in which both k and r are greater than 1. It is the rule for determining how many _____ *degrees*
of _____ a particular table contains. *freedom*

Review

7-40 *The number of degrees of freedom in a table is the number of _____ frequencies which must be independently determined* *expected*
by the _____ . *null hypothesis*

7-41 *In a 2 x 2 table, the number of degrees of freedom (d.f.) equals _____ . In a 3 x 2 table, d.f. = _____ ; and in a* *one — 2*
4 x 3 table, d.f. = _____ . *6*

7-42 The general rule for determining the number of degrees of freedom in a table with k columns and r rows is _____. In an 8 x 10 table, d.f. = _____.

C. Computation of Chi-square

7-43 The chi-square test is based upon the difference between the _____ and _____ frequencies. If the null hypothesis is correct, these frequencies will be almost alike for any cell.

7-44 Table 7-5 contains the observed frequencies from Table 7-1, with the expected frequencies also shown (in italics). Let the letter O represent "observed frequency" and the letter E represent "expected frequency." If the null hypothesis is correct, the difference $O - E$ for any cell will be approximately _____.

7-45 In general, as the difference $O - E$ becomes larger for each of the cells, the chance of *rejecting the null hypothesis* becomes _____.

7-46 It makes sense, therefore, to test the null hypothesis by a method which depends upon the difference $O - E$. For this purpose, a quantity $(O - E)^2/E$ is computed for each cell. This quantity will increase as the difference $O - E$ grows _____.

7-47 Notice that the difference $O - E$ is *squared* in the computation of the quantity $(O - E)^2/E$. As $O - E$ increases, its square will increase at a _____ rate than $O - E$ itself.

7-48 Notice, further, that the *squared difference* $(O - E)^2$ is considered *relative* to the value of E, for the quantity $(O - E)^2$ is

Table 7-5 **Observed and Expected Frequencies**

	Number Improved		Number Not Improved		Totals
Drug Group	45	*30.9*	8	*22.1*	53
Control Group	18	*32.1*	37	*22.9*	55
Totals	63		45		108

_____ by E in the formula. In this way, some allowance is made for variations in the absolute size of the frequencies involved. This arrangement recognizes that the difference between an observed frequency of 40 and an expected frequency of 35 is _____ significant than the same difference occurring between 940 and 935.

7-49   The first step in making a chi-square test, therefore, is to take each cell in the table and compute $(O - E)^2/E$ for that cell. Do this for the upper left-hand cell in Table 7-5. The quantity computed for this cell is _____ .

7-50   When the quantity $(O - E)^2/E$ has been calculated for each cell in a table, the *sum* of these quantities is called CHI-SQUARE. The quantity 6.43 computed for the upper left-hand cell represents the *contribution* of that cell to the value of _____ for Table 7-5.

7-51   Now calculate the contributions of the remaining three cells, and write each in the corresponding position in the table below:

6.43	____
____	____

7-52   The sum of these four contributions is _____ . This number is the value of _____ for the entire table.

7-53   When the differences between observed frequencies and expected frequencies are large, the resulting value of chi-square will tend to be _____ than for cases in which these differences are small.

7-54   Table 7-6 is a table of critical values of chi-square. According to the caption in the table, such a table tells the _____ of obtaining a chi-square greater than or equal to a certain size when the _____ hypothesis is assumed.

7-55   We have a chi-square of 30.30 for Table 7-5, which is a table with _____ degree(s) of freedom. We must therefore look for the nearest value to 30.30 in the _____ row of Table 7-6.

7-56   The value nearest to 30.30 is 10.83, corresponding to a probability of _____ . Therefore, the probability of getting such a large value of chi-square if the null hypothesis is valid is _____ than 0.001. Therefore, we would _____ the null hypothesis.

divided

more

6.43

chi-square

6.43	*9.00*
6.19	*8.68*

30.30
chi-square

larger

probability

null

one
first

0.001
less
reject

Table 7-6 Critical Values of Chi-square*

d.f.	Probability under the Null Hypothesis of Obtaining Chi-square Greater than or Equal to the Value Entered in the Table									
	0.99	0.95	0.90	0.70	0.50	0.30	0.10	0.05	0.01	0.001
1	0.00016	0.0039	0.016	0.15	0.46	1.07	2.71	3.84	6.64	10.83
2	0.02	0.10	0.21	0.71	1.39	2.41	4.60	5.99	9.21	13.82
3	0.12	0.35	0.58	1.42	2.37	3.66	6.25	7.82	11.34	16.27
4	0.30	0.71	1.06	2.20	3.36	4.88	7.78	9.49	13.28	18.46

* A complete table of chi-square values will be found on the foldout in this book.

7-57 If our chi-square value for Table 7-5 had been 10.83, we would say, "Assuming that the null hypothesis is correct and there is no difference between the populations from which our two groups were drawn, we should get a chi-square as large as this only once in _____ experiments of this kind."

1,000

7-58 In other words, large values of chi-square *can* sometimes occur even when the null hypothesis is correct. When they occur, they are due to sampling variability. Small values would occur most frequently, and the larger the value of chi-square, the _____ likely it is to occur as a result of sampling variability alone.

less

7-59 Notice in Table 7-6 that the critical values of chi-square for a probability of 0.001 grow _____ as the number of degrees of freedom increases. The same is true for all the other columns in the table. It is very important, therefore, to determine correctly the number of _____ for your data before you refer to the chi-square table.

larger

degrees of freedom

Review

7-60 *The contribution of any cell to chi-square is given by the quantity _____. The total value of chi-square for the table is equal to the _____ of the contributions of all the individual cells.*

$\dfrac{(O - E)^2}{E}$

sum

7-61 *A table of critical values of chi-square tells the _____ of obtaining a value of chi-square that is at least as _____ as the value computed from the frequency table when the _____ is assumed.*

probability
large
null hypothesis

7-62   *Before referring to a table of critical values of chi-square, it is very important to determine correctly the number of _____ for the frequency table you are testing.*

D.   Chi-square For the Single Sample

In each of the examples so far considered, at least two samples were being compared. The drug experiment (Section A) included a drug group and a control group, with the null hypothesis that the two samples really came from the same population. In the example of Section B, Table 7-4, we had four samples, one from each of four college classes. The null hypothesis stated that there was no significant difference among these samples with respect to scores on a social science test.

It is also common to use chi-square for testing whether a single sample can be considered as belonging to a population which is defined in some logical or theoretical way. In such a case, the frequency table contains only one row of observed frequencies, and the expected frequencies are calculated from the characteristics of the theoretical population to which the sample is being compared. The null hypothesis states that there is no significant difference between the frequency distribution of the actual sample and that of the theoretical population. Section D gives two examples to illustrate this application of chi-square.

7-63   The distribution of the variable "IQ score" within the general population has been carefully studied. If a large sample were drawn from the general population, one would expect to find approximately 34.1 per cent of the IQ scores between 100.1 and 116, approximately 13.6 per cent between 116.1 and 132, and approximately 2.3 per cent above 132.

Since the distribution is *symmetrical,* the number of scores between 84.1 and 100 should be about _____ per cent; between 68.1 and 84, about _____ per cent; and below 68.1, about _____ per cent.

7-64   This kind of distribution is called a "normal distribution," and it will be discussed in detail in Lesson 10. You may be interested to note, in passing, that a person with an IQ score above 132 has a higher score than at least 97.7 per cent of the general population, since only _____ per cent of the scores are above 132. You can also show from these figures that only 15.9 per cent of the population have scores above 116.

Table 7-7 **Hypothetical Tenth-grade IQ Scores**

Below 68.1	68.1–84	84.1–100	100.1–116	116.1–132	Above 132	Total
0	8	25	45	17	5	100

7-65   While IQ is distributed in this way in the population as a whole, it is not necessarily true that IQ scores for special subgroups will have a normal distribution: For example, since the less bright students tend to drop out of school earlier than the brighter ones, a sample of IQs from tenth-grade students would be expected to contain proportionately more _____ IQ scores and fewer _____ scores than are found in the general population.

high — low

7-66   In such a case, chi-square could be used to test whether the deviation from a normal distribution is *significant*. Table 7-7 contains hypothetical frequencies of tenth-grade IQ scores classified into _____ categories.

six

7-67   The *expected* frequencies are to be determined on the null hypothesis that this distribution is not different from a normal distribution. According to the percentages given in frame 7-63 for the normal distribution, _____ per cent of the 100 students are expected to have IQs below 68.1. The expected frequency for the category "below 68.1" is therefore _____.

2.3

2.3

7-68   Write in the remaining expected frequencies in the table below (answers in Table 7-8):

Below 68.1	68.1–84	84.1–100	100.1–116	116.1–132	Above 132	Total
0 2.3	8	25	45	17	5	100

Table 7-8 **Observed and Expected Frequencies**

Below 68.1	68.1–84	84.1–100	100.1–116	116.1–132	Above 132	Total
0 2.3	8 13.6	25 34.1	45 34.1	17 13.6	5 2.3	100

7-69   Table 7-8 contains the observed and expected frequencies for this example. Notice that there is only _____ row in this table because there is only _____ sample.

one

one

Table 7-9   **Observed and Expected Frequencies Reclassified**

Below 84.1	84.1–100	100.1–116	Above 116	Total
8 _15.9_	25 _34.1_	45 _34.1_	22 _15.9_	100

7-70   Before you compute chi-square for this example, one modification must be made. It is a basic rule in using the chi-square test that *no more than* 20 per cent *of the expected frequencies may be less than* 5.* Table 7-8 has six expected frequencies, _____ of which are less than 5; this proportion is greater than 20 per cent.

two

* Some authors recommend that *all* expected frequencies less than 5 be eliminated.

7-71   This difficulty can easily be remedied by combining categories. In our example, the first two categories can be combined; likewise, the last two can be combined. Table 7-9 shows the reclassification, which eliminates the expected frequencies less than 5. Table 7-9 has only _____ categories.

four

7-72   Calculate the contributions to chi-square for each of the four cells, and write them in the table below. Write their sum at the bottom.

Category	Contribution to Chi-square
Below 84.1	_____
84.1–100	_____
100.1–116	_____
Above 116	_____
Total chi-square	_____

3.9
2.4
3.5
2.3
12.1

7-73   Before looking this value up in a table of chi-square, it is necessary to determine the number of _____ . The rule $(k - 1)$ $(r - 1)$ cannot be applied to Table 7-9 because the number of rows is only _____ in this case.

degrees of freedom

one

7-74   When chi-square is applied to a single sample, the table of frequencies has only one row and the rule for degrees of freedom is simply $k - 1$. For Table 7-9, d.f. = _____ .

3

7-75   This rule is consistent with our earlier discussion of degrees of freedom. With four categories, only _____ expected fre-

three

quencies need to be determined by multiplication of the number of observations by the expected *proportion*. The last expected frequency can be determined by _____ the sum of all the others from the total number of observations.

subtracting

7-76 Look up the chi-square for Table 7-9 in the table of critical values of chi-square (Table 7-6 or the complete table on the foldout). Use the row for which d.f. $= 3$. What is the probability that we would obtain such a large value of chi-square if the tenth-grade sample is really drawn from a population with a normal distribution? _____. Do you accept or reject the null hypothesis? _____ .

Between 0.01 and 0.001
Reject (beyond the .01 level)

7-77 One more example will be provided for practice. In this example, we shall compare observed frequencies with a "rectangular distribution," that is, with a distribution in which *all* the categories have the same frequency. Such a distribution, if drawn as a frequency polygon, would have a _____ shape.

rectangular

Table 7-10. **Family Position of Children Brought For Treatment**

Oldest Child in Family	Youngest Child in Family	Middle Child	Only Child	Total
32 30	29 30	27 30	32 30	120

7-78 Table 7-10 gives some hypothetical observations on children brought for treatment to a mental hygiene clinic. The four categories represent different positions in the family, and the null hypothesis is that this distribution is not different from a rectangular distribution. In other words, we shall test the hypothesis that the clinic sample includes oldest, youngest, middle, and only children in _____ numbers.

equal

7-79 Compute chi-square for this example. The value of chi-square is _____. There are _____ degrees of freedom.

0.6 — three

7-80 The table of chi-square values indicates a probability of _____ that a chi-square this large or larger would be obtained from a sample that is in fact drawn from a rectangular population. The null hypothesis should therefore be _____ .

0.90

accepted

7-81   *To test whether a single sample is likely to have come from a population with a particular frequency distribution, the expected frequencies must be calculated from the frequency distribution characteristic of that* _____ .

population

7-82   *Frequency tables for a single sample have only* _____ *row. If there are k categories in the row, there will be* _____ *degrees of freedom in the table.*

one
k − 1

E.   Limitations on the Use of Chi-square Tests

7-83   The chi-square test can be used only when the observations can be classified into two or more _____ . The data for the chi-square test therefore consist of observed _____ falling into distinct _____ .

categories
frequencies
categories

7-84   An important assumption made in the chi-square test is the assumption that the *individual observations which make up the frequency in any one cell are independent of one another.* In all the examples discussed in this lesson, the individual observations have been scores and each score has been taken from a separate person. Therefore, the assumption that the observations were _____ of one another was justified in these cases.

independent

7-85   Suppose, however, that 100 observations were to be collected by taking 10 scores from each of 10 individuals. Such a set of observations would not meet the requirement that all the observations must be _____ .

independent

7-86   Observations coming from the same individual would be _____ likely to fall into the same category than observations coming from different individuals. A set of observations containing such groups of *interrelated* observations would not have the same characteristics as sets of independent observations.

more

7-87   A further limitation on the application of the chi-square test has already been mentioned in Section D. It is the basic rule that no more than 20 per cent of the expected frequencies may have values less than _____ .

5

7-88   The value 5 is an arbitrary rule of thumb. The chi-square test is most effective when the expected frequencies are relatively large. They can be made larger by reclassifying the data into categories that are _____ inclusive .

more

7-89   Because of the required size of expected frequencies, it is necessary to have a relatively large number of _____ when one wishes to employ a large number of categories.

observations

7-90   If the available number of observations is small, then one must be content with a relatively _____ number of categories.

small

7-91   In the IQ example of Section D, two of the six expected frequencies were equal to 2.3. In order to bring these expected frequencies up to at least five, we regrouped the observations. If we had retained all six categories, how many observations would we have needed to have in order to bring these expected frequencies up to five? Since 2.3 must be multiplied by _____ to make 5, the number of observations available (100) must be multiplied by _____ to make an expected frequency of 5. With a total of _____ observations, therefore, the expected frequency in the two extreme categories would be 5.

2.17
2.17
217

Review

7-92   *The chi-square test can be used only with observations which can be classified into _____ and which are _____ of one another.*

categories — independen

7-93   *The chi-square test cannot be used when more than _____ per cent of the _____ frequencies have a value less than 5.*

20
expected

7-94   *In order to meet this minimum value, it may be necessary to decrease the number of _____ or to increase the number of _____ .*

categories
observations

Problems for Lesson 7

7-1   Use chi-square to test whether the zoology class (Problem 5-1) with 50 women and 40 men enrolled in it will support the null hypothesis that women and men tend to elect zoology equally often. The student population is made up of 500 women and 1,000 men, and these proportions also hold for each individual class (freshman, sophomore, etc.)

7-2   Use chi-square to test whether your friend can tell the difference between instant and "real" coffee if he gets 8 out of 10 samples correct. Then suppose that he is given 100 samples and gets 80 out of 100 correct; compute chi-square for this result also. What is the effect of the increased number of observations even though he is correct on 8 out of every 10 samples in *both* cases?

7-3   A college suspects that its rising tuition rate has changed the composition of its student body with respect to economic level. It classifies the students of the class of 1963 into three groups according to their fathers' incomes (high, middle, and low), and taking into account the nationwide change in salary levels during the intervening 10 years, it classifies the students of the class of 1953 into three comparable groups.

The frequencies in these three categories for each of the two classes are shown in the table below. Using chi-square, determine whether it is possible to reject, at the .05 level, the hypothesis that these two groups came from the *same* population with regard to economic composition.

Fathers' Incomes

	High	*Middle*	*Low*	*Total*
Class of 1953	450	750	400	1,600
Class of 1963	1,050	1,650	500	3,200
Total	1,500	2,400	900	4,800

Lesson 8.   Indicators of Central Tendency

This lesson is the second lesson on frequency distributions. In Lesson 6, it was shown how large sets of numbers could be simplified by the construction of frequency distributions, either in the form of tables or in the form of graphs. The discussion of such frequency distributions can be further simplified by using certain convenient methods for stating their principal characteristics. For many purposes it is sufficient to state just two of these characteristics: the location of the center of the distribution and the extent to which the distribution spreads out around its center. Lesson 8 provides the most common methods for describing the center, or central tendency, of a distribution. Lesson 9 provides the methods for stating its degree of spread or dispersion.

Lessons 8 and 9 may be studied with only Lesson 6 as preparation. Students who began the book at Lesson 6 may therefore go directly on to Lessons 8 and 9 before studying Lessons 1 to 5 and 7. For students who are following the lessons in the order in which they have been arranged in this book, the study of central tendency and dispersion is introduced at this point because these ideas will be needed for the further discussion of statistical inference.

A.   Modal Class

8-1   Figure 8-1 is a simple bar graph showing the number of autobiographical books written between 1950 and 1959 by former mental patients. The variable "author's illness" assumes values which are of the _____ type.

nominal

8-2   Since nominal values cannot be arranged in an order from lowest to highest, these five classes can be displayed in *any* arbitrary order. Therefore, one can hardly speak of a "center" for this distribution. However, the distribution does tend to *cluster* at certain points where the frequency is greatest. The class with the greatest frequency in Figure 8-1 is _____ .

paranoid schizophrenia

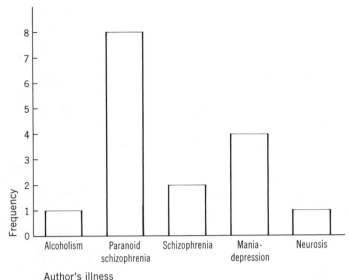

Figure 8-1. Number of autobiographies of former mental patients which appeared from 1950 to 1959. (*Data from R. Sommer and H. Osmond, Autobiographies of Former Mental Patients, Journal of Mental Science, 106:653, 1960.*)

8-3 A class whose frequency is not exceeded by that of any other class in a distribution is called a MODAL CLASS. The class "paranoid schizophrenia" is a _____ class for the distribution of Figure 8-1.

modal

8-4 Figure 8-2 shows the *total* number of such autobiographies available in English in 1959, again divided into the same classes. In the distribution of Figure 8-1, the number of modal classes was _____. In the distribution of Figure 8-2, the number of modal classes is _____, since there is more than one class whose frequency is not exceeded by that of any other class.

one

two

8-5 A distribution with *two* modal classes is said to be BIMODAL. A distribution with only one modal class is UNIMODAL. The distribution in Figure 8-1 is a _____ distribution, while the distribution in Figure 8-2 is a _____ distribution.

unimodal

bimodal

8-6 Distributions in which there is only one modal class are called _____ distributions. Distributions in which there are two modal classes are called _____ distributions. Even when the two largest classes have only *approximately* equal frequencies, the distribution is often referred to as a _____ distribution,

unimodal

bimodal

bimodal

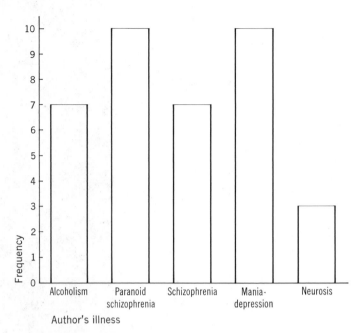

Figure 8-2. Total number of autobiographies of former mental patients available in English in 1959. (*Data from R. Sommer and H. Osmond, Autobiographies of Former Mental Patients, Journal of Mental Science, 106:653, 1960.*)

provided both these classes have distinctly higher frequencies than all the other classes.

8-7 In looking for the class with the greatest frequency, one occasionally finds that a distribution has *more than two* modal classes. Such a distribution is MULTIMODAL. However, the idea of a modal class becomes less and less useful the greater the number of such classes becomes. A statement about the _____ may be very useful in a unimodal distribution, but it is not very meaningful in a multimodal distribution.

modal class

8-8 Figure 8-3 shows the frequencies, per hundred individuals, of persons with schizophrenia for each of six classes of the variable "degree of relationship to a schizophrenic patient." Although the values of this variable cannot be placed along an equal interval scale, they can nevertheless be arranged in an _____ from lowest to highest degree of relationship; they are therefore _____ values.

order
ordinal

8-9 The class "monozygotic co-twins" refers to persons having an *identical twin* who is schizophrenic. The frequency of schizophrenia among persons of this group is _____ per 100. This class is the _____ of the distribution.

86.2

modal class

8-10 Because we are dealing now with *ordinal* values, we can say in this case that the modal class is the class with the _____ degree of relationship to schizophrenics. In the examples of Figures 8-1 and 8-2, we could not make any such statement about the *position* of the modal class among the other classes because we were dealing with _____ values.

highest

nominal

8-11 The idea of the modal class can also be applied to *interval* values. Figure 8-4 shows an example of such an application. The variable whose values are being considered is the _____ , in milligrams per liter, of a certain bitter substance PTC (phenylthiocarbamide). For each class of the variable, the figure shows the _____ of persons in a sample of English males who were able to *taste the bitterness* at that concentration but at no lower concentration.

concentration

frequency (number)

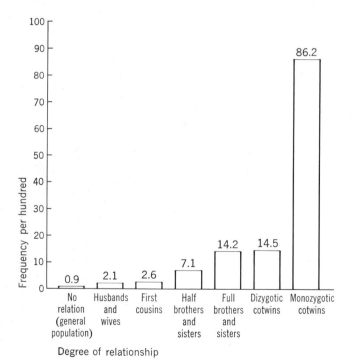

Figure 8-3.   Frequency of schizophrenia per hundred persons among relatives of schizophrenics. (*Data from F. J. Kallmann, The Genetic Theory of Schizophrenia, American Journal of Psychiatry, 103:309–322, 1946, and personal communication.*)

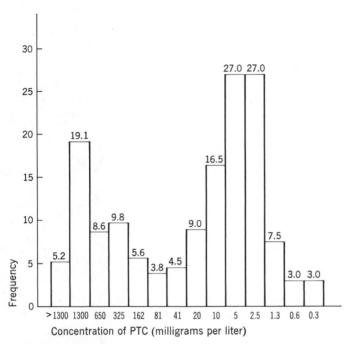

Figure 8-4. Number of persons first able to taste PTC at particular concentrations. (*Data from N. A. Barnicott, Taste Deficiency for Phenylthiourea in African Negroes and Chinese, Annals of Eugenics, 15:248–254, 1950.*)

Students of psychology will recognize that the *lowest* concentration at which a person is able to taste the substance is his *taste threshold* for that substance. Therefore, the figure shows the numbers of persons whose *threshold* fell into each of the 14 different classes. Because the thresholds varied over an enormous range—from 0.3 to over 1,300 milligrams per liter—the X axis has been given a logarithmic scale. We shall not discuss such scales in detail, but even if they are not familiar to you, you may be interested to note that *each successive midpoint is approximately one-half the value of the preceding one.* In this way, it is possible to get all the values on one scale, without confining the six or eight lowest values to an infinitesimally small part of the scale.

8-12   This distribution would be called "bimodal," and it would be said that the modal classes are at 1,300 milligrams per liter and at 2.5 to 5 milligrams per liter. Actually, there are _____ classes at the second of these points—both 5 and 2.5 milligrams per liter have the same frequency (about 27). These two classes are treated as a single modal class because they are exactly side by side on an equal (logarithmic) interval scale.

two

8-13   Although the frequency of the class at 1,300 milligrams per liter is considerably _____ than 27, it is still considered to be a _____ because it does have a distinctly higher frequency than any other class in its neighborhood.

less

modal class

Such a bimodal distribution of sensitivity to the bitter taste of PTC is taken as evidence that the sample of English males is not *homogeneous* with respect to this sensitivity. The sample appears to contain *two* different groups, one with a generally *low* sensitivity (requiring hundreds of milligrams per liter), another with a *high* sensitivity (requiring only about 2 to 5 milligrams per liter). Indeed, ability to taste this substance is known to be dependent on heredity, and low sensitivity is thought to depend upon possession of a recessive gene. *Obtaining a bimodal distribution for a certain variable may be the first clue that one is dealing with more than one group, each with different characteristics.*

Review

8-14 *With nominal values of a variable, the class or classes in which frequencies tend to cluster can be stated in terms of the concept of a _____ class. With ordinal or interval values, it is also possible to speak about the position of a _____ among the other classes.*

modal
modal class

8-15 *A unimodal distribution has _____ modal class(es). A bimodal distribution has _____ modal class(es). A multimodal distribution has _____ modal class(es).*

one
two
more than two

B. The Mode for Interval Values

8-16 The MODE is defined as the *most frequently occurring observation* in a set of observations. We shall discuss the mode only in connection with observations that are *interval* values. Table 8-1 presents a set of scores which lie on an equal interval scale from 1 to 11.

In Table 8-1, the score of 6 occurs with greater frequency than any other score. Therefore, 6 is the _____ for this set of scores.

mode

8-17 Instead of the scores in Table 8-1 being thought of as a set of discrete numbers, each score can be considered as the midpoint of a class interval. The class interval in which the *mode* is found has a lower limit of _____ and an upper limit of _____. The mode itself is the _____ of this interval.

5.5 — 6.5
midpoint

8-18 The variable in Table 8-2 is again "test scores." This variable has continuous values along an equal interval scale. Since there is only one class whose frequency is not exceeded by that of any other class, this distribution is _____; it has only one _____ class. *The mode is always taken to be the midpoint of such a class.*

unimodal — modal

Table 8-1 **Frequency Distribution of Test Scores (N = 50)**

X_i	f_i
11	1
10	2
9	3
8	6
7	8
6	10
5	8
4	6
3	3
2	2
1	1

8-19 The class interval in Table 8-2 is equal to _____ score units. The modal class is the class of scores from _____ to _____. The mode is the _____ of this class.

10
109.5—119.49
midpoint

8-20 Compute the mode for the distribution in Table 8-2 by taking one-half of the difference between the lower limit of the modal class and the lower limit of the next higher class; then add this number

Table 8-2 **Frequency Distribution of Test Scores (N = 110)**

Class	f_i
159.5–169.49	1
149.5–159.49	2
139.5–149.49	6
129.5–139.49	10
119.5–129.49	16
109.5–119.49	20
99.5–109.49	19
89.5–99.49	18
79.5–89.49	12
69.5–79.49	3
59.5–69.49	2
49.5–59.49	1

to the exact lower limit of the modal class. The mode is equal
to _____ .

114.5

8-21 When the mode is used to describe such interval values, some
irregularities can arise. Because it is conventional to take the *midpoint
of the modal class* as the value of the mode, the mode will depend somewhat on the way the interval values have been classified. For example,
compare distributions A and B in Table 8-3. The distributions are
drawn from the same set of scores, and distribution A is copied from
Table 8-2. The class interval for B is _____ as large as the

twice

class interval for A. The mode of distribution A is 114.5. Distribution
B has a mode of _____ .

99.5

8-22 This discrepancy is a consequence of the conventional rule by
which we take the _____ as the value of the mode for

*midpoint of a
modal class*

observations of interval values which are grouped into classes. Such
irregularities do not arise when the values are not grouped. They also
do not arise when the concept of a *modal class* is applied to *nominal*
values, for which the concept is particularly appropriate.

8-23 When there is a single modal class, there is only one value for
the *mode* of the distribution, and this value can be used to indicate the
point around which the values cluster most heavily. Thus the
_____ can be used to indicate the central tendency of such

mode

a distribution.

Table 8-3 **Two Frequency Distributions for the Same 110 Test
Scores Based upon Different Class Intervals**

A		B	
Class	f_i	*Class*	f_i
159.5–169.49	1	149.5–169.49	3
149.5–159.49	2		
139.5–149.49	6	129.5–149.49	16
129.5–139.49	10		
119.5–129.49	16	109.5–129.49	36
109.5–119.49	20		
99.5–109.49	19	89.5–109.49	37
89.5–99.49	18		
79.5–89.49	12	69.5–89.49	15
69.5–79.49	3		
59.5–69.49	2	49.5–69.49	3
49.5–59.49	1		

8-24   In bimodal distributions, there is more than one _____
class and therefore there is also more than one _____.
In Figure 8-4, the bimodal distribution of taste sensitivity, the number
of modes is _____, since the distribution is bimodal.

modal
mode

two

8-25   The mode is easy to determine, and in unimodal distributions
it is representative of the typical case. In distributions that are not unimodal, however, the mode may not represent any reasonable middle
or central score, and it is therefore not a good description of the
_____ of the distribution. In such cases, it is often most
important simply to state that the distribution is bimodal or multimodal in form.

central tendency

8-26   Some frequency distributions are SYMMETRICAL around a single
modal class. Figure 8-5 (drawn from Table 8-1) is an example of such a
_____ distribution. Notice that the frequencies in the classes
to the right of the modal class form a mirror image of the frequencies
in the classes to the _____ of the modal class.

symmetrical

left

8-27   In this distribution, the exact lower limit of the modal class is
_____ and the lower limit of the next higher class is
_____. Notice that the scores 5 and 7, which are the mid-
points of the class intervals adjoining the modal class, both occur with
a frequency of _____. The scores 4 and 8 both occur with
a frequency of _____, and in general the frequencies of
pairs of intervals lying at equal distances to the left and right of the

5.5
6.5

8
6

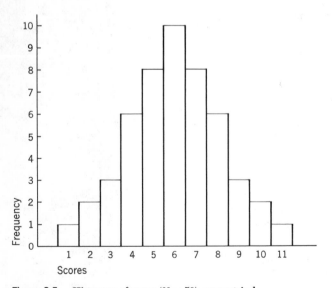

Figure 8-5.   Histogram of scores ($N = 50$): symmetrical.

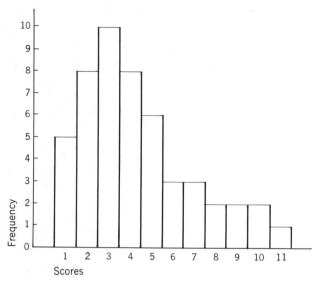

Figure 8-6. Histogram of scores ($N = 50$): asymmetrical.

modal class are identical. For this reason, the distribution is said to be

_____ .

symmetrical

8-28 Not all distributions are symmetrical. Some distributions have a single modal class which is not in the center of the distribution; it is displaced toward one end of the distribution. Such distributions are called *asymmetrical* distributions. Figure 8-6 is an example of an _____ distribution; its modal class has a midpoint of

_____ .

asymmetrical

3

8-29 The modal class lies in the center of the distribution when the distribution is _____ . The modal class is displaced toward one end of the distribution when the distribution is _____ .

symmetrical

asymmetrical

Review

8-30 *The class whose frequency is not exceeded by that of any other class in a distribution is called a* _____ . *When there is only one such class, it describes the* _____ *of the distribution.*

modal class

central tendency

8-31 *With variables which assume values on an equal interval scale, the* _____ *of the modal class defines a particular value called the* _____ . *The concept of a* _____ *can be used with values of all three sorts: nominal, ordinal, and interval. The concept of a* _____ *is appropriate for interval values only.*

midpoint

mode — modal class

mode

8-32 With interval or ordinal values, we can speak of a distribution as symmetrical or asymmetrical. In an asymmetrical distribution, the _____ does not fall in the _____ of the distribution.

C.   The Median

8-33 The concept of the modal class, which requires only counting frequencies, has a logical relation to *nominal* values. There is a second indicator of central tendency which is logically related to *ordinal* values. It is called the MEDIAN. The *median* is the middle value in a set of values which have been arranged in order, from highest to lowest. For such a middle value, the number of values lying above it will be _____ the number of values lying below it.

8-34 The rule for selecting the middle value in an ordered series of values will vary slightly depending upon whether the series contains an *even* number of values or an *odd* number. When the series contains an odd number of values, the _____ is literally the "middle" value. For example, in the ordered series 2, 5, 7, 8, 9, 10, 17, the middle value is _____ because there are an equal number of values above and below it. There are _____ values greater than this value and _____ values less than this value.

8-35 When the series contains an *even* number of values, the median is taken as the point halfway between the *two* middle values. In the series 2, 5, 7, 9, 11, 17, 20, 25, the two middle values are _____ and _____. The median lies halfway between these two values; therefore, the median is _____.

8-36 Notice that in the example given in frame 8-35, which contains an _____ number of values, the selection of 10 as the median is consistent with the definition of the median. There are eight values in the series; _____ of them lie below 10, and _____ are greater than 10.

> Series of scores such as the following require special treatment: 2, 3, 5, 5, 6, 7, 8. The value of the middle score is 5, but there are three scores above 5 and two scores below 5. The problem raised by such a series can be solved if the series is treated by the rules for *grouped values* (see frames 8-40 to 8-50).

8-37 The median is a very natural indicator of central position for a set of *ordinal* values, such as ranks in a graduating class. If there are 101 students, the ranks will be numbered 1 through 101 and the median rank will, of course, be _____, with 50 ranks above it and 50 below it. With 100 students, the median would have to be taken as _____, according to the rule for an even number of values.

51

50.5

8-38 The median could not be applied to values which are only _____ values because there is no way to arrange such values in an ordered series from lowest to highest.

nominal

8-39 Although the median is particularly related to ordinal values, it can also be used for _____ values, since such values can be arranged in an ordered series from lowest to highest.

interval

8-40 When interval values have been grouped into classes to form a frequency distribution, the determination of the median is sometimes a little tricky. The median is still defined as that value which has exactly _____ per cent of the scores below it and exactly _____ per cent above it. But when that value lies somewhere *within* a particular class interval, a special convention is required for computing it.

50 — 50

8-41 Although we shall not usually go into the details of computing procedures, an important point can be made clear if we illustrate the procedure which is necessary in this case. Figure 8-7 shows a frequency distribution of 100 scores, and the median is indicated by a vertical arrow drawn from the top of the polygon to a point on the X axis. The value of the median in this distribution can be read from the graph; it is equal to _____ .

68

8-42 Since there are 100 scores, there must be _____ scores greater than 68 and _____ scores less than 68. Let us see whether this is indeed true by adding up the frequencies of the classes to either side of 68.

50

50

8-43 Evidently the class interval in Figure 8-7 is _____ score units. Since the *midpoint* of the lowest class interval is 40, the *limits of the class interval* for that class must be _____ and _____ .

5

37.5

42.5

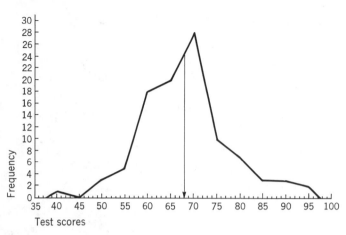

Figure 8-7. Frequency polygon of essay test scores ($N = 100$) showing the location of the median.

8-44   Add up the frequencies of the first six classes, starting with the class whose midpoint is 40 and ending with the class whose midpoint is 65. The total frequency of these six classes is _____ .

47

8-45   The *lower limit* of the seventh class is 67.5. Therefore, we know that, when we reach 67.5 on the scale, we have reached a point below which _____ of the 100 scores lie. But we need to know the point below which 50 of the 100 lie in order to find the median.

47

8-46   If we had the original scores, it would, of course, be easy to locate the fiftieth score by counting. But we have only the frequency distribution. Therefore, we know only that the fiftieth score must lie in the interval between _____ and _____ . There are _____ scores in this class.

67.5 — 72.5

28

8-47   The conventional procedure requires that we now make a somewhat unrealistic assumption, which is justified only because we do not have enough information about the scores to make a better assumption. The assumption is *that the 28 scores are evenly spread over the five units of this class interval.* If they were evenly spread, then the third lowest score in the 28—which is the _____ th score in the whole set—would lie $\frac{3}{28}$ of the way from 67.5 to 72.5. This fraction $\frac{3}{28}$, if divided out to one decimal place, is approximately equal to

_____ .

50

0.1

8-48   So if the scores were evenly spread over this interval, the fiftieth score would lie $\frac{1}{10}$ of the way between 67.5 and 72.5. The total distance between these limits is _____ units; $\frac{1}{10}$ of this

5

distance is _____. Add this distance to the lower limit (67.5), and you find that the value of the median is _____.

8-49   Thus, we have verified that 68 is the point *below* which 50 scores lie. Is it also the point *above* which 50 scores lie? If we add up the frequencies of the classes above 72.5, we get a total of _____. The fiftieth score from the top must lie between 72.5 and 67.5, and it must be the _____th of the 28 scores in that class, *counting from the top of the interval.*

8-50   The fraction $^{25}/_{28}$ is about 0.9. If we *subtract* $^9/_{10}$ of 5 from 72.5, we obtain, again, 68. Therefore, the point 68 must have _____ scores above it as well as 50 scores below it.

> Although you will not need to compute medians again in working out these lessons, it may be helpful to you to know that there is a formula for computing the median for grouped values. The formula is
>
> $$\text{Median} = L_c + \left[\frac{(N/2) - f_L}{f_c} \right] W$$
>
> where L_c is the lower limit of the class in which the median must lie, f_c is the frequency of that class, f_L is the total frequency of all classes *below* that class, W is the size of the class interval, and N is, as usual, the total number of values. In our example, $L_c = 67.5$, $f_c = 28$, $f_L = 47$, $W = 5$, and $N = 100$. The series, 2, 3, 5, 5, 6, 7, 8, given in the note following frame 8-36, is handled as follows by regarding the scores as members of classes with lower limits 1.5, 2.5, and so on:
>
> $$\text{Median} = 4.5 + \left(\frac{3.5 - 2}{2} \right) 1 = 5.25$$

8-51   This example is intended only to illustrate the *principle* involved in locating the median for observations which have been grouped into classes. Notice that there is an *important difference* from the procedure for determining the mode: The mode for grouped data is always the _____ of the class in which it lies.

8-52   The median, however, is *not* the midpoint of the class in which the middle score falls unless by chance the frequency of the classes above that class is exactly _____ to the frequency in the classes below it. In all other cases, the median will be some point other than the _____ of the class within which it falls.

Review

8-53   *The median of a set of values is always that value of which it can be said that _____ of the values lie below it and _____ lie above it. The values must be arranged in _____ of value,* and the median is therefore particularly suited for values of the sort we have called _____ values.

8-54 *The median of the series of scores, 1, 3, 7, 8, 9, 10, 13, 15, 20, 27, is equal to _____ . For the series 40, 43, 47, 52, 58, 65, 90, the median is _____ . When the values are grouped into classes, the median (unlike the mode) will only rarely be the _____ of the class interval in which it falls.*

D. The Arithmetic Mean

We now come to the indicator of central tendency which is logically related to interval values, the ARITHMETIC MEAN. *From your study of arithmetic, you are already very familiar with the arithmetic mean, which is commonly (but loosely) called "the average." Actually, there are many kinds of average, since any number used to indicate central tendency is in a way an average. When it is necessary to be quite specific, one must say "arithmetic mean," for there are other kinds of "means" (for example, the geometric mean, which we shall not study). In most cases, however, when the word "mean" alone is used, the arithmetic mean is understood.*

8-55 For a series of 11 observations, 10, 9, 8, 8, 7, 7, 7, 6, 6, 5, 4, the arithmetic mean is determined as follows:

$$\frac{10 + 9 + 8 + 8 + 7 + 7 + 7 + 6 + 6 + 5 + 4}{11} = \underline{\hspace{3cm}}$$

(Write down the mean for this series.)

8-56 The rule for determining the mean of a set of observations is therefore, "Take the _____ of the values, and divide it by the _____ of observations in the set."

8-57 For convenience, we use the symbol $\overline{X}$ ("X-bar") to represent the mean. We shall use the symbol N to represent the number of observations in a set. If the mean of a set of 10 observations is 24, we can write in symbols that _____ = 10 and that _____ = 24.

8-58 When we want to indicate that we are referring to several individual scores, we shall think of the individual scores as being numbered and we shall put subscripts on the letter X and write X_1 for the first score, X_2 for the second, and so on. Thus, for the set of scores in frame 8-55, $X_1 = 10$, $X_2 = $ _____, $X_3 = $ _____, $X_4 = $ _____, and so on, up to _____ $= 4$.

8-59   We could write the rule for finding the mean in symbols:

$$\bar{X} = \frac{X_1 + X_2 + X_3 + X_4 + X_5 + X_6 + X_7 + X_8 + X_9 + X_{10} + X_{11}}{N}$$

In this equation, $\bar{X}$ stands for _____ and N stands for _____.

8-60   In order to represent each of these 11 scores in a single symbol, we shall write simply X_i, where the subscript i is thought of as taking each of the values from 1 to 11. For any set of N scores, we can therefore write _____ instead of writing out the whole set, and the subscript _____ will be understood as taking each of the values from _____ to _____.

8-61   Instead of using many plus signs, we can use the Greek capital letter S, sigma, written Σ, to indicate the operation of adding or *summation*. Whenever you find this symbol, regard it as an instruction to *take the sum of that which follows it*. Thus, ΣX_i means "take the _____ of all the _____ from the first to the Nth."

8-62   Using all these symbols, the definition of the arithmetic mean can be written very simply:

$$\bar{X} = \frac{\Sigma X_i}{N}$$

where $\bar{X}$ represents the _____ of the set of scores, ΣX_i stands for the _____, and N stands for the _____ of scores in the set.

8-63   Since a score is a particular value of a variable, such as IQ, this equation is, of course, suitable for any set of interval values (whether they are "scores" or some other sort of values). When X is the variable being considered, then X_1, X_2, and so on, are particular values of the _____ X and X_i stands for each of the particular values which the _____ assumes in that set of observations.

8-64   Note that the equation $\bar{X} = \Sigma X_i / N$ is both a *definition* of the mean and a set of directions indicating what must be done in order to determine its value. If the equation is put into words, it reads, "The _____ of the set of observations is equal to the _____ of all the observed values of the variable X divided by the _____ of observations."

the mean
the number of scores

X_i
i
$1 - N$

sum — scores

mean
sum of all the scores —
  number

variable
variable

arithmetic mean — sum
  number

$9 - 8$
$8 - X_{11}$

8-65   Suppose that the numbers of words in the vocabularies of six two-year-old children were determined and the following values were obtained: 105 words, 95 words, 150 words, 90 words, 60 words, and 100 words. The variable X in this case is "number of words in vocabulary." For these six values of the variable, $\Sigma X_i = $ _____,
$N = $ _____, and $\bar{X} = $ _____ .

8-66   When values are grouped into classes, the procedure for finding the mean is slightly different. Table 8-4 shows the 11 scores from frame 8-55 arranged in the form of a frequency distribution. Notice that the second column is labeled f_i. The letter f stands for *frequency,* and f_i means the _____ of each particular class, from the first to the _____ .

8-67   The symbol at the top of the third column, $f_i X_i$, means the *product* of a particular value X_i and the _____ (f_i) with which it occurs. In this distribution, each X_i has a frequency of 1, except for the scores 6, 7, and 8, which have frequencies of _____ , _____ , and _____ , respectively.

8-68   In frequency distributions where some values of the variable X occur more than once, it is necessary to begin by computing the sum of X_i *within* each class. If the value 8, which occurs twice in Table 8-4, is multiplied by its frequency 2, the result is the same as the result obtained by *adding* the two values of 8. Therefore, the summation *within* each class is accomplished by _____ each value X_i by its _____ .

Table 8-4   **Frequency Distribution of 11 Scores**

X_i	f_i	$f_i X_i$
10	1	10
9	1	9
8	2	16
7	3	21
6	2	12
5	1	5
4	1	4
	$N = 11$	$\Sigma f_i X_i = 77$

8-69 Keep in mind that the first step in computing the mean is to obtain the total sum of all the values in the frequency distribution. When the value X_i for each class is multiplied by its frequency, the product (which appears in the _____ column of Table 8-4) is the sum of the scores for that _____ . The symbol for this product is _____ .

third (f_iX_i)
class
f_iX_i

8-70 For a particular value of the variable X, such as X_1, which occurs with the particular frequency _____ , the product _____ is identically equal to the *sum* $X_1 + X_1 + \cdots + X_1$, in which the number of terms equals _____ .

f_1
f_1X_1
f_1

8-71 When the value f_iX_i has been obtained for each class, the total sum of X_i for the entire distribution is obtained by adding the numbers in the third column. In Table 8-4, this sum is equal to 77. It is represented by the symbol _____ .

Σf_iX_i

8-72 The number Σf_iX_i is the sum of all the _____ in the distribution. This value must now be divided by _____ to obtain the arithmetic mean of the distribution. In Table 8-4, $\overline{X} =$ _____ .

values (scores)
N

7

8-73 Again, now, we are going to illustrate what happens when we deal with large numbers of values grouped into classes. In Table 8-4, the class interval was equal to _____ score unit, and each score was therefore also the midpoint of its class interval. The mean as computed from the frequency distribution was *exactly* the same as the mean computed directly from the raw scores.

1

8-74 In Table 8-3, 110 scores were displayed in two separate frequency distributions with two different class intervals. This table has been repeated on page 120 to show how the mean is computed when the class interval is greater than 1. Notice that X_i for each class is taken as the *midpoint of the class interval*. The sum of all the values within a class is therefore taken to be the _____ of the class times the _____ of the class, or f_iX_i. *Since not all the values in the class are equal to the midpoint, this sum is an approximation.* The mean computed from such a table will not be *exact*.

frequency
midpoint

Table 8-3 (repeated)

Distribution A				Distribution B			
Class	X_i	f_i	f_iX_i	Class	X_i	f_i	f_iX_i
159.5–169.49	164.5	1	_____	149.5–169.49	159.5	3	_____
149.5–159.49	154.5	2	_____				
139.5–149.49	144.5	6	_____	129.5–149.49	139.5	16	_____
129.5–139.49	134.5	10	_____				
119.5–129.49	124.5	16	_____	109.5–129.49	119.5	36	_____
109.5–119.49	114.5	20	_____				
99.5–109.49	104.5	19	_____	89.5–109.49	99.5	37	_____
89.5–99.49	94.5	18	_____				
79.5–89.49	84.5	12	_____	69.5–89.49	79.5	15	_____
69.5–79.49	74.5	3	_____				
59.5–69.49	64.5	2	_____	49.5–69.49	59.5	3	_____
49.5–59.49	54.5	1	_____				

8-75 Compute some or all of the values to fill in the blanks in Table 8-3. If you care to do so, you may then take their sum Σf_iX_i and divide it by $N = 110$ to obtain the mean *as estimated from each of the two different distributions.* The completed table, with means, follows.

Table 8-3 (repeated)

Distribution A				Distribution B			
Class	X_i	f_i	f_iX_i	Class	X_i	f_i	f_iX_i
159.5–169.49	164.5	1	164.5	149.5–169.49	159.5	3	478.5
149.5–159.49	154.5	2	309.0				
139.5–149.49	144.5	6	867.0	129.5–149.49	139.5	16	2232.0
129.5–139.49	134.5	10	1345.0				
119.5–129.49	124.5	16	1992.0	109.5–129.49	119.5	36	4302.0
109.5–119.49	114.5	20	2290.0				
99.5–109.49	104.4	19	1985.5	89.5–109.49	99.5	37	3681.5
89.5–99.49	94.5	18	1701.0				
79.5–89.49	84.5	12	1014.0	69.5–89.49	79.5	15	1192.5
69.5–79.49	74.5	3	223.5				
59.5–69.49	64.5	2	129.0	49.5–69.49	59.5	3	178.5
49.5–59.49	54.5	1	54.5				

$$\Sigma f_iX_i = 12075.0 \qquad\qquad \Sigma f_iX_i = 12065.0$$
$$\bar{X} = 109.77 \qquad\qquad\qquad \bar{X} = 109.68$$

8-76   Compare the two values of $\Sigma f_i X_i$ computed from the two distributions, and notice that they are slightly different. The means obtained are also slightly different, but if both were rounded off to whole numbers, both would equal _____ . The difference is not great, therefore, and the procedure is somewhat easier than adding up a large number of different scores, especially when the number of scores is very large.

110

Review

8-77   *The arithmetic mean of a set of values is defined as the _____ of all the values _____ by the number of values in the set.*

sum — divided

8-78   *When the values are grouped into classes, each value in a particular class is regarded as having the value of the _____ of that class. Consequently, the mean calculated from grouped values will be approximate rather than _____ .*

midpoint

exact

8-79   *When the values are grouped into classes, the first step in computing the mean is to determine the product _____ for each class. The definition of the mean, in symbols appropriate to values grouped into classes, is _____ .*

$f_i X_i$

$\bar{X} = \dfrac{\Sigma f_i X_i}{N}$

E.   Comparison of the Mean, Median, and Mode

8-80   Compare Table 8-4 with Table 8-5. Table 8-5 is the same set of scores shown in Table 8-4, except that four more scores of 4 have been

Table 8-4   **Frequency Distribution of 11 Scores**

X_i	f_i	$f_i X_i$
10	1	10
9	1	9
8	2	16
7	3	21
6	2	12
5	1	5
4	1	4
	$N = 11$	$\Sigma f_i X_i = 77$

Table 8-5   **Frequency Distribution of 15 Scores**

X_i	f_i	$f_i X_i$
10	1	10
9	1	9
8	2	16
7	3	21
6	2	12
5	1	5
4	5	20
	$N = 15$	$\Sigma f_i X_i = 93$

added in Table 8-5 (repeated here) so that the frequency of the score of 4 is _____. In Table 8-5, $N =$ _____, $\Sigma f_i X_i =$ _____, and $\overline{X} =$ _____. The addition of these four low scores has considerably *reduced* the value of the mean.

5 — 15

93 — 6.2

	Table 8-5 *(repeated)*		Table 8-6	Frequency Distribution of 15 Scores	
X_i	f_i	f_iX_i	X_i	f_i	f_iX_i
10	1	10	10	5	50
9	1	9	9	1	9
8	2	16	8	2	16
7	3	21	7	3	21
6	2	12	6	2	12
5	1	5	5	1	5
4	5	20	4	1	4
	$N = 15$ $\Sigma f_iX_i = 93$			$N = 15$ $\Sigma f_iX_i = 117$	

8-81 Imagine, instead, that the four additional scores had all been scores of 10 instead of scores of 4. Then, the distribution would have been that of Table 8-6, where the frequency of the score of 10 is 5 while the frequency of 4 is again _____. In Table 8-6, $N =$ _____, $\Sigma f_i X_i =$ _____, and $\overline{X} =$ _____. The addition of these four high scores to the distribution of Table 8-4 has considerably _____ the value of the mean.

1

15 — 117 — 7.8

increased

8-82 On the other hand, increasing the frequency of the score of 7 in Table 8-4 would not change the value of the mean. Even if the frequency of this score were 100, making $N = 108$, $\Sigma f_i X_i = 756$, the value of $\overline{X}$ would still be $^{756}/_{108}$ or _____. Increasing the frequency of *that score which is equal to the mean* does not change the value of the mean.

7

8-83 We can see, therefore, that the mean is strongly affected by the occurrence of scores at the *extremes* of the distribution. If the frequency of a value which lies *above* the mean is increased, the value of the mean will _____. If the frequency of a value which lies *below* the mean is increased, the value of the mean will _____.

increase

decrease

8-84 But increasing the frequency of the score which is _____ does not change the value of the mean. Furthermore, increasing the frequencies of values which lie *close* to the mean will change the value of the mean *less* than increasing the frequencies of

equal to the mean

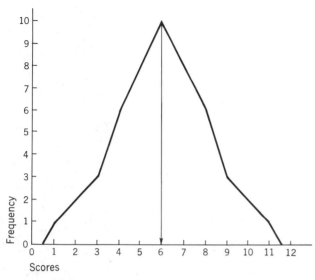

Figure 8-8. A symmetrical frequency polygon of test scores ($N = 50$) showing the location of the mean.

scores which lie _____ from the mean at the extreme ends of the distribution.

far

8-85 Figure 8-8 is a frequency polygon of the distribution which was shown as a histogram in Figure 8-5. Notice that the mean of this distribution, indicated by the vertical arrow, lies exactly at the midpoint of the modal class; the value of the mean corresponds to the value of the _____. Furthermore, the mean lies exactly in the _____ of the range of scores.

mode
middle

8-86 In this case, since the frequencies on both sides of the middle score are equal, the mean also corresponds to the value of the _____ of the distribution. Thus, in distributions which are symmetrical, the values of the _____ , _____ , and _____ are identical.

median
mean ↔ median
↔ mode

8-87 Certain distributions show a preponderance of observations near one end of the range, with a few observations lying in the tail at the other end of the range. These are called SKEWED distributions. In Figure 8-9, distribution B is a _____ distribution.

skewed

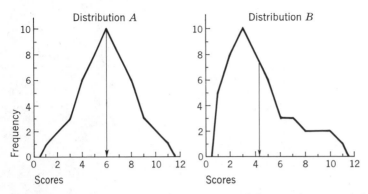

Figure 8-9. Comparison of the relative positions of the mean in symmetrical (Distribution A) and positively skewed (Distribution B) distributions.

8-88 In Figure 8-9, the observations in distribution B are concentrated near the *lower* end of the range and the longer tail of the distribution extends toward the right, where the scores are larger. Such distributions are POSITIVELY skewed. Thus, when the longer tail of the distribution extends toward the larger values, it is called a _____ skewed distribution.

8-89 Larger scores appear at the _____ end of the X axis in conventional graphs; hence, positively skewed distributions are sometimes said to be "skewed to the right." When the longer tail of the distribution extends toward values larger than the mean value, the distribution is very likely to be _____ to the _____ .

8-90 On the other hand, when the observations are concentrated near the *upper* end of the range, with the longer tail extending toward the lower values, the distribution is said to be NEGATIVELY skewed. It is conventional to place the lower values toward the left on the X axis; distributions which are _____ skewed are therefore skewed to the left.

8-91 There is a mathematical measure of the degree to which a distribution is skewed with respect to its mean. In this book, however, we shall notice merely certain relations between the *direction* of the skew and the position of the mean. Look again at Figure 8-9. The mean of the symmetrical distribution coincides with the mode and with the center of the range, but the mean of the skewed distribution lies _____ these two points.

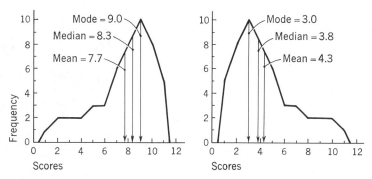

Figure 8-10. Comparative positions of the mean and median relative to the position of the mode in two skewed distributions ($N = 50$, each distribution).

8-92 Figure 8-10 shows two frequency polygons. The distribution on the left is skewed to the _____; the distribution on the right is skewed to the _____ .

left
right

8-93 The positions of the mean, median, and mode are indicated for each distribution in Figure 8-10. The mean does not coincide with the mode. It is displaced to the _____ of the mode in the distribution which is skewed to the left; in the distribution which is skewed to the right, the mean lies to the _____ of the mode. In each case, the mean is displaced away from the mode *in the same direction as the skew.* This observation holds true in practice for *nearly all* skewed distributions.

left

right

8-94 The median is also displaced away from the mode in both distributions. The direction of displacement of the median is _____ the direction of displacement of the mean, but the extent of its displacement is _____ than that of the mean. The mean is influenced _____ than the median by the occurrence of extreme scores lying out in the tail of the skewed distribution.

the same as
less
more

8-95 When a distribution is not badly skewed, the three measures of central tendency will not be very different from one another. The distribution for which we determined the median in Section C of this lesson can be used to illustrate this kind of case. Figure 8-11 shows the position of the mean in that distribution. Since $N = 100$ and $\Sigma f_i X_i = 7{,}050$, $\bar{X} = $ _____ , as indicated in the figure. We know from Section C that the median is 68, and you can tell from the figure that the mode is _____ . These values are not identical, but they are closely similar to each other. Notice that this example is one of the instances in which the median does not lie between the mean and the mode.

70.5

70

Comparison of the Mean, Median, and Mode **125**

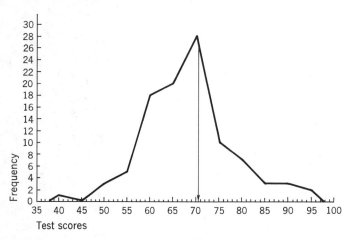

Frequency

Figure 8-11. Frequency polygon of essay test scores ($N = 100$) showing the location of the mean.

8-96 The three measures of central tendency which we have discussed in Lesson 8 have different uses. With respect to the *three kinds of values* which variables can assume, we can make the following statements: The modal class is particularly suited for _____ values but can also be used for variables with _____ values. When it is used with _____ values, it can be used to identify a particular point, called the _____. The *median* is particularly suited for _____ values, and it can also be used with _____ values. However, it cannot be applied to variables with only _____ values.

nominal
ordinal and interval
interval
mode
ordinal
interval
nominal

8-97 The arithmetic mean is suited only for variables with _____ values. It cannot be applied to either _____ or _____ values.

interval — nominal
ordinal

8-98 When a variable has interval values, we can choose any one of the three measures of central tendency. Ordinarily, we would choose the mean, because it lends itself to numerical manipulation somewhat more easily than the other measures. When the distribution is not badly skewed, the three measures will have _____ values.

approximately equal

8-99 When the distribution is badly skewed, we may wish to state the median or the mode as well as (or instead of) the mean. This would be true if we are particularly interested in describing "typical" behavior. Figure 8-12 shows the number of Oberlin College students in a particular sample who arrived at various times *after* the scheduled class hour. To describe the *typical* behavior of students in this sample, one would

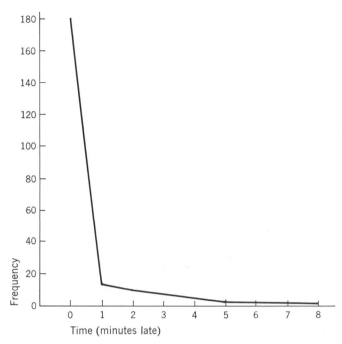

Figure 8-12. A distribution ($N = 212$) showing the number of Oberlin College students in a sample who arrived at various times after the scheduled class hour.

choose the _____ as his measure of central tendency,
even though the variable is "time," which assumes _____
values.

8-100   The distribution of personal incomes in the United States is very badly skewed in a positive direction; there are many high incomes which occur with relatively low frequency. In such a distribution, the median income will have a _____ value than the mean
income and the mode will be _____ than either of these.
Because of the skewness, the median is usually taken as a better indicator of central tendency ("average" income) than the mean.

Review

8-101   *With nominal values, one must use the _____ as his*
measure of central tendency. With ordinal values, one may use either the
_____ or the _____ . With interval values, one
would ordinarily use the _____ unless the distribution is
badly _____; in that event, he might choose to use the
_____ or the _____ .

Problems for Lesson 8

8-1 If a variable is measured in terms of a nominal scale, can the modal class (assuming one exists) be interpreted as an indicator of the *relative scale position* of the maximum frequency in the distribution? Why or why not? For what kinds of values, (nominal, ordinal, or interval), can a numerical value of the mode be computed?

8-2 What steps are necessary to determine the mode of interval values grouped into the classes of a frequency distribution?

8-3 In this lesson, we have described four indicators of central tendency: **(a)** identification of the modal class, **(b)** computation of the mode, **(c)** computation of the median, and **(d)** computation of the mean. Which one (or ones) of these can be used when the distribution is made up of nominal values? Ordinal values? Interval values?

8-4 Which of the four indicators of central tendency could be used in each of the following situations? (If more than one measure is possible, mention all of them).

(a) The frequency of alcoholism among various national groups, such as French, Norwegians, Poles, Americans, etc.

(b) The frequency of alcoholism among economic classes of Americans divided into various annual income groups, such as $0.00 to $999.99, $1,000.00 to $1,999.99, and so forth.

(c) A group of 20 wine tasters are asked to assign a rank from 1 (highest quality) to 5 (lowest quality) to a particular brand of sherry. A distribution is made up showing the frequency of ratings 1, 2, 3, 4, and 5.

8-5 Compute the mean, median, and mode for the following distribution of scores:

Scores	Frequency
110–119	1
100–109	0
90–99	2
80–89	5
70–79	10
60–69	13
50–59	9
40–49	4
30–39	5
20–29	0
10–19	1

Which of these three measures would be most strongly influenced by the occurrence of extreme scores in the distribution? Which the least influenced by extreme scores?

Lesson 9. Measuring Dispersion

Following our discussion of indicators of central tendency in Lesson 8, our next step is to measure the degree of spread or dispersion *around the central position. We shall now be concerned only with variables which assume interval values; nominal and ordinal values will not enter into our discussion of dispersion. Keep in mind, therefore, that we are now dealing* only *with variables whose values can be stated in terms of some scale which has equal intervals.*

A. The Range as a Measure of Dispersion

9-1   Figure 9-1 shows two distributions which differ from each other chiefly in their degree of DISPERSION. The figure shows two frequency distributions of IQ scores of six-year-old children. Both distributions have the same value of $\overline{X}$, which is _____ . Both are *symmetrical* around the mean.

100

9-2   The two groups of children are alike in mean IQ, but the groups are very different in degree of _____ . Group *B* is spread out around the mean IQ of 100 very much _____ than Group *A* is.

dispersion
more

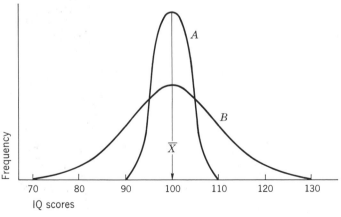

Figure 9-1.   Symmetrical distributions with the same mean, having different degrees of dispersion.

9-3   In Group _____, there are some very high IQs and some very low ones, but Group _____ is quite homogeneous with respect to IQ. A greater degree of *homogeneity* means a _____ degree of dispersion or variability.

B
A

lesser

9-4   The word "variability" can be used instead of the word "dispersion," and the words "degree of" can be omitted. Thus, one can speak of a low degree of dispersion as a low _____. The adjective form VARIABLE is also frequently used; since Group *A* has a lower variability than *B*, we can say that Group *A* is *less* _____ than *B*. This is the same as saying that Group *A* is more _____ than *B*.

variability

variable
homogeneous

9-5   In spite of the fact that both groups have the same mean, they are different with respect to the RANGE of scores which they contain. Group *A* contains no scores below _____ or above _____, while Group *B* contains IQs ranging from a low of _____ to a high of _____ .

90
110
70 — 130

9-6   We shall define the *range* of a distribution as the distance between the highest and the lowest value in the distribution. Thus, Group *A* has a mean of 100 and a _____ of 20. Correspondingly, Group *B* has a mean of 100 and a _____ of _____ .

range
range — 60

9-7   The distance between the highest value and the lowest value in a distribution is called the _____. This distance can be calculated by _____ the lowest value from the _____ value.

range
subtracting — highest

9-8   The range of a set of values can be determined quickly and easily. It provides a rough idea of the degree of _____ of a distribution. If we know both the mean and the range, then we know where the _____ of the distribution lies and how much the distribution spreads out around that point.

dispersion (variability)

center

9-9   If we know the mean and the range, we can even form an idea of the shape of the distribution. When the distribution is approximately *symmetrical*, the mean will lie approximately in the _____ of the range.

center

9-10   If the mean is nearer to the *upper* end of the range, we can guess that the distribution is probably somewhat _____ to

skewed

the _____. (If you are in doubt about your answer, look back at Figure 8-10 on page 125.)

(If you are in doubt about your answer, look back at Figure 8-10 on page 125.)

9-11   If the mean is nearer to the *lower* end of the range, then the distribution is probably _____ to the _____.

9-12   The range is a convenient indicator of dispersion, but it is a very rough and approximate one. There are two facts we shall point out in order to emphasize that the range is only a _____ indicator of dispersion.

9-13   First, note what would happen to the range of Group A, in Figure 9-1, if the group were to contain just *one* individual with an IQ of 130. Instead of having a range of 20, the distribution would now have a range of _____. Yet intuitively one feels that a single extreme score ought not to make so much difference. *The range is a rough measure, because it does not tell whether many or only a few scores lie near the _____ of the range.*

9-14   Second, consider how the range will be affected by the *size of the sample* that is drawn from a population. Suppose the population contains a few extreme values. The chance of obtaining any of these values will be _____ with a *large* sample than with a *small* sample. Therefore, *the range of a small sample is likely to be _____ than the range of a large sample even when both samples are drawn from the same population.*

9-15   This second fact ought to make us particularly cautious when we want to *compare* the dispersions of two different samples. If we use the *range* as an indicator of dispersion, we must remember that the range is likely to be greatly affected by the _____ of the sample.

Review

9-16   *Three words are used in referring to the tendency of a set of scores to spread out around their center. A distribution which does not spread very much may be said to have a low degree of _____ or a low degree of _____; it is a relatively _____ distribution.*

left
skewed — right
rough
40
ends (extremes)
greater
smaller
size
dispersion variability — homogeneous

9-17   A quick but rough indication of dispersion can be obtained by calculating the _____ of the distribution. This measure is obtained by _____ the _____ value in the distribution from the _____ value.

range
subtracting — lowest
highest

B.   The Deviation Score

We shall now turn to the most common and most useful measure of dispersion, the STANDARD DEVIATION. *Our first step will be to develop the idea of the* DEVIATION SCORE, *which must be understood before the standard deviation can be discussed.*

9-18   Let us recall the notation which we used in Lesson 8. When we are considering a variable X, the values of this variable can be indicated as X_1, X_2, and so on, up to X_N, where $N =$ _____. The whole set of values can be written simply as _____, where the subscript is understood as taking each value from _____ to _____.

number of values
X_i

1 — N

9-19   The symbol for the arithmetic mean is _____. Each of the values symbolized by X_i is greater than, equal to, or less than the value of the mean. In other words, each value *deviates* from the mean by some amount; this amount of deviation will be 0 for any particular X_i which happens to equal _____.

$\overline{X}$

$\overline{X}$

9-20   If we subtract the value $\overline{X}$ from each X_i, we shall convert each value in the distribution into a DEVIATION SCORE. Thus, the quantity $X_i - \overline{X}$ defines the _____ for any particular value X_i.

deviation score

9-21   The quantity $X_i - \overline{X}$ will equal 0 if $X_i =$ _____. If X_i is greater than $\overline{X}$, then $X_i - \overline{X}$ will be _____ than 0 and its algebraic sign will be _____. If X_i is less than $\overline{X}$, then $X_i - \overline{X}$ will be _____ than 0 and its algebraic sign will be _____.

$\overline{X}$
greater
positive
less
negative

9-22   The deviation score for a particular value X_1 is found by _____ the value of _____ from the value of _____. In symbols, this deviation score is written _____.

subtracting — $\overline{X}$
X_1
$X_1 - \overline{X}$

Table 9-1 Frequency Distribution of Test Scores ($N = 50$) Illustrating Deviation Scores

X_i	f_i	$f_i X_i$	x_i $(X_i - \bar{X})$	$f_i x_i$
11	1	11	+5	+5
10	2	20	+4	+8
9	3	27	+3	+9
8	6	48	+2	+12
7	8	56	+1	+8
6	10	60	0	0
5	8	40	−1	−8
4	6	24	−2	−12
3	3	9	−3	−9
2	2	4	−4	−8
1	1	1	−5	−5
$N = \Sigma f_i = 50$		$\Sigma f_i X_i = 300$ $\bar{X} = 6$	$\Sigma x_i = 0$	$\Sigma f_i x_i = 0$

9-23   It is common to represent the deviation score for a particular value X_i by the lower-case symbol x_i. Thus, X_1 is the first score in the set, and x_1 is the same score expressed as a _____ from the mean. Therefore, $x_1 =$ _____ .

9-24   Similarly, $X_2 - \bar{X} =$ _____ and $X_N - \bar{X} =$ _____ . Both of these values are _____ scores.

9-25   Table 9-1 shows the scores which appeared as a histogram in Figure 8-5. The deviation scores appear in the _____ column. There are 11 deviation scores; 1 is equal to 0, _____ have positive signs, and _____ have negative signs.

9-26   The deviation score x_1 is equal to +5. It is positive because the raw score X_1 is _____ than _____ . The devia- tion score x_{11} is equal to −5. It is negative because the raw score X_{11} is _____ than _____ .

9-27   The symbol Σx_i means "take the _____ of all the values x_i from the first to the Nth." In Table 9-1, Σx_i is computed by way of $\Sigma f_i x_i$, and it equals _____ .

9-28   It can easily be proved that the sum of all the deviation scores in a distribution is *always* equal to 0. The sum of the deviation scores with positive signs is always exactly _____ the sum of the deviation scores with negative signs.

9-29 When a distribution is relatively *homogeneous,* its variability or dispersion is _____. In such a distribution, you would expect the size of the deviation scores to be relatively _____.

9-30 If we compare two distributions such as *A* and *B* in Figure 9-1, where *B* is more variable than *A*, we would expect the size of the deviation scores in *A* to be in general rather _____ than the deviation scores in *B*.

9-31 If we were to compute some kind of *average* deviation score for each distribution, then, this average might give us a way of comparing the _____ of the two distributions. But since the sum of the deviation scores is equal to _____, we cannot use the simple arithmetic mean of the deviation scores.

9-32 Sometimes this problem is solved by taking the ABSOLUTE VALUES of the deviation scores and calculating the arithmetic mean of these values. The *absolute value* of a quantity is its *numerical* value without regard to its algebraic sign. Thus, the absolute value of $+5$ is _____, and the absolute value of -5 is _____.

9-33 If the deviation scores in distribution *B* tend to be larger than the deviation scores in distribution *A*, then the arithmetic mean of the _____ values of the deviation scores ought to be greater for distribution _____ than for distribution _____.

9-34 The arithmetic mean of the absolute values of the deviation scores is called the *average deviation.* The average deviation can be used as a measure of _____, but since it is not very often used, we shall not emphasize it here.

9-35 In Section C, we shall discuss the *standard deviation,* the measure of dispersion most often used. We shall then be able to compare the *standard* deviation with the *average* deviation, and we shall find that both involve taking an arithmetic mean based on deviation scores. The *average* deviation is the arithmetic mean of the _____ values of the _____.

equal to (the same as)

low
small

smaller

variability
0

5 — 5

absolute
B — A

dispersion (variability)

absolute
deviation scores

9-36 If we subtract the mean $\bar{X}$ from a particular raw score X_5, we obtain a _____ score which can be symbolized as _____. If X_5 is greater than _____, then _____ will have a positive sign.

deviation — x_5
$\bar{X} - x_5$

9-37 The quantity Σx_i is always equal to _____ for any distribution.

0

9-38 The average deviation, *which is a kind of measure of dispersion, is* equal to the _____ of the _____ of the deviation scores.

arithmetic mean
  — absolute values

C. The Standard Deviation

9-39 The *standard deviation* is the measure of dispersion which is most commonly used. It does not have the disadvantages which make the _____ a very rough measure of dispersion, and it is more satisfactory for mathematical reasons than the average deviation. We shall represent the standard deviation by the lower-case letter s.

range

9-40 In computing the value of s, or the _____ of a distribution, we begin by converting the raw scores X_i into deviation scores. The deviation scores are symbolized by _____.

standard deviation

x_i

9-41 The standard deviation of a distribution is defined by the equation

$$s = \sqrt{\frac{\Sigma x_i{}^2}{N}}$$

where each value x_i must be _____ before the summation is performed. Notice that the equation requires that we take the *square root* of the quantity $\Sigma x_i{}^2/N$.

squared

9-42 You will understand the meaning of this equation best if you actually work out a simple example. Take a blank sheet of paper (ruled paper will be best), and copy the equation for s at the top of the sheet. Divide the sheet into three vertical columns. Then write X_i at the head of the left-hand column, and put the following scores in that column: 10, 9, 8, 6, 5, 4, 3, 2, 2, 1. Determine ΣX_i and $\bar{X}$, and write these values at the bottom of the column.

$\Sigma X_i = 50, \bar{X} = 5$

9-43   At the top of the second column, write x_i. Then determine x_i for each X_i by _____ the value of _____ from the value of X_i. This column now contains the _____ scores. Be sure to write the proper *sign* in front of each score in column 2. Check your result by determining Σx_i. Does it equal 0?

subtracting — $\bar{X}$
deviation
Top to bottom: $+5, +4,$
  $+3, +1, 0, -1, -2,$
  $-3, -3, -4$

9-44   At the top of the third column, write x_i^2. Fill in the column by multiplying each x_i by itself. Notice that all the signs in this column will be _____ .

Top to bottom: $25, 16, 9,$
  $1, 0, 1, 4, 9, 9, 16$

positive

9-45   At the bottom of the third column write the value of Σx_i^2. The next step is to divide this sum by _____ . Write the result of this division.

$\Sigma x_i^2 = 90$
N
$\dfrac{\Sigma x_i^2}{N} = 9$

9-46   Now, the final step indicated by the equation is to take the _____ of $\Sigma x_i^2/N$. In this case, you can write the result with-out referring to a table; the value of s for this set of scores is _____ .

square root

3

9-47   Since $s = \sqrt{\Sigma x_i^2/N}$, $s^2 = $ _____ . There is a name for s^2. It is called the VARIANCE of the distribution. We shall discuss the variance in greater detail in Lessons 21 and 22, where the idea of "analysis of variance" is introduced.

$\dfrac{\Sigma x_i^2}{N}$

9-48   Both s and s^2 are measures of variability. The name for s is _____ ; the name for s^2 is _____ .

standard deviation —
variance

9-49   When you take the square root of $\Sigma x_i^2/N$, you obtain the value of _____ (symbol). When you leave $\Sigma x_i^2/N$ without taking the square root, you have the value of _____ (symbol). The _____ is the square root of the _____ .

s
s^2
standard deviation
— variance

9-50   Carefully compare the following two equations:

$$\bar{X} = \frac{\Sigma X_i}{N} \qquad (a)$$

$$s^2 = \frac{\Sigma x_i^2}{N} \qquad (b)$$

Equation (*a*) is the equation for finding the _____ of a distribution. Equation (*b*) is the equation for finding the _____ of a distribution. Both equations require division by the same factor, _____ .

mean
variance

N

9-51   If $\Sigma X_i/N$ gives the arithmetic mean of a set of *scores*, then we can say that $\Sigma x_i^2/N$ gives the arithmetic _____ of a set of *squared deviation scores. The variance is nothing other than the arithmetic mean of the squared deviation scores.*

mean

9-52   In Section B, we said that the "average deviation" is the arithmetic mean of the _____ values of the deviation scores. The variance is therefore analogous to the average deviation, but to obtain the variance, we take the _____ of each deviation score instead of taking the _____ of each deviation score.

absolute

square
absolute value

9-53   The variance and its square root (the standard deviation) are used more than the average deviation because their mathematical properties are more convenient. But in determining any one of the three measures—the mean, the average deviation, or the variance—we divide a sum by the factor _____ , thus obtaining the arithmetic *mean* of some quantity.

N

9-54   Now examine the equation for *s* once again. Put the equation into words: The standard deviation is the square _____ of the arithmetic _____ of the _____ deviation scores. Notice the key words which you have supplied in this verbal definition. The standard deviation is sometimes called the ROOT-MEAN-SQUARE DEVIATION.

root
mean — squared

9-55   The name "root-mean-square deviation" may help you to recall the way to determine the standard deviation, for the steps in computing *s* are contained *in reverse order* in that name. The first step (deviation) is to obtain the _____ of each score from the _____ .

deviation
mean

9-56   The second step (square) is to _____ these _____ . The third step (mean) is to _____ the _____ together and divide them by _____ .

square
deviation scores — add
squared deviation scores
— N

9-57   The final step (root) is to take the _____ of the _____ of the _____ .

square root
mean — squared
deviation scores

9-58 *The standard deviation is symbolized by the letter _____,
and it is often called the _____-_____-_____
deviation. This name contains the steps required for its computation, in
_____ order.*

s

root — mean — square

reverse

9-59 *The quantity s^2 is called the _____, and it is the
_____ of the standard deviation. It is also the _____
of the squared deviation scores.*

variance
square — mean

9-60 *We have already noted that an increase in variability will produce
an _____ in the size of the deviation scores. The standard
deviation is an indicator of dispersion, since its size will increase whenever
the size of the deviation scores _____.*

increase

increases

D. The Standard Deviation of the Normal Distribution

9-61 Figure 6-5 is repeated here to remind you of what you learned
earlier about the area under a frequency polygon. In Lesson 6, you
learned that the total area under a frequency polygon is equal to the

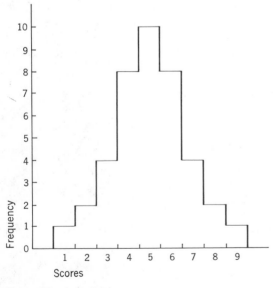

Figure 6-5 repeated

quantity _____, or total _____. It makes no difference whether the distribution in Figure 6-5 is drawn as a frequency polygon or as a histogram; the total area in the distribution remains the same.

N — frequency

9-62   Remember that the area of a bar in a histogram is equal to the _____ for that class. Therefore, the sum of the areas of several bars, e.g., those representing the classes 4, 5, and 6, is equal to the _____ of the classes _____ , which is equal to _____ .

frequency

frequency — 4 through 6
26

9-63   The total area in the histogram in Figure 6-5 is equal to 40, and the area included within the bars representing the classes 4, 5, and 6 is equal to 26. If you divide the area representing classes 4, 5, and 6 by the total area, you will obtain the number _____ . This number is the *proportion* of the total area represented by the combined areas of classes 4, 5, and 6. It is called a PROPORTIONAL FREQUENCY.

0.65

9-64   The proportional frequency of a particular set of classes is the frequency of those _____ divided by the _____ . Since area represents frequency in all graphs of frequency distributions, the proportional *area* in a particular set of classes is therefore the same as the _____ of those classes.

classes — total
frequency

proportional frequency

9-65   Figure 9-2 is a symmetrical frequency distribution with a very large N and a very small class interval. The frequency polygon for such a distribution usually approximates a smooth curve; in such cases, we

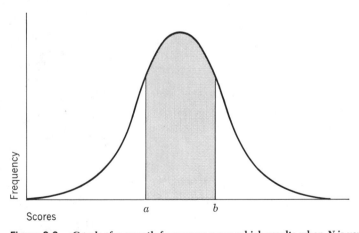

Figure 9-2.   Graph of a smooth frequency curve which results when N is very large and the size of the class interval is very small.

can speak of a *frequency curve*. The histogram for such a distribution will also approximate a smooth _____ .

frequency curve

9-66   In Figure 9-2, vertical lines have been drawn at the points *a* and *b*, and the area under the curve between these lines has been shaded. Consider that $N = 10,000$ and that the sum of the frequencies between *a* and *b* is 5,000. The 5,000 observations in the area between *a* and *b* represent a *proportional* frequency of _____ ; they occupy a proportional area of _____ , since area represents frequency.

0.5

0.5

9-67   If the area under the curve from *a* to *b* is 5,000 units and the total area is 10,000 units, then the combined area of the *unshaded* regions is _____ . The *proportional* area belonging to the unshaded regions is _____ .

5,000 units

0.5

9-68   The sum of the two proportional areas—0.5 for the shaded region and 0.5 for the unshaded region—is _____ . The sum of all the proportional areas under a frequency curve must always equal _____ .

1.0

1.0

9-69   Let the sum of the frequencies in the unshaded region to the right of *b* equal 2,500. Since the sum of the frequencies from *a* to *b* is 5,000, the sum of *all* the frequencies to the right of *a* under the curve must equal _____ . The *proportional* frequency to the right of *a* must equal _____ ; the proportional *area* of this region also equals _____ .

7,500

0.75

0.75

9-70   When $N = 10,000$, *any* set of classes with a proportional frequency of 0.75 must have a *frequency* of _____ . When we know the value of N and the proportional area for a set of classes, we can determine the actual _____ for that set of classes.

7,500

frequency

9-71   The total of all the proportional areas under any frequency curve must always equal 1. When we express areas under a frequency curve as *proportional* areas, we can regard the total area under any such curve as equal to _____ .

1

9-72   Now we are ready to turn back to the *standard deviation*. In the example worked out in Section C, $s = 3$ scale units and $\bar{X} = 6$. The distance between 6 and 9 is a *distance along the X axis*, and it is equal to the size of 1 standard deviation. We talked about the shaded area in Figure 9-2 as the area under the curve from *a* to *b*; we can talk now about the area under this other curve from 6 to 9. This area can also be called the area under the curve from the *mean* to a point which is 1 _____ above the mean.

standard deviation

9-73   The distance between 6 and 3 is also equal to 1 standard deviation, on the other side of the mean. It is natural to take the mean as a center point because the standard deviation is based on deviation scores, which are the deviations of the raw scores from the _____ . The area under the curve from 6 to 3 is the same as the area under the curve from the _____ to a point which is 1 standard deviation _____ the mean.

mean
mean
below

9-74   Let us take a new example. The distribution of IQ scores in the general population, as measured by the Stanford-Binet test, has a mean IQ of 100 and an s of 16. The distance along the X axis from 100 to 116 is equal to 1 standard deviation. *The score 116 is therefore said to lie 1 standard deviation above the mean.* The distance from 100 to 84 is also equal to s. The score 84 therefore can be said to lie _____ the mean.

*1 standard deviation
below*

9-75   All the scores between 100 and 116 are said to lie *within* 1 *standard deviation above the mean.* Likewise, all the scores between 100 and 84 are said to lie _____ .

within 1 standard deviation below the mean

9-76   All the scores between 84 and 116 are said to lie *within* ±1 *standard deviation of the mean.* This statement means that none of the scores between 84 and 116 deviate from the mean by a distance along the _____ that is greater than _____ .

X axis — s (or 16)

9-77   We can speak of an area under the frequency curve which lies between the mean and 1 standard deviation above the mean. This would be the area between the IQ scores _____ and _____ .

*100 ↔
116*

9-78   The area under the frequency curve between 84 and 100 is the area under the curve between the _____ and _____ . The area under the curve between 84 and 116 is the same as the area within _____ or _____ 1 standard deviation of the mean.

*mean — 1 s below the
mean*
plus — minus

9-79   For Stanford-Binet IQ scores from the general population, the *proportional area* under the frequency curve between 100 and 116 is known to be 0.3413. The distribution is perfectly symmetrical, so the

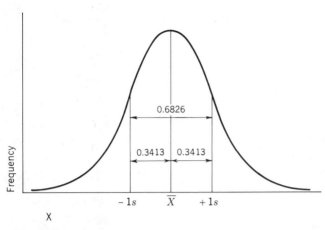

Figure 9-3. A normal distribution.

proportional area under the frequency curve between 100 and 84 is also _____ . The proportional area between 84 and 116 is

_____ .

9-80   The distribution of Stanford-Binet IQ scores is a good example of the NORMAL DISTRIBUTION, a symmetrical, bell-shaped distribution which is of great importance in statistics. Figure 9-3 shows such a distribution. The figure indicates that the proportional area within _____ of the mean is 0.6826.

9-81   We can consider other distances along the X axis and other areas. The distance between 100 and 132, for example, includes all scores within _____ standard deviations *above* the mean. The corresponding distance between 100 and 68 includes all scores

_____ .

9-82   The distance between 68 and 132 includes all scores which lie _____ . Figure 9-4 shows that the proportional area between these limits is _____ , since the distribution is a _____ distribution.

9-83   Since the curve is symmetrical, and since we know that the proportional area within ±2 standard deviations of the mean is 0.9544, we can tell that the proportional area between the mean and 2 standard deviations above the mean is _____ .

9-84   We can even determine the proportional area which lies between +1 standard deviation (116) and +2 standard deviations (132). The area between the mean and 1 standard deviation above the

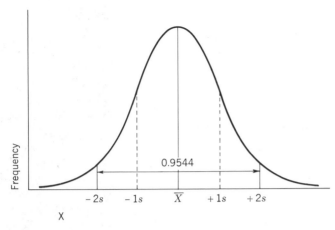

Figure 9-4. A normal distribution.

mean is 0.3413. The area between the mean and 2 standard deviations above the mean is 0.4772. The area between +1 and +2 standard deviations, therefore, is _____.

9-85 Figure 9-5 shows the area under the normal distribution curve which lies within ± _____ standard deviations of the mean. This area is _____ and includes very nearly the entire area under the curve. The proportional area outside this region is only 0.0026.

9-86 One of the great values of the normal distribution is that we know quite specifically the proportional areas associated with regions along the X axis. When an observed distribution, such as the distribu-

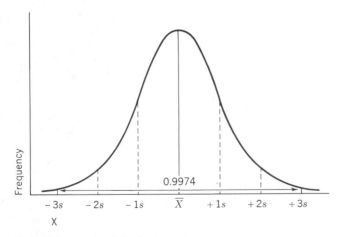

Figure 9-5. A normal distribution.

tion of Stanford-Binet IQs in the general population, turns out to be very similar to the normal distribution, we can determine the proportional areas in that distribution for any range of scores; we need only to know the mean and the _____ of the distribution.

s (standard deviation)

9-87 These properties of the normal distribution have already been used in an example in Lesson 7D. They will be used very extensively in later lessons on significance tests (Lessons 11 to 14). However, very few variables in psychology and the social sciences have a truly normal distribution; the variable IQ is one of the best examples of a _____ which does have a distribution like that of the _____ distribution.

variable
normal

9-88 Even when a variable does *not* have a normal distribution, we can talk about the s as a distance along the _____. We can also talk about proportional areas under the curve between the mean and 1, 2, 3, and more _____ above or below the mean. But these areas will not be equal to the corresponding areas under the normal distribution curve unless the distribution is _____.

X axis

standard deviations

normal

9-89 Figure 9-6 is a distribution of 100 test scores, with $s = 2.4$. The mean of this distribution is indicated by a vertical arrow; it is equal to _____. The point on the X axis which lies $1s$ above the

56

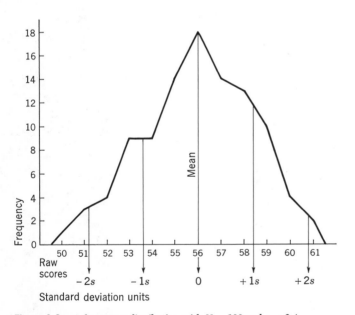

Figure 9-6. A frequency distribution with $N = 100$ and $s = 2.4$.

mean can be found by adding _____ to _____ ;
this point is _____ .

9-90   To determine the point which lies $2s$ above the mean (or $+2s$ from the mean), add $2s$ to the mean. The point is _____ .
For the corresponding point $2s$ below the mean (or $-2s$ from the mean), you must _____ the same quantity from 56. The point is _____ .

9-91   This distribution appears to be *approximately* normal. Let us see whether it has the areas expected to appear in the normal distribution. If it is approximately normal, we expect approximately 68 per cent of the scores to lie within _____ standard deviation of the mean, approximately 95 per cent to lie within _____ standard deviations of the mean, and approximately 100 per cent to lie within _____ standard deviations of the mean.

9-92   The distribution in Figure 9-6 contains 100 scores. If the distribution is normal, it should have about _____ of those 100 scores within $\pm 1s$ of the mean. There are actually 67 scores within this range; the distribution comes close to the normal distribution in this region.

9-93   If the distribution is normal, we should find _____ scores within $\pm 2s$ of the mean; there are actually 94. There should be about _____ scores within $\pm 3s$ of the mean; there are actually 100. The distribution is therefore approximately a _____ distribution.

In making this judgment, we have taken into consideration also the fact that the shape is symmetrical and that there are no peculiar "humps" in the polygon. It would be possible for a distribution to meet the simple requirements for which we have just tested it yet *not* have a normal shape. In Lesson 7D, a better test—the chi-square test—was applied to determine whether a distribution could be said to be normal.

9-94   Suppose that we were to examine a positively skewed distribution. Sketch such a distribution for yourself (Figure 8-6, page 111, is such a distribution). The area between the mean and $+1s$ will not be equal to the area between the mean and $-1s$, in such an asymmetrical distribution. Which of these areas is larger? _____ . (You do not need to know the size of s in order to answer this question.)

2.4 — 56
58.4

60.8

subtract
51.2

± 1
± 2

± 3

68

95

100

normal

The area between the mean and $-1s$

9-95 *We may speak of certain scores as lying between the mean and 1 standard deviation above the mean. The proportional frequency of these scores is the same as the _____ in the frequency polygon between the mean and _____ s.*

proportional area

+1

9-96 *The normal distribution has a fixed set of proportional areas under different parts of its distribution curve. About 68 per cent of its total area lies _____ . Almost 100 per cent of its total area lies _____ .*

within ±1s of the mean

within ±3s of the mean

9-97 *The proportional areas in a distribution will correspond to the areas characteristic of the normal distribution only when the distribution is approximately _____ . An example of a variable which does have such a distribution is _____ .*

normal

IQ (Stanford-Binet)

Problems for Lesson 9

9-1 Compute the range, average deviation (AD), and standard deviation (s) of the distribution of scores given below:

X_i	f_i	f_iX_i
20	1	20
19	4	76
18	6	108
17	9	153
16	10	160
15	16	240
14	10	140
13	8	104
12	5	60
11	4	44
10	2	20
	$N = 75$	$\Sigma = 1{,}125$

9-2 Give two reasons why the range should be regarded as a rough and approximate measure of the dispersion of a distribution.

9-3 What is the value of the variance of the distribution in Problem 9-1? State, in a few words, what the variance of a distribution is.

9-4 The distribution of scores in Problem 9-1 is approximately symmetrical. Assuming that the distribution does not deviate greatly from the form of a normal distribution, how many scores would you expect to find between the following limits:

(a) Between $+1s$ and $-1s$?

(b) Between $+2s$ and $-2s$?

(c) Between $+1s$ and $+2s$?

How many scores *actually* fall within each of the areas given above?

9-5 If a normal distribution has a mean $= 118$ and $s = 11$,

(a) What percentage of the scores will be found between the score limits 107 and 118?

(b) What percentage will lie below a score of 129?

(c) What percentage will be expected to lie above 140?

Lesson 10. Cumulative Distributions, Percentiles, and Standard Scores

The study of central tendency and dispersion has now put us in a position to discuss some of the most useful terms in psychological and educational measurement: percentiles, norms, and standard scores. After you have studied this lesson, you should have a much clearer idea about those terms which are commonly used to describe your relative standing on aptitude and achievement tests. Lesson 10 has a largely practical significance. However, a good sense of the meaning of standard scores will be necessary also in the later discussion of certain methods of statistical inference.

A. Cumulative Frequencies

Table 10-1 **Cumulative Frequency Distribution of Test Scores ($N = 40$)**

Class	f_i	Exact Upper Limits of Class Intervals	Cumulative Frequency (cum f_i)
33.5–36.49	1	36.5	40
30.5–33.49	2	33.5	39
27.5–30.49	4	30.5	37
24.5–27.49	8	27.5	33
21.5–24.49	10	24.5	25
18.5–21.49	8	21.5	15
15.5–18.49	4	18.5	7
12.5–15.49	2	15.5	3
9.5–12.49	1	12.5	1

10-1   Table 10-1 is a frequency distribution of 40 test scores made up as an illustration. Note the fourth column headed "Cumulative Frequency." The values in this column are frequencies, but they are different from the frequencies in the column f_i. These frequencies in column 4 are called _____ frequencies. The lowest numbers in the column are at the _____ of the column, and the

cumulative

bottom

numbers become steadily larger toward the _____ of the column.

10-2 Compare the second and fourth columns. Column 2 is the column of f_i. The class 9.5–12.49 has a frequency of _____ and a cumulative frequency of _____. The class 12.5–15.49 has a frequency of _____ and a cumulative frequency of _____. Where did the number 3 come from? It is the _____ of the *frequencies* in the lowest two classes.

10-3 The cumulative frequency for the class 15.5–18.49 is the sum of the frequencies in the lowest _____ classes. It therefore includes the frequencies in the class 15.5–18.49 as well as all the frequencies in classes *below* the class _____.

10-4 The exact upper limit of the class interval for scores 15.5 to 18.49 is _____. The number 7 thus represents the sum of all the frequencies which lie below the limit, _____, since there are 7 scores to be found in the three lowest classes.

10-5 The cumulative frequency 15 represents the sum of all the frequencies which lie below the limit, _____, since there are 15 scores to be found in the _____ lowest classes.

10-6 The *cumulative frequency* for any class is the sum of the _____ for that class and the _____ of the next lower class.

10-7 The cumulative frequency at the top of column 4 is 40. The value of N for this set of scores is _____. The cumulative frequency for the highest interval in a distribution must always equal _____ because it must include *all* the scores in the distribution.

10-8 If we graph the cumulative frequencies, we obtain a CUMULATIVE FREQUENCY CURVE. Figure 10-1 shows such a graph for the cumulative frequencies of Table 10-1. Notice that the X axis value at which each cumulative frequency is plotted is the value of the _____ for the class interval. This point is different from the point that is used in constructing a frequency polygon. In a frequency polygon, the frequencies are plotted at the _____ of the class intervals.

10-9 In plotting a _____, the exact upper limit of each

---

top

1
1
2
3
sum

3

15.5 — 18.49

18.5
18.5

21.5
four

frequency — cumulative frequency

40

N

exact upper limit

midpoints

cumulative frequency curve

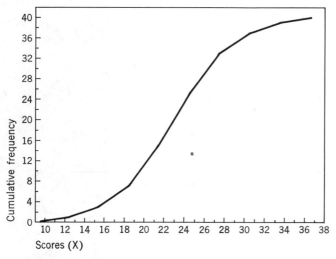

Figure 10-1. A graph of cumulative frequencies from Table 10-1.

class interval is used because the cumulative frequency through any class represents the number of scores which lie _____ the exact upper limit of that interval.

below

10-10   Recall that in Lesson 8C we determined one such cumulative frequency point (although we did not call it this) when we calculated the *median* for a distribution of 100 scores (see page 114). We had to find out the total number of _____ which lay below the lower limit of the class containing the middle score.

scores

10-11   If we have the entire cumulative frequency curve for those essay scores, as in Figure 10-2, finding the median is quite easy. The middle score in 100 scores must be between scores _____ and _____; we could say that it is score 50.5. Find 50.5 on the Y axis in Figure 10-2. The horizontal arrow starting at this point indicates that point on the _____ curve at which the middle score is found, and the vertical arrow from that point tells the position on the _____ axis for that middle score. As in Lesson 8C, we find the median to be 68.

50 ↔
51

cumulative frequency

X

10-12   The cumulative frequency curves in Figures 10-1 and 10-2 both have somewhat the shape of the letter _____. This shape arises whenever the *frequency distribution* itself is approximately *normal.* For a perfectly normal frequency distribution, the cumulative frequency curve is called an OGIVE (oh' jive). The curves in Figures 10-1 and 10-2 have approximately the shape of an _____.

S

ogive

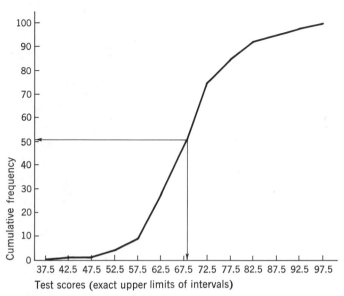

Figure 10-2. Cumulative frequencies for the distribution presented as Figure 8-7.

10-13 *Cumulative frequencies are added up, starting with the* _____ *class in a distribution. The cumulative frequency of any particular class is the* _____ *of the* _____ *of that class and the* _____ *of the* _____ *. The highest cumulative frequency in a distribution is always equal to* _____ *.*

10-14 *A cumulative frequency curve is drawn by taking the exact* _____ *of each class interval and plotting the* _____ *of that class at this point. If the frequency distribution is approximately normal, the cumulative frequency curve will be approximately* _____ *-shaped, like an* _____ *.*

lowest

sum — frequency
cumulative frequency
— next lower class

N

upper limit —
cumulative frequency

S — ogive

B. Cumulative Proportions and Percentiles

10-15 In Table 10-2, the distribution from Table 10-1 is repeated, with the addition of a new column of CUMULATIVE PROPORTIONS. You already know that a frequency is converted into a proportional frequency when it is divided by total frequency N. Similarly, a *cumulative*

Table 10-2 Cumulative Frequencies and Cumulative Proportions for a Distribution of Test Scores ($N = 40$)

Class	f_i	Exact Upper Limit	Cum f_i	Cumulative Proportion
33.5–36.49	1	36.5	40	1.000
30.5–33.49	2	33.5	39	0.975
27.5–30.49	4	30.5	37	0.925
24.5–27.49	8	27.5	33	0.825
21.5–24.49	10	24.5	25	0.625
18.5–21.49	8	21.5	15	0.375
15.5–18.49	4	18.5	7	0.175
12.5–15.49	2	15.5	3	0.075
9.5–12.49	1	12.5	1	0.025

frequency is converted into a *cumulative proportional frequency* when it is divided by the same factor _____ .

N

10-16 We shall use the shorter name *cumulative proportions* for these cumulative proportional frequencies. For the class 9.5–12.49, the cumulative proportion is _____ . This number is obtained by dividing _____ by _____ .

0.025

1 — 40

10-17 The highest cumulative frequency in column 4 is equal to the total frequency 40. The highest cumulative proportion in column 5 is equal to _____ . You know already that the sum of *all* the proportions is equal to 1.00.

1.00

10-18 Figure 10-3 is a graph of the cumulative proportions from Table 10-2. At the same time, it is a graph of the cumulative frequencies. The Y axis has two scales. One scale, from 0 to 40, is the scale of cumulative _____ ; the other scale, from 0 to 1.000, is the scale of cumulative _____ . The same curve can be drawn against both these scales because the change to cumulative proportions is only a *change in the units in which cumulative frequency is measured.*

frequencies

proportions

10-19 The cumulative proportion scale will be still more convenient than the cumulative frequency scale for finding out about *percentiles*. Determining a percentile is much like determining a median, so let us first determine the *median* in Figure 10-3. Since half the scores must lie below the median, we can say that the *proportion* of scores below the median must be _____ .

0.5

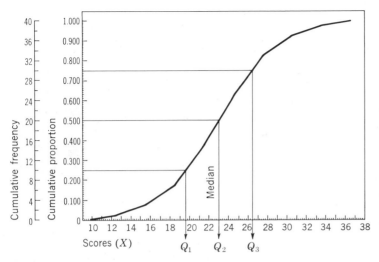

Figure 10-3. Cumulative proportions from Table 10-2.

10-20 Find the point which is 0.5 on the Y axis. The horizontal line from this point indicates the point on the curve at which the _____ lies. The vertical arrow shows the value on the X axis to be _____ .

10-21 The cumulative proportion curve makes it very easy to find the median because the Y axis is marked off in proportional units. The median score divides the upper _____ per cent of the scores from the lower _____ per cent. Any person in the group of 40 who made a score greater than the median is in the upper _____ per cent of the group.

10-22 Suppose now that you wanted to learn which score divides the *lower* 25 per cent from the remainder of the group. What position on the Y axis would you choose? _____ . What X value corresponds to the curve at this position? _____ .

10-23 Determine from the same curve what the score is which divides the *upper* 25 per cent from the remainder. You must choose the position _____ on the Y axis. The proper score is _____ .

10-24 These scores which divide the distribution into *quarters* are called QUARTILES. They are numbered from 1 to 3, starting at the low end of the scale, and indicated on Figure 10-3 as Q_1, Q_2, and Q_3. Thus, the score marking the top of the lowest 25 per cent is the _____

Cumulative Proportions and Percentiles   **153**

quartile, the score marking the top of the next 25 per cent is the
_____, and the score dividing the lower 75 per cent from
the upper 25 per cent is the _____ . Which one of these is
the same as the *median?* The _____ quartile.

10-25 In Figure 10-3, the score 19.6 is the _____ quartile.
Any person in the group of 40 making a score lower than 19.6 is in the
bottom _____ per cent of the group. The score 26.4 is the
_____ quartile. Scores above 26.4 are in the _____
per cent.

10-26 Similarly, if one takes successive *tenths* of the distribution,
one can obtain the first, second, and so on, up to the ninth and tenth
DECILE. The *first decile* score is that score dividing the lowest
_____ per cent from the upper _____ per cent.
In Figure 10-2, repeated below with cumulative proportions on the *Y*
axis, the first decile score, as read from the graph, is closest to the
score _____ .

10-27 The median can be called the second quartile. It could also be
called the _____ decile.

10-28 Quartiles and deciles are less frequently used than PERCEN-
TILES (or *centiles*). *Percentiles* divide the distribution into *hundredths.*

second quartile
third quartile
second

first

25
third — upper 25

10 — 90

58

fifth

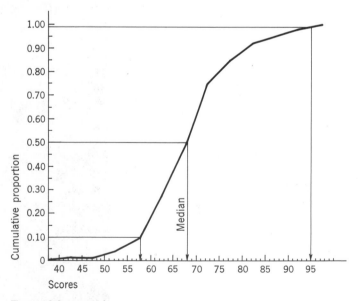

Figure 10-2 repeated

The first quartile is also the _____th percentile, and the median is the _____th percentile.

25
50

10-29   The score below which 76 per cent of the values in a distribution fall is called the 76th _____. That score *equals or exceeds* 76 per cent of the scores in the distribution.

percentile

10-30   The score which equals or exceeds 99 per cent of the scores in the distribution is the _____. In Figure 10-2, this score is equal to _____.

99th percentile
95

10-31   Any score can be expressed in terms of a percentile for a given distribution. For the distribution in Figure 10-2, the score 75 is the same as the 80th percentile. You determine this by drawing or imagining a vertical arrow up to the cumulative proportion curve from the score 80 and a horizontal arrow from that point on the curve to the Y axis. The score 72.5 is the same as the _____ percentile.

75th

10-32   Percentiles are principally used in establishing NORMS for comparing the test score of an individual person with the scores made by a large group of persons. The College Entrance Examination Board provides a test which is taken each year by a large number of applicants to colleges and universities. The scores of all these applicants form a frequency distribution from which a cumulative proportion curve can be drawn and percentiles can be calculated. The table of percentiles is a table of *norms*. When you know the score of a particular student, you can use the _____ of _____ in order to determine his standing relative to the entire group of applicants.

table — norms

10-33   If you were told that a student received 39 points on a history test, 76 points on a test of arithmetic, and 135 points on a test of vocabulary and English grammar, you would not be able to say whether the student was high, low, or average in any of these subjects. You would need to know also the _____ for these three tests.

norms

10-34   If you were told that 39 in history was the 48th percentile, 76 in arithmetic was the 29th percentile, and 135 in English was the 97th percentile for a large group of students, you could then say that the student ranks relatively *high* in _____, close to the median in _____, and relatively *low* in _____.

English
history — arithmetic

10-35   Note carefully that a percentile point for a given raw score is *not* the same as a percentage of total points on the test. If there were 150 points possible on the English test, the student who earned 135 points has earned 90 per cent of the total possible points. *But this does not mean that* 135 *is the 90th percentile.* You cannot determine the percentile score for a given raw score without knowing the _____ for the test, which are based on the distribution of scores earned by some particular group.

Review

10-36   *The 50th percentile is the same as the _____ quartile, the _____ decile, and the _____. It is the score below which _____ of the scores in a particular frequency distribution fall.*

10-37   *A table of percentiles for a particular test, based on the scores of a large group of persons, is called a table of _____.*

10-38   *When you hear that a person made 95 per cent on a particular test, you know only that he came near to earning all the points possible. If nearly everyone else scored low on the test, his percentile standing may be even _____ than the 95th percentile, but if nearly everyone else also scored very high, then his percentile standing may be quite _____. You cannot tell what percentile 95 per cent represents without a table of _____.*

C.   Standard Scores

10-39   You are already familiar with the equation $x_i = X_i - \bar{X}$, which defined the _____ score. In this definition, the symbol _____ stands for any particular raw score and the symbol _____ stands for the arithmetic mean of the distribution.

10-40   We shall use the letter z to represent the STANDARD SCORE. Just as we can obtain a deviation score x_i for every raw score X_i, we can also obtain a _____ score z_i for every X_i.

10-41 The *standard score* is defined by the equation,

$$z_i = \frac{x_i}{s}$$

To convert a deviation score into a standard score, we divide the _____ score by the _____ of the distribution.

10-42 To find the standard score for any X_i, we first convert X_i into a deviation score, then divide by s. It is necessary that we know *two* characteristics of the frequency distribution from which our score comes: We must know the _____ in order to convert X_i into a deviation score, and we must know the _____ in order to convert x_i into a standard score.

10-43 Let $\bar{X} = 100$ and $s = 10$. If $X_i = 120$, then $x_i = $ _____ and $z_i = $ _____ .

10-44 Watch the *algebraic sign* in this next example. Let $\bar{X}$ again equal 100 and $s = 10$. If $X_i = 90$, then $x_i = $ _____ and $z_i = $ _____ .

10-45 When the deviation score is positive in sign, the standard score, or z score, is _____ . When the deviation score is negative, the z score is _____ .

10-46 The deviation score and z score will be negative whenever _____ is smaller than _____ . The deviation score will equal 0 whenever _____ , and (since zero divided by any number is zero) in this case the z score will also be _____ .

10-47 All negative z scores fall below the _____ , and all positive z scores fall above the _____ . A z score of 0 coincides with the _____ .

10-48 The z score for $\bar{X}$ always equals _____ . If X_j falls 1 *standard deviation above the mean*, z_j must equal _____ .

10-49 Similarly, if X_k lies 2 *standard deviations below the mean*, z_k must equal _____ .

10-50 The x score expresses any *raw* score as a _____ from the mean. The z score expresses any *deviation* score *in units equal to s.* Therefore, the z score expresses any *raw* score as a _____ score in *units* equal to _____ .

Review

10-51 *A deviation score is defined by the equation* _____ .
A standard score is defined by the equation _____ .

10-52 *A standard score expresses a raw score as a* _____ *from the* _____ *of the distribution in units equal to* _____ .

10-53 *Let* $\bar{X} = 16$ *and* $s = 2.4$. *If* $X_j = 10$, $x_j =$ _____
and $z_j =$ _____ . *If* $z_k = +1$, *then* $x_k =$ _____
and $X_k =$ _____ .

D. The z-score Distribution

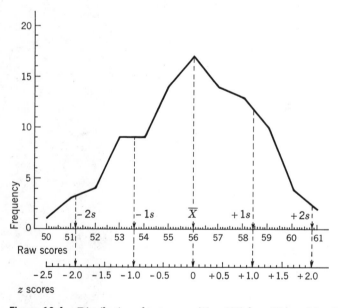

Figure 10-4. Distribution of test scores ($N = 100$) from Figure 9-6, with the addition of a scale of z scores.

10-54 Figure 10-4 has *two* scales for its X axis. The upper scale is in _____ scores; the lower scale is in _____ scores.

10-55 If you use the raw-score scale in reading this figure, this is a frequency distribution of raw scores. If you use the z-score scale, it is a distribution of standard scores. The raw-score distribution has $\bar{X} =$ _____ and $s =$ _____. The z-score distribution has a mean of _____ and a standard deviation of _____.

10-56 When the z-score scale is used, Figure 10-4 is the frequency distribution which is obtained when every X_i is converted into a _____. Notice that the *form* of the frequency distribution is not changed by this transformation. For $X_j = 56$, $z_j = 0$. The frequency of X_j is 17, and the frequency of z_j is _____. The same is true of each X_i and its z_i.

10-57 *Any* raw-score distribution can be transformed into a z-score distribution. The mean of any z-score distribution will always be _____, and s will always be _____. The *form* of the z-score distribution will always be like that of the _____ distribution from which it comes.

10-58 The z-score transformation of a *normal* raw-score distribution (such as the distribution of Stanford-Binet IQs from the general population) will have the shape of a _____ distribution.

10-59 The normal distribution whose X axis is in z-score units is called a NORMAL PROBABILITY DISTRIBUTION. The graph of this distribution is called the NORMAL CURVE, and it has the bell shape characteristic of all normal distributions. It is symmetrical around a mean of _____, and its standard deviation is _____. Because of its mathematical properties, this distribution is very important, and it will be used a great deal in Lessons 11 to 14.

The normal probability distribution is also called the Gaussian distribution after the mathematician Gauss, although he was actually not the very first mathematician to use it. The normal curve can be expressed as an equation with y (the distance on the Y axis) and z as variables:

$$y = \frac{1}{\sqrt{2\pi}} e^{-z^2/2}$$

In this equation, e is the number 2.7183, which is the base of natural logarithms.

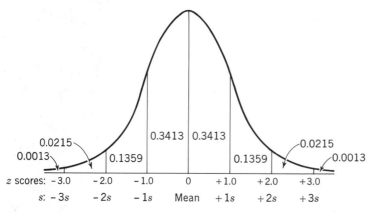

Figure 10-5. A normal distribution with a scale of z scores and a scale of standard deviation units.

10-60 Since we already know something about areas between certain limits in the normal frequency distribution, we can apply this knowledge also to the normal probability distribution. Figure 10.5 can be compared with Figures 9-3, 9-4, and 9-5. Since the proportional area in a normal distribution which lies between the mean and $1s$ above the mean is 0.3413, we know that the area in a normal probability distribution which lies between $z = 0$ and $z = +1$ is _____ of the total area.

0.3413

10-61 The area between $z = -1$ and $z = +1$ is the same as the area which lies within _____ 1 standard deviation of the mean. This area is _____ of the total area.

plus or minus
0.6826

10-62 We can *combine* proportional areas under the curve, shown in Figure 10-5, in order to answer various questions such as the following. What proportion of the area in the distribution lies between $z = 0$ and $z = +2$? _____ . Between $z = 0$ and $z = +3$? _____ .

0.4772 — 0.4987

10-63 What proportion of the total area lies above the mean and *beyond* $z = +3$? _____ . What is the total area which lies above the mean? _____ .

0.0013
0.5

10-64 *In a normally distributed set of 10,000 IQ scores with a mean of 100 and an s of 16, a z score of +3 represents an IQ score of _____ . A z score of −3 represents an IQ score of _____ .*

148 — 52

10-65   *Only 0.0013 (or 13/10,000) of the total area lies beyond z $= +3$. How many of the 10,000 IQ scores shall we therefore expect to find which are equal to or greater than 148?* _____.

E.   Percentiles and Standard Scores Compared

10-66   Since this lesson has dealt with both percentiles and standard scores, it may be helpful to discuss the relation between these two types of scores. When you know the raw score X_j made by a particular person, you can determine his *percentile* standing only if you also have information about the _____ for the test.

norms

10-67   These norms may be given in the form of a cumulative proportion graph (like Figure 10-3) or as a table of percentiles. If you are using a graph, you determine his percentile standing by finding his raw score on the _____ axis, imagining a line from that point to the cumulative proportion curve, and reading the position on the _____ axis which corresponds to that point.

X

Y

10-68   In this way, you find out what _____ of the scores made by a large group of persons have been found to fall _____ the score you are interested in.

proportion (percentage)
below

10-69   In order to determine the standard score z_j for a particular X_j, you need to know the _____ and _____ of a distribution of scores made by a large group of persons. In effect, then, you also need to know the *norms*, but in this case the norms must be put in terms of the _____ and _____ of the distribution.

mean — s

mean — s

10-70   With a cumulative proportion graph, you could compute the mean and standard deviation even if they were not given to you directly. For such a computation, you need to know the frequency distribution; the cumulative proportion graph is a graph of cumulative proportions which have been derived from the original frequencies. It would be inconvenient, but you could derive the original _____ from the _____ if you had to do so.

frequencies
cumulative   proportions

10-71   On the other hand, given only the mean and standard deviation of the distribution, you could determine the percentile norms *only* if you could assume that the shape of the distribution is _____ .

normal

Only in that case would you know the proportional areas lying within particular regions of the distribution.

10-72   If you knew that the distribution was a normal distribution, then you could say that the 50th percentile lies at the point where $X_i =$ _____ . Half of the scores in a normal distribution lie below the _____ , and the median therefore coincides with the _____ .

$\bar{X}$

mean

mean

10-73   Also, since you know that 0.34 of the normal distribution lies between $z = 0$ and $z = +1$, you can quickly determine that 84 per cent of the scores in the normal distribution lie below the point that is _____ above the mean. If $\bar{X}$ is given as 100 and s as 16, then the IQ which represents the 84th percentile must be _____ .

1 standard deviation

116

10-74   But if you could *not* assume that the distribution is a normal distribution, percentile norms could not be calculated from the mean and standard deviation. You could tell the value of z_j for any particular X_j, but you would not be able to determine the _____ standing of persons making that score.

percentile

10-75   The basic difference, then, is that the percentile score is an extension of the idea of the *median*, which is logically related to *ordinal* positions, while the standard score is based on the *mean*. When you want to determine *rank* or *relative standing*, you are interested in the *ordinal position* of scores, and the more useful measure of central tendency is the _____ .

median

10-76   Because percentiles have the same *ordinal* quality that the median possesses, _____ are likely to be more useful than _____ scores when you are interested in relative standing.

percentiles

standard

10-77   However, in those cases in which the distribution is normal, it is quicker and more convenient to use standard scores. In such cases, the whole table of norms can be reduced to just two numbers, the _____ and the _____ .

mean — s

Review

10-78   *In order to determine the relative standing of a person on a particular test, it is not sufficient to know only his score on the test. You must also know the _____ for the test. If the distribution is normal,*

norms

it will be sufficient to know the _____ *. But if the distribution is not normal, you will need a* _____ *.*

mean and s

table of percentiles or
    cumulative proportion
    distribution

10-79 *Relative standings can be described in terms of standard scores when the distribution is* _____ *. Relative standings are better given in percentiles when the distribution is* _____ *.*

normal
nonnormal

Problems for Lesson 10

10-1 The distribution of values below is the same as that given in Problem 1, Lesson 9. Compute the cumulative frequencies and cumulative proportions for this distribution by completing the following table:

X_i	f_i	Exact Upper Limits of Class Intervals	Cum f_i	Cum Proportions
20	1	20.5	_____	_____
19	4	19.5	_____	_____
18	6	18.5	_____	_____
17	9	17.5	_____	_____
16	10	16.5	_____	_____
15	16	15.5	_____	_____
14	10	14.5	_____	_____
13	8	13.5	_____	_____
12	5	12.5	_____	_____
11	4	11.5	_____	_____
10	2	10.5	_____	_____

10-2 **(a)** What is the percentile point corresponding to the score 15.5 in the distribution above?

(b) What score falls approximately at the 1st quartile?

(c) Optional: Obtain a piece of graph paper ruled 20 squares to the inch, and plot the curve of cumulative proportions for the distribution. Graphically determine the score values corresponding to the 1st through 10th deciles.

10-3 If a distribution has a mean $= 118$ and $s = 11$, what z scores correspond to raw scores of 115, 134, and 99?

10-4 For a particular normal distribution of scores, the following facts are known: **(a)** 16 per cent of the scores fall below 57, and **(b)** a z score of $+0.5$ corresponds to a raw score of 69. What is the mean of the distribution? What is the standard deviation? What raw score corresponds to the 98th percentile?

10-5 In a normal distribution, what is the z score equivalent of the 50th percentile? Of the 84th percentile? What percentile point corresponds to a z score of $+2.0$?

Lesson 11. The Normal Curve and Probability

We are now at a point of connecting the two lines of study which have been so far developed independently: the methods of describing frequency distributions (Lessons 6, 8, 9, and 10) and the use of probability in significance testing (Lessons 1 through 5). In the next six lessons (Lessons 11 through 16), our treatment of the common significance tests will be completed by making use of the concepts derived from frequency distributions.

As we return to the problems of significance testing, we take up again the familiar alternation experiment introduced in Lesson 2, where each observation can be classified as either a repetition or an alternation, with $p_R = p_A = \frac{1}{2}$ according to the null hypothesis. At the end of Lesson 5, we were using the triangular table from Lesson 4 in order to calculate the probabilities of obtaining certain particular kinds of results in such an experiment. This table is helpful for experiments having as many as 10 observations, but larger numbers of observations make the work of computing probabilities by that method very tedious. Therefore, we shall now begin to make use of a more efficient procedure based on the properties of the normal probability distribution introduced in Lesson 10.

A. The Histogram for Groups of 10 Observations

11-1 Figure 11-1 treats a set of *expected frequencies* in the way you are now accustomed to treat *frequencies*, that is, by presenting them in the form of a graph called a _____ . For ordinary frequency distributions, such as those in Lesson 6, you are accustomed to find along the X axis the values of the X variable, often "scores." In this graph of expected frequencies, the X axis shows the different kinds of outcomes that can occur in an alternation experiment containing _____ observations.

histogram

10

11-2 Since this is a histogram for groups of 10 observations, you know from the triangular table that the total number of combinations is 1,024. Therefore, the area in this histogram is also

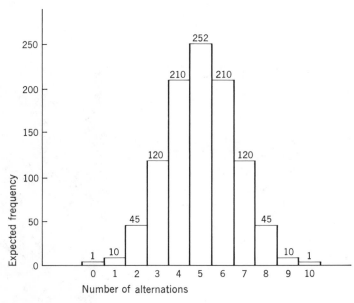

Figure 11-1. Histogram of expected frequencies of outcomes in a 10-observation alternation experiment ($p_A = p_R = \frac{1}{2}$).

_____. All the expected frequencies will add up to this number.

1,024

11-3 Figure 11-2 is exactly like Figure 11-1 except that the scale on the Y axis has been changed. Instead of representing _____, the Y axis now represents _____ .

expected frequency
probability

11-4 Actually, this transformation is one already familiar to you, for it is the same as the transformation from *frequencies* to *proportional frequencies*. To obtain a proportional frequency, you divided the frequency by the total _____ in the frequency distribution. To obtain probability, you divide expected frequency by _____ .

frequency
total frequency

11-5 The numbers at the tops of the bars in Figure 11-1 represented _____ . The numbers at the tops of the bars in Figure 11-2 are these same numbers, *each divided by* 1,024. Therefore, they have become _____ .

expected frequencies

probabilities

11-6 The modal class in this histogram is the outcome which has _____ alternations and _____ repetitions. Its probability is 252/1,024, or _____ .

five — five
0.246

11-7 The total area in the histogram in Figure 11-2 must equal

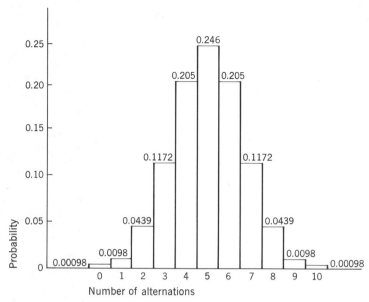

Figure 11-2. Histogram of probabilities of outcomes in a 10-observation alternation experiment $(p_A = p_R = \frac{1}{2})$.

_____. The total area represents the sum of the _____ of all the possible combinations of 10 observations, and this sum is always equal to _____. From Lesson 9, you also know that the sum of all the proportional _____ in such a figure must equal _____.

11-8 The probability of any event or group of events can thus be visualized as an _____ making up part of the total area in this histogram.

11-9 The area of the column for 8 alterations is 45/1,024, or 0.044. The area of the column for 9 alternations is 10/1,024, or 0.0098. The area of the column for 10 alternations is 1/1,024, or 0.00098. What is the total area which corresponds to the probability of getting 8, 9, or 10 alternations in a 10-observation experiment? _____.

11-10 From this parallel between frequency distributions and *expected frequency* distributions, we can obtain a new notion about the meaning of probability. A probability distribution is related to an _____ frequency distribution in the same way that a proportional frequency distribution is related to an ordinary frequency distribution.

11-11   Thus, a _____ distribution is a *proportional expected frequency distribution.*

probability

Review

11-12   *When histograms are representations of ordinary frequency distributions, the height of a column represents the* _____ *of values in a certain class. The total area in the histogram is the* _____ *frequency, symbolized by* _____.

frequency

total — N

11-13   *When histograms are representations of probability distributions, the height of a column represents the* _____ *of a certain kind of outcome. It also represents the* _____ *expected* _____ *of that outcome. The total area in the histogram in such a case is equal to* _____.

probability
proportional —
  frequency
1

B.   The Histogram for Groups of 100 Observations

11-14   The histogram in Figure 11-3 shows the probabilities of obtaining different numbers of alternations in an experiment with 100 rats (assuming the null hypothesis). From the histogram, you can determine that the probability of obtaining *exactly 50 alternations* is 0.08. The expected frequency of the outcome "50 alternations and 50 repetitions" is therefore _____ in 100 experiments where

8

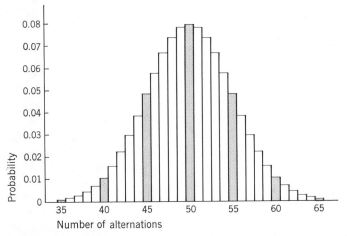

Figure 11-3.   Histogram of probabilities of outcomes in a 100-observation alternation experiment $(p_A = p_R = \frac{1}{2})$.

each experiment involves 100 rats. In 200 such experiments, this out-come is expected to occur approximately _____ times.

11-15 It may surprise you that the probability of exactly 50 alterna-tions is so low, since this outcome is the _____ class in the probability distribution and occurs _____ frequently than any other kind of outcome. The lowness of the probability reflects the fact that there are quite a large number of different outcomes which can occur when $N = 100$. No *one* of these can therefore occur very frequently.

11-16 From Figure 11-3, you can see that *two* of the kinds of out-comes have an expected frequency of 3 in 100 experiments: the out-come "43 alternations" and the outcome "_____ alternations."

11-17 The probability of getting more than 65 alternations is so small that it does not even appear on the graph. The same is true of the probability of getting fewer than _____ alternations. The absence of these kinds of outcomes from the figure does not mean that they will never occur in a nonsystematic population of observa-tions, but their expected frequency is so _____ that it might take *several thousand* 100-rat experiments before either event would occur at all.

11-18 In order to determine each of these probabilities in the histo-gram, one could extend the triangular table to the one-hundredth row. The total number of combinations in a 10-rat experiment is 2 to the 10th power, or 1,024. The total number in a 100-rat experiment would be 2 to the _____ th power, which is an astronomical num-ber that would require about 30 figures to write out!

11-19 You can already see that the procedure used for 10 observa-tions would be out of the question for 100 observations. But imagine further: To find the probability of getting 60 alternations, you would take ½ to the 100th power, which is the probability of getting any *one* of the 2^{100} _____ , and multiply this infinitesimal probability by the number of combinations in which 60 alternations and 40 repeti-tions could occur. This number of combinations is given by the fac-torial fraction which has 100! in the numerator and _____ in the denominator.

11-20 Computing this factorial fraction would obviously be very laborious. But it would be even more laborious to answer the question

"Is it a rare event if we obtain *as many as* 60 alternations in a 100-rat experiment?" Let us assume that our alternate hypothesis is "Rats will show more alternation behavior." To answer the question, we would have to know not only the probability of obtaining 60 alternations but also all the probabilities of the various numbers of alternations _____ than 60, up to 100.

greater

11-21   From the histogram in Figure 11-3 or 11-4, you can estimate the probability of 60 or more alternations quite easily. You know that this probability is represented by the total area at the _____-hand end of the figure, starting with the column for _____ alternations.

right
60

11-22   The area of the column for 60 alternations is about 0.01. The areas of the columns to the right of 60 alternations are all _____ than 0.01.

less

11-23   With such an alternate hypothesis as we supposed, an outcome of 60 alternations in a 100-rat experiment is therefore _____ at the .05 level because the probability of at least 60 alternations is obviously _____ than 0.05.

significant
less

Review

11-24   *We say that the expected frequency of alternations in a 100-rat experiment is _____ when the population is nonsystematic. Yet this expected frequency is expected to occur only about _____ times in every 100 replications of a 100-rat experiment.*

50
eight

11-25   *When we say "The expected frequency of alternations is 50 in a 100-rat experiment," we do not mean that 50 alternations and 50 repetitions should occur all or even most of the time. We mean that 50 alternations should occur more _____ than any other kind of outcome of 100 observations and that the numbers of alternations which do occur should usually be quite close to _____.*

frequently (often)

50

C.   The Normal Probability Curve for Large Values of N

11-26   Figure 11-4 is the histogram from Figure 11-3 with a smooth curve drawn through the middle of the top of each column. This curve

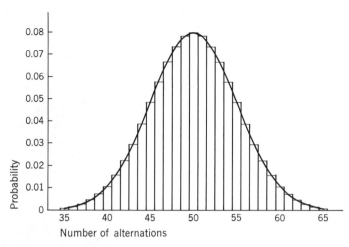

Figure 11-4. Histogram of probabilities of outcomes in a 100-observation alternation experiment.

is _____ around the midpoint, and it has the bell shape which is characteristic of the _____ distribution.

symmetrical

normal

11-27 Look back at Figure 11-2 (page 167) and Figure 11-3 (page 168). Figure 11-2 is for experiments with _____ rats, and Figure 11-3 for experiments with _____ rats. Both these histograms have the same general shape, but the shape is nearer to a smooth curve in Figure _____ .

10

100

11-3

11-28 The smoothness of the shape of the probability histogram increases as the number of _____ in the experiment increases—in other words, as the value of _____ increases.

rats

N

11-29 The histogram for 100 rats is smoother than that for 10 rats; a histogram for 1,000 rats would be even _____ . With a *very* large number of rats, the histogram would be indistinguishable from the smooth curve shown in Figure 11-5. The curve in Figure 11-5 is the *normal probability curve* discussed in Lesson 10D.

smoother

11-30 The histogram of probabilities becomes more and more like a normal curve as the number of _____ in an experiment becomes very large. We can use our knowledge about the shape and area of the normal curve to compute probabilities when we have very large values of _____ .

rats (observations)

N

11-31 Notice that the normal curve in Figure 11-5 has its X axis

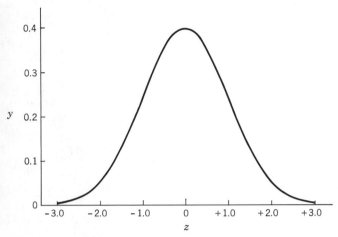

Figure 11-5. The normal probability curve.

z-score

labeled in _____ units. From Lesson 10, you know that the normal probability distribution is a normal frequency distribution with its X axis in _____ units.

z-score

11-32   The value of z at the mean of the distribution is always _____. Its value at 1 standard deviation above the mean is always _____, and its value at 1 standard deviation below the mean is always _____ .

0
+1
−1

11-33   The Y axis in Figure 11-5 is labeled simply _____, whereas the Y axis in the probability histogram of Figure 11-4 was labeled "probability."

y

11-34   This is an important difference between the *probability histogram* and the *normal probability curve*. In the histogram, the height measured along the Y axis represented the actual _____ of a particular kind of outcome of 100 observations. *This is no longer true with the normal curve.* In the normal probability distribution, only the _____ under the curve represents probability.

probability

area

11-35   The meaning of y in the normal curve comes from the equation for this curve, which was given in Lesson 10D as

$$y = \frac{1}{\sqrt{2\pi}} e^{-z^2/2}$$

where π and e are numbers, not variables. You do not need to study this equation. All you need to remember is that the histogram of probabilities *tends to resemble such a curve as* _____ gets very large.

N

11-36 *A probability distribution is a distribution of* _____ *expected* _____. *As the number of observations in an experiment becomes very large, the* _____ *distribution tends to take on the shape of the* _____ *curve.*

proportional
frequencies
probability
normal

11-37 *The normal curve is not a frequency distribution of any sort. It is a line represented by a particular equation. The Y axis of the normal curve does not represent* _____ *as the Y axis of a probability distribution does. The X axis also has a different scale; it is marked off in units which are symbolized by the letter* _____, *each one of which equals one* _____.

probability

z
standard deviation

D. Determining Probabilities by Means of the Normal Curve

11-38 In Section B, we estimated the probability of 60 or more alternations from an examination of the probability histogram. Since an N of 100 is sufficiently large to make the probability distribution approximately like a _____, we can now calculate this probability more precisely.

normal curve

11-39 The probability we are interested in is represented by an _____ under the normal curve lying to the right of a certain point, namely, 60 alternations. But we need to know what point along the normal curve axis corresponds to the point _____.

area

60 alternations

11-40 The X axis of the normal curve is marked off in z-score units. Therefore, we need to convert 60 alternations to a _____. For this conversion, we need to know two things about our probability distribution: We need to know its _____, and then we need to know its _____.

z score

mean
standard deviation

11-41 The *mean* of a probability distribution of this kind is always the *expected frequency*—in this case, the expected frequency of alternations. The mean of our probability distribution is therefore _____.

50

11-42 Notice how you arrived at this expected frequency of 50: You multiplied the _____ of alternation p_A by _____.

The general definition of the mean of a probability distribution is

$$\overline{X} = Np$$

where p represents the probability of a certain outcome (e.g., alternation).

probability — N

11-43 Now for the standard deviation. In a probability distribution of this kind, the *standard deviation* is defined as

$$s = \sqrt{Npq}$$

where q now stands for the probability of the *other* outcome (e.g., repetition). For our example, therefore, we can substitute for the symbols p and q the symbols _____ and _____ . In symbols, for our example,

$$s = \underline{\hspace{3cm}}$$

$p_A - p_R$

$\sqrt{Np_A p_R}$

11-44 Since $N = 100$ and $p_A = p_R = \frac{1}{2}$, the standard deviation of our probability distribution is _____ .

5

11-45 Now that we know the mean and standard deviation for our probability distribution, we can determine that the z score for 60 alternations is _____ because this kind of outcome lies _____ standard deviations *above* the mean in the probability distribution.

$+2$

2

11-46 Now recall that we are interested in the area under the normal curve which lies *beyond* our result, 60 alternations. We are not interested in the area to the left of this point, nor are we concerned about the area beyond 60 repetitions at the bottom of the distributions because our _____ hypothesis states "Rats will show more *alternation* behavior."

alternate

11-47 You can determine the probability of 60 or more alternations from Figure 11-6, which shows the _____ of the area under the normal curve which lies beyond $z = +2$. The probability is _____ . We were not wrong when we estimated that the probability was less than 0.05.

proportion

0.0228

11-48 One other example should be tried to make sure the procedure is clear. Consider an experiment involving 900 rats. The value of

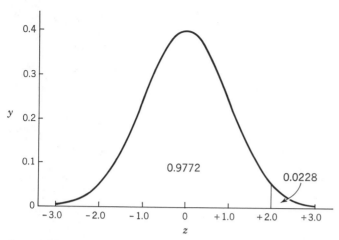

Figure 11-6. Areas under the normal probability curve.

N for such an experiment is _____. The mean of the probability distribution is _____.

900
450

11-49 The standard deviation of the probability distribution is the square root of _____ x _____. It is equal to _____.

900 — ¼
15

11-50 With a mean of 450 and an s of 15, the z score for 465 alternations is _____. The z score for 426 alternations is _____ (watch the algebraic sign).

+1
−1.6

Review

11-51 *Since the shape of the normal probability distribution for large values of N is like the shape of the normal curve, we can use our knowledge of areas under the normal curve to determine the _____ of any particular outcome.*

probability

11-52 *In order to find the probability of an outcome, we must be able to express that outcome as a _____, and this requires that we know the _____ and _____ for our _____.*

z score
mean — s —
probability distribution

11-53 *The mean of a probability distribution of this kind is defined as $\bar{X} =$ _____. The standard deviation is defined as $s =$ _____.*

Np
√Npq

E. Practice in Determining Probabilities as Proportional Areas

11-54 The total area in a probability distribution is equal to _____. The area above the mean is equal to _____, and the area below the mean is equal to _____ .

11-55 Since the shape of a probability distribution for large N is like a normal curve, we can apply what we know about proportional areas under the normal curve to our probability distribution. Probabilities are also _____ areas.

11-56 In Section D, we determined that the probability of 60 or more alternations is 0.0228. If 60 alternations were observed in a 100-observation experiment, we would _____ the null hypothesis that the population is nonsystematic.

11-57 Remember that our alternate hypothesis is "Rats will show more alternation behavior." Suppose that, having committed ourselves to such an alternate hypothesis, we have the bad luck to observe 45 alternations in 100. Let us, for practice, determine the probability of 45 *or more* alternations in 100 observations. The z score for 45 alternations is _____, since the mean is 50 and $s = 5$.

11-58 We are interested in the area which lies _____ $z = -1$. Think of this area as having two parts: the area between $z = -1$ and $z = 0$ and the area _____ $z = 0$.

11-59 The area above (to the right of) $z = 0$ is _____ of the total area. From Figure 11-7, you will be reminded that the area between the mean and $1s$ below the mean is _____ . The total area above $z = -1$ is therefore _____ .

11-60 Thus, the probability of getting 45 *or more alternations* from a nonsystematic population, is _____ . We would expect to get *at least* 45 *alternations* in _____ out of every 100 replications of the 100-rat experiment.

11-61 If we had held the alternate hypothesis "Rats will show more repetition behavior," we would have been interested in the probability of 45 or _____ alternations. This probability is given by the area under the curve which is _____ the z score of −1.

11-62 If the area above $z = -1$ is 0.8413, then the area below that

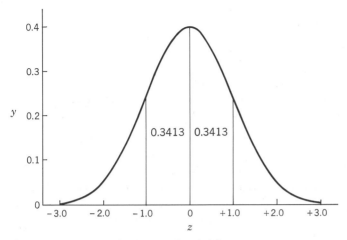

Figure 11-7. Areas under the normal probability curve.

point is _____. The probability of getting 45 or fewer alternations is _____.

0.1587

0.1587

11-63 The z score for the outcome, 55 alternations, is _____. The probability of 55 or more alternations is the same as the proportional area under the normal curve which lies _____.

+1

above z = +1

11-64 Since the proportional area above $z = 0$ is equal to _____ and the area between $z = 0$ and $z = +1$ is _____, the probability of 55 or more alternations is _____.

0.5

0.3413

0.1587

Problems for Lesson 11

11-1 Determine the mean and standard deviation for the normal probability distribution for 900 tosses of an unbiased coin. What is the probability in 900 tosses of obtaining between 435 and 465 heads? Between 465 and 480 heads? More than 495 heads?

11-2 Just before a national election, Republicans and Democrats each claim that the odds are 50:50 for their party to carry a particular state. A random sample of 400 voters contains 220 who say that they plan to vote Republican and 180 who say that they plan to vote Democratic. What is the probability of getting at least this large a number of Republican responses in the sample of 400 if the population of the state *is* equally divided between people intending to vote Republican and people intending to vote Democratic?

11-3 For this set of 400 observations, convert the following results into z scores. Consider that the probability distribution is drawn with the x axis labeled "number of Republicans."

(a) 215 Republicans, 185 Democrats

(b) 150 Republicans, 250 Democrats

(c) 190 Republicans, 210 Democrats

Lesson 12. Significance Tests Using the Normal Curve Table— I: Testing Dichotomized Data

In Lesson 11, it was shown how areas under the normal curve correspond to probabilities. You have probably already memorized some proportional areas under the normal curve, namely, those which are associated with distances of 1 or 2 standard deviations along the X axis. You know that 0.6826 of the total area under the normal curve lies within ± 1 standard deviation of the mean and that 0.9544 of the total area lies within ± 2 standard deviations of the mean.

Tables have been worked out which show the areas under the normal curve for all the possible z scores, even those which are not whole numbers like 1 or 2. In Lesson 12, the use of these tables will be explained. A table of normal curve areas appears on the foldout between pages 336 and 337; the page can be opened out so that the table is visible while you are working through this lesson.

You will notice from the title of Lesson 12 that this is the first of two lessons in which the normal curve table will be applied to problems of significance-testing. In this lesson, we will be concerned only with those applications in which the observed frequencies can be separated into two classes, that is, in which they can be dichotomized. The alternation experiment is an example of experiments providing dichotomized frequencies; all the observations can be classified into one of two classes: "alternation" and "repetition." We shall later study the use of the normal curve table in significance tests on other kinds of experimental observations.

A.   Using the Normal Curve Table

Turn to the foldout and refer to the Table of Areas under the Normal Curve.

12-1   In the normal curve table, the columns containing values of z are also labeled x/σ. This symbol is identical with our definition of z as x/s, for the Greek lower-case sigma, written σ, is frequently used in statistics tables to represent the _____ , which we represent by s.

standard deviation

12-2 The letter x in the expression x/σ stands for the _____ score, which we have defined earlier as $x_i =$ _____ . Therefore, when the table states that $z = x/\sigma$, this statement is equivalent to our statement that $z_i =$ _____ .

deviation
$X_i - \overline{X}$
$\dfrac{x_i}{s}$

12-3 For any value of z, the adjacent column of the table gives the area from the _____ to _____ . The "mean" referred to is the point 0 on the z scale. The mean of a z distribution is always _____ .

mean — z

0

12-4 Look at the first line of the table. What is the area from the mean to z when $z = +1$? According to the table, it is _____ ; this number is already familiar to you.

0.3413

12-5 At $z = 2$, the table shows another familiar number; the area from the mean to $z = 2$ is _____ . If this value is multiplied by 2, the result is _____ , which is the area you already know to lie within ± 2 standard deviations of the mean.

0.4772
0.9544

12-6 The areas in the table are all areas between z and _____ . Therefore, they all refer to only *one-half* of the area under the normal curve. If z is negative, the areas are areas on the _____ side of the mean. If z is positive, the areas refer to the _____ half.

the mean

left
right

12-7 The highest value in the table for the area from the mean to z is nearly _____ . Because the table refers to only one-half of the area under the normal curve, and not to the whole area, the maximum value of the area from the mean to z is *half* of _____ .

0.5

1.0

12-8 Using this table, you can find probabilities for z scores other than 1 or 2. Return to the example of the 100-rat alternation experiment. The mean of the probability distribution is 50, and $s = 5$. The value of z for the outcome, 58 alternations, is _____ .

+1.6

12-9 The probability of getting *between* 50 *and* 58 alternations is equal to the area between the mean and a z of $+1.6$. This area can be found in the normal curve table by looking in the row opposite $z = 1.6$. The area is _____ .

0.4452

12-10 The probability of getting 58 *or more alternations* is equal to 0.4452 subtracted from the total area under the right half of the curve. The probability is _____. You would expect to get as many as 58 alternations in about _____ out of 100 replications of the 100-rat experiment.

Review

12-11 *The normal curve table lists _____ for all values of z. In order to look up a result from the alternation experiment in such a table, you have to determine the _____ which corresponds to that result. You can do this if you know the _____ and _____ of the probability distribution.*

12-12 *The areas in the normal curve table refer to only _____ of the total area under the normal curve. One edge of the area listed in the table is at the _____ of the distribution. To find the area under the curve which lies* beyond *a particular value of z, one must subtract the area listed in the table from _____ .*

B.   One- and Two-tailed Tests

12-13 In testing the significance of results from the alternation experiment, we start by assuming the null hypothesis. We then decide on an alternate hypothesis, that is, a hypothesis we expect to *accept* if we find that we can _____ the _____ hypothesis.

12-14 Alternate hypotheses may be of two kinds, as we showed in Lesson 5. A hypothesis that "Rats will show more alternation behavior" or that "Rats will show more repetition behavior" states explicitly the _____ in which the difference is expected to occur.

12-15 The other sort of alternate hypothesis is "Rats will show some systematic behavior in one or the other direction (but I don't know which)." This hypothesis does not specify the _____ of the expected _____ .

12-16 Suppose the outcome in a 100-rat experiment is 59 alternations. If your alternate hypothesis is "Rats will show more alternations," then you must consider only the probability of obtaining _____ from rats whose behavior is really nonsystematic.

12-17 Since the z score for 59 alternations in a 100-rat experiment is _____, the probability of obtaining 59 or more alterna-tions is _____. The probability is _____ than 0.05, and the result is therefore _____ beyond the .05 level.

1.8
0.0359 — less
significant

12-18 Suppose you had an alternate hypothesis which did *not* specify the direction of the expected difference. If you obtained the same result, 59 alternations, you would have to consider the proba-bility of obtaining _____ in addition to the probability of obtaining 59 or more alternations.

59 or more
repetitions

12-19 In this case, the probability you are interested in is exactly _____ times as large as the probability under the other kind of alternate hypothesis. The probability is _____, which is _____ at the .05 level.

two
0.0718
not significant

12-20 The extremes of the probability distribution are called *tails* because they stretch out to very narrow terminals. The alternate hypothesis which does not specify direction requires consideration of both extremes, or _____, of the probability distribution. *A test of the null hypothesis must be a* TWO-TAILED TEST *whenever the alternate hypothesis does not specify the direction of the expected difference.*

tails

12-21 The alternate hypothesis "Rats will show more alternations" requires consideration of only one tail, and it is correspondingly called a _____-tailed test.

one

12-22 Thus, an alternate hypothesis which specifies the direction of the expected difference requires only a _____ for testing the significance of an observed result. When the alternate hypothesis does *not* specify the direction, a _____ must be applied.

one-tailed test

two-tailed test

Review

12-23 *The "tail" in a one-tailed test is one of the extreme ends of the* _____. *The probability which is calculated in such a test corresponds to the* _____ *beyond* _____ *on one side only.*

probability distribution
(normal curve)
area — z

12-24 *In a two-tailed test, the probability which is calculated includes the area beyond z in* _____ *of the probability distribution.*

both tails

This probability is exactly _____ as large as the probability *calculated when a one-tailed test is applied with the same value of z.*

C. Applying One- and Two-tailed Tests

12-25 We can apply the same reasoning to the coin-tossing example introduced at the end of Lesson 2. If one is interested in determining whether a particular coin is fair, he can proceed to test the null hypothesis that results obtained with this coin are *not different* from what would be expected of a _____ .

12-26 The hypothesis "The coin gives more *heads* than a fair coin" is one of the two kinds of _____ hypotheses which one might hold. A test of the null hypothesis would then be a _____-tailed test because the probability of getting a large number of tails _____ (is, is not) relevant to the test.

12-27 With the hypothesis "The coin is biased in one or the other direction," a _____-tailed test would be required, and the probability to be determined is the probability of getting the observed deviation from expected frequency in _____ direction.

12-28 The probability of getting the observed number of heads or more is _____ than the probability of getting at least that many *heads or tails*. The null hypothesis is more likely to be rejected when the probability is relatively _____ . Therefore, the null hypothesis is more likely to be rejected when a _____-tailed test is used.

12-29 Suppose that a friend offers to sell you a certain nickel for $1 on the grounds that it is a *biased* nickel with which you can easily make a great deal of money through bets. You want to be sure that it is really _____ , so you toss it ten times and get nine tails.

12-30 If your friend has not told you whether the coin is biased toward heads or toward tails, you will have to consider the probability of getting at least nine tails *plus* the probability of getting at least nine heads. Either kind of extreme result would support the hypothesis "The coin is biased," provided that the probability turns out to be _____ enough.

12-31   On the other hand, if your friend claims that the coin is biased toward *tails* and you toss it ten times and get nine tails, you would consider only the probability that an unbiased coin would give _____. A consideration of the probability of getting _____ would be irrelevant and unnecessary.

at least nine tails
at least nine heads

12-32   The probability of *at least nine tails* is _____ than the probability of *at least nine heads or at least nine tails.* You would be _____ likely to believe your friend's assertion if you got nine tails after he had said "The coin is biased toward tails" than after he simply claimed "The coin is biased."

lower (smaller)

more

12-33   If your friend really has evidence that the coin is biased toward tails, it will be _____ advantageous for him if he says so than if he says simply that it is biased.

more

12-34   If he has no such evidence but is trying to trick you, it will be _____ advantageous for him if he says simply that it is biased. An *unbiased* coin is as likely to give a preponderance of heads as a preponderance of tails. If he claimed it to be biased toward tails, there would be a good chance he might be embarrassed by having it give a large number of *heads.*

more

Review

12-35   *For any observed result, the probability calculated by a two-tailed test will always be _____ than the probability calculated by a one-tailed test. The probability calculated by the one-tailed test is always exactly _____ as large as that calculated by the two-tailed test.*

higher (larger)

half

12-36   *The observed result, whatever it may be, is more likely to be found significant when the probability of that result is _____ . The result is therefore more likely to be found significant if a _____-tailed test is used.*

low (small)
one

D.   The Sign Test

12-37   The alternation experiment and the coin-tossing example have certain characteristics in common with a great many experimental situations. In both cases, the observations can be classified into exactly _____ categories. When observations are classified in this way, they are said to be DICHOTOMIZED. Alternation and coin-tossing are examples of observations that can be _____ .

two

dichotomized

12-38 Many kinds of experimental data can be classified into two categories. In particular, whenever the effectiveness of a *change* in some variable is being tested, the observations following the change can be _____ as follows: those showing a *positive* change, or increase, and those showing a *negative* change, or decrease.

dichotomized

12-39 The alternation and coin-tossing examples are alike in another respect: The null hypothesis is similar in both cases. In both examples, it is the hypothesis that the *frequencies* in the two categories will be _____ . Likewise, with observations of the effect of the changed variable, the null hypothesis is that the changed variable made _____ difference and the observations of an increase or of a decrease should occur with _____ frequency.

equal

no
equal

12-40 For example, the effectiveness of information about lung cancer upon attitudes toward smoking could be measured in terms of scores on an attitude scale before and after receiving the information. If the message has no effect, then the "after" scores should some-times be higher (more favorable) and sometimes lower (less favorable) than the "before" scores. The *differences* in scores ("before" minus "after") can be dichotomized into *positive* differences and *negative* differences, and the null hypothesis requires that _____ .

the frequencies in the
two groups are equal

12-41 Another example: If one were testing the effect of high noise level on number of pages read per hour, some of the persons serving as subjects might read more pages in high noise and other persons might read fewer pages. The *difference* in number of pages read ("with noise" minus "without noise") might therefore be either _____ or _____ . The null hypothesis would require that the fre-quencies in these categories should be about equal if the noise really makes no difference.

positive ↔
negative

12-42 Whenever a set of observations is dichotomized according to the algebraic _____ of the observations, the test of significance can be called a SIGN TEST. Once the observations are classified, one can make use of a variety of procedures for testing the null hypothesis that this population is one in which the frequency of observations with _____ is equal to the frequency of obser-vations with _____ .

sign

positive sign
negative sign

12-43   The observations can be put into a 2 x 2 table and tested by the chi-square test. Or the normal curve test described in Sections A and B of this lesson can be applied. With 64 persons in the noise experiment, the value of N in the normal curve test would be _____. The null hypothesis requires that the frequencies of positive and negative differences be _____ .

12-44   If 39 observations were in the positive-difference category, the z score for this result would be _____ . (You will have to determine the mean and s before you can find this z score.) The probability of this result, on the null hypothesis and using a two-tailed test, is 0.08 (as you can determine for yourself, from the normal curve table). The null hypothesis cannot be rejected at the .05 level.

12-45   The alternate hypothesis which would require such a two-tailed test is the hypothesis that _____ . There are two possible ways of stating an alternate hypothesis which would require only a one-tailed test. Give *one* of these.

12-46   The probability of 39 of our 64 persons falling in the positive-difference category is 0.08 when a two-tailed test is used. If the alternate hypothesis is "Noise will *increase* pages read per hour," then a one-tailed test could be used and the probability of the result would be _____ . Could the null hypothesis then be rejected at the .05 level? _____ .

Review

12-47   *Any test applied to observations which have been classified into two hypothetically equal categories according to algebraic sign is called a _____ . Various procedures can be used to make the test, including the _____ test and the test for dichotomized observations which employs the _____ table.*

12-48   *When the alternate hypothesis specifies which sign is expected to predominate, then a _____ test is applied. When the alternate hypothesis indicates only that the frequencies in positive and negative categories will not be equal, then a _____ test is required.*

E. Testing Hypotheses with Probabilities Other than ½

12-49 Suppose that an alternation experiment were to be carried out with a *four-choice maze* instead of a T maze. There would be four possible end boxes instead of two. It would then be inappropriate to consider $p_A = $ ½ and $p_R = $ ½ on the null hypothesis because the animal, having chosen one of the four pathways on the first run, can show alternation behavior by choosing any one of the _____ pathways which he did *not* choose on the first run.

three

12-50 On the null hypothesis that behavior is nonsystematic, all four pathways must be considered equally likely to be chosen on the second run. Since three of the four possible choices will be called "alternation," p_A must be _____ times as large as p_R. In this case, then, p_A will equal _____ and p_R will equal _____.

three

¾ *(0.75)* — ¼ *(0.25)*

12-51 Fortunately, the procedure which we have been using for dichotomized observations is not limited to the case in which $p_A = p_R = $ ½. Recall from Lesson 11D that the mean of the probability distribution for the alternation experiment is Np. *This statement is true for all probability distributions provided only that the observations can be dichotomized.* Since $p_A = $ ¾, the mean of the probability distribution for $N = 100$ is _____.

75

12-52 Since the observations are still dichotomized, the equation for the standard deviation will also hold. For $N = 100$, $s = \sqrt{Npq} = $ _____.

$\sqrt{18.75} = 4.3$

12-53 The probability distribution when $p_A = $ ½ and $N = 100$ is approximately a _____ curve with mean of _____ and standard deviation of _____. The probability distribution when $p_A = $ ¾ and $N = 100$ is also approximately _____ in shape, with a mean of _____ and a standard deviation of _____. As long as p does not deviate very far from ½, the probability distribution (when N is large) will be approximately like that for $p = $ ½.

normal — 50

5

normal

75

4.3

12-54 When a set of values have approximately the same shape as the graph of a certain mathematical equation, we say that the values can be FITTED by that equation. The normal curve is the graph of a particular mathematical equation. *Every probability distribution for dichotomized data can be* _____ *by a normal curve provided*

fitted

only that the value of N is sufficiently large. The fit is best for values of p close to ½.

12-55   The mean and the standard deviation of the *particular* normal curve fitting a particular probability distribution will be determined by two values, which appear in the definition of the mean of the distribution. These values are _____ and _____. (The value of q is also determined by the value of _____.)

12-56   Once the _____ and _____ of the fitted normal curve are known, any observed result of an experiment can be expressed in terms of a _____ and the probability of that result can be determined from the *normal probability distribution,* whose mean is _____ and whose standard deviation is _____ .

12-57   When $N = 100$ and $p_A = $ ½, an outcome of 60 alternations is 2 standard deviations above the mean. When $p_A = $ ¾, what outcome would be 2 standard deviations above the mean? _____ alternations.

12-58   The probability of getting a result which is at least 2 standard deviations above the mean of a normal curve is 0.0228. Therefore, when $N = 100$ and $p_A = $ ¾, the probability of obtaining at least 83.6 alternations is _____ . This probability is the same as that of getting at least _____ alternations when $p_A = $ ½.

Review

12-59   *The procedure for significance testing which is described in this lesson is appropriate for any case in which the observations can be classified into exactly* _____ *categories. Such observations are said to be* _____ .

12-60   *In many such cases, the null hypothesis is the hypothesis that* $p = $ ½. *The alternation experiment in the two-choice T maze is such a case. Likewise, the hypothesis that* $p = $ ½ *is appropriate in cases where the observations are divided into categories according to their algebraic* _____ .

12-61   *However, regardless of the value of p, a normal curve can be* _____ *to the probability distribution for any set of dichotomized observations provided only that the value of* _____ *is* large enough. The mean and standard deviation of the normal curve will be determined by the values of _____ and _____ .

$N \leftrightarrow p$

12-62   To test for significance by this procedure, one must first determine the value of p for his particular experiment. This value is determined by the _____ hypothesis. In the case of a sign test, p is usually equal to _____ .

null
½

12-63   The value of p, together with the value of N, must then be used to determine the _____ and _____ of the normal curve which fits the probability distribution. Then it is possible to convert the observed result to a _____ score, and this score is looked up in a table of _____ .

mean — standard deviation
z
normal curve areas

12-64   One decides whether to use a one-tailed test or a two-tailed test on the basis of his _____ hypothesis. A one-tailed test may be used only when _____ .

alternate
the alternate hypothesis specifies the direction of the expected difference

Problems for Lesson 12

12-1 A coin is tossed 900 times. The owner of the coin alleges that the coin is biased. How many heads must turn up in 900 tosses for the null hypothesis to be rejected at the .05 level?

12-2 Which of the following hypotheses require a two-tailed test?

(a) That the number of men in the snack bar at 4:30 P.M. is significantly different from the number of women in that place at that time.

(b) That students with averages of B or better study significantly more hours per day than students with averages less than B.

(c) That the average number of words in the *correct* alternatives on a multiple-choice examination is significantly different from the average number of words in the incorrect alternatives.

(d) That professors give significantly higher marks to essay answers which are long than to those which are of short or medium length.

12-3 Out of 57 men at a weekly college dance, 36 were found to have been at the dance also the previous week. Of these 36, 23 had brought the same date on both weeks and 13 had brought a different date or had come alone. Test whether the number of men who came both weeks with the same date is significantly different from the number who came both weeks but *not* with the same date.

12-4 Of 64 students in a mathematics class, 35 made *higher* grades on the second examination than on the first and 29 made *lower* grades. If the professor gave the same number of A's, B's, etc., on the second examination as he gave on the first examination, then for every student whose grade went up to A on the second examination there must be a student whose grade went down from A. Apply a sign test, using the normal curve, to test whether the number of students whose grades increased is significantly different from the number of students whose grades decreased.

12-5 In a college of 1,000 students, 400 came from large high schools and 600 came from small high schools. The honor roll listed 50 students in a particular year, of whom 25 came from large high schools. Use a normal curve test to determine whether the number of honor roll students coming from large high schools is significantly *larger* than the number coming from small high schools.

How would the result differ if the hypothesis being tested were "The number of honor roll students coming from large high schools is significantly *different* from the number coming from small high schools"? Since this hypothesis requires a two-tailed test, it can also be tested by chi-square. Test it in this way if you studied Lesson 7, and compare the conclusion drawn from chi-square with the conclusion drawn from the normal curve test.

Lesson 13. Inferring the Population Mean from a Sample Mean

The characteristics of a sample, such as its mean and standard deviation, are called the STATISTICS *of the sample; this special use of the word statistics was mentioned in Lesson 1C. The characteristics of the population from which the sample was drawn are called the population* PARAMETERS. *Random sampling procedures do not as a rule provide us with samples whose statistics coincide with the values of the population parameters. At best, these statistics represent* approximations *to the "true" population values. Lesson 13 tells how sample statistics should be used in order to obtain the best estimate of one population parameter, the population mean. It will also tell how to determine the amount of error involved in this estimate.*

Many occasions arise on which an investigator would like to make statements about the parameters of a particular population. On the basis of questions put to a relatively small number of persons, the social psychologist seeks to provide information about opinions or attitudes of a much larger population. Educational and psychological measurements made on samples can be used to give information about the characteristics of whole populations and to compare two populations with each other.

Besides these practical applications of the concepts to be discussed in Lesson 13, you will find that the concepts themselves form part of the logic behind a very important test for significance of differences to be discussed in Lessons 15 and 16.

A. A Sampling Distribution of Means

13-1 The sample statistics represent only approximations to the population _____. They are only approximations because many different samples, all of the same size, could be drawn randomly from the same population and these samples would not all have the same mean and standard deviation. The variation among samples

parameters

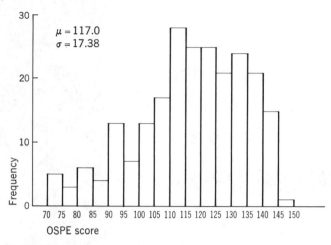

$\mu = 117.0$
$\sigma = 17.38$

Figure 13-1. Frequency distribution of scores on the OSPE for 228 freshman men entering Oberlin College in September, 1956.

drawn in the same way from the same population has already been given the name of _____ .

sampling variability

13-2   The only case in which this discrepancy between statistics and parameters does not arise is the case of the so-called "exhaustive sample," where the entire population of observations is included in the sample. Figure 13-1 is a histogram of college aptitude scores from the 228 freshman men in the class of 1960 at Oberlin College. With respect to the population of men entering Oberlin College as freshmen in 1956, this set of scores constitutes the entire population, or an _____ sample.

exhaustive

13-3   A set of 20 scores randomly drawn from this population of 228 would be a random _____ from the population. Two such sets of 20 scores would not be likely to have identical means because of sampling variability. Neither of the means could be taken as an exact indication of the value of the _____ mean.

sample

population

13-4   In Figure 13-2, the means of 50 such 20-score samples are shown as a frequency distribution. Each sample was randomly drawn from the population of 228, with the use of a *table of random numbers.* In this frequency distribution, the individual members are not scores but the _____ of samples. The value of N for the distribution is _____ .

means
50

A random number table is a published list of numbers in random order obtained by a random procedure such as drawing digits out of a container

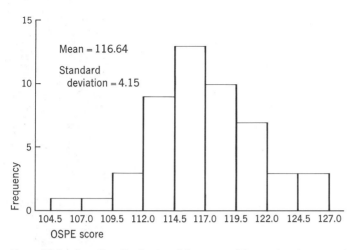

Figure 13-2. Sampling distribution of the means of 50 samples of $N = 20$, drawn randomly from a population of 228 OSPE scores.

or performing certain operations on a modern high-speed computer. In order to obtain the 50 samples whose means appear in Figure 13-2, each of the 228 scores in the population was assigned a number from 1 to 228 according to its rank in the population, the lowest number corresponding to the lowest score. Successive triplets in the random number table were read, and when a triplet constituted a number between 001 and 228, that number determined a member for inclusion in the sample. Any triplet not between 001 and 228 was ignored. By taking successive triplets in this way until 20 different members were chosen, the first sample was determined; then the second was selected in the same way, and so on. In this case, triplets were read starting at the top right of a page of random numbers and traveling down the first column on the right, then down the second column from the right, and so on. Random number tables can be read in any direction from any starting point, however, provided the procedure decided upon is consistent and carefully carried out. Notice that, since there are 50 samples of 20 and 50 x 20 = 1,000, some members of the population of 228 must appear in more than one sample. For a helpful discussion of procedures in drawing random samples, see Chapter 6 in *Introduction to Statistical Reasoning* by Philip J. McCarthy.

13-5 Classes for this frequency distribution can be designated by their midpoints. The sample means range between the class whose midpoint is _____ and the class whose midpoint is _____. The total range, subtracting the lower midpoint from the higher, is _____ score points.

105.75

125.75

20

13-6 The raw scores, on the other hand, range from the class with a midpoint of _____ to the class with a midpoint of _____ (see Figure 13-1). The total range of the raw-score distribution is _____.

72.5

147.5

75

13-7 The means of the samples differ from one another by a con-

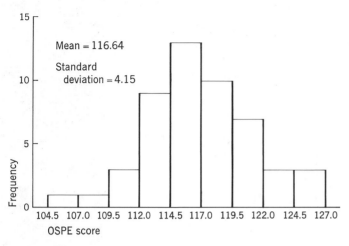

Figure 13-2 repeated

siderable amount, but they differ over a _____ range than
the raw scores in the population.

narrower (smaller)

13-8 The mean of the distribution of sample means is shown in
Figure 13-2 as equal to _____ . The mean of the raw score
distribution is 117.0. *The mean of the distribution of sample means is*
approximately equal to the mean of the population. With a still larger
number of samples than the 50 samples used in this example, the
approximation would be even closer.

116.64

13-9 The frequency distribution of Figure 13-2 is called a SAMPLING
DISTRIBUTION OF MEANS. When a large number of samples are actually
drawn for study, a *mean* for the distribution of means of samples can
be computed. This mean is the mean of a _____ , and it
will be approximately equal to the mean of the _____ .

sampling distri-
bution of means
population

13-10 One can also determine a *standard deviation* of the sampling
distribution of means. When this standard deviation is *small*, the degree of dispersion of the sample means is _____ and the
difference between the population mean and any sample mean is
relatively _____ .

small

small

Review

13-11 *The sampling distribution of means is a frequency distribution of*
the _____ of _____ all of a particular size and
all drawn randomly from the same _____ .

means — samples
population

13-12 *The mean of the sampling distribution of means tends to be very close to the* _____ , *although individual sample means may vary quite widely from this value. However, their variability, as indicated by the range in our example, is likely to be much* _____ *than the variability of the observations in the population.*

population mean

smaller

B. The Standard Deviation of the Sampling Distribution of Means

13-13 The standard deviation of the sampling distribution in Figure 13-2 has been calculated, and it is shown in the figure as equal to _____ . The standard deviation of the population of raw scores is 17.38, roughly _____ times as great as the standard deviation of the sampling distribution.

4.15
four

13-14 Now, since we are going to want to refer to several *different* standard deviations, it will be well to have a distinct symbol for each. The standard deviation which we have discussed extensively in Lessons 9 and 10 is the standard deviation of *a particular sample;* for it, we use the symbol _____ . The standard deviation of an entire population (like that of Figure 13-1) we shall designate by the Greek lower-case s, sigma, written σ.

s

13-15 The standard deviation of the sampling distribution of means will be designated as $\sigma_{\bar{X}}$. This name is logical, since $\bar{X}$ refers to the _____ of a sample. When we refer to the number of observations in a *sample* from now on, we shall use the small letter n in order to distinguish it from the population size N.

mean

13-16 The symbol $\sigma_{\bar{X}}$ stands for the _____ of the _____ . This quantity is commonly called the STANDARD ERROR OF THE MEAN. The logical reason for this name will become clearer with further discussion.

standard deviation
sampling distribution
  of means

13-17 It has been shown by rigorous mathematical proof that the value of $\sigma_{\bar{X}}$ will approach the value $\sigma/\sqrt{n}$ as the number of *samples* becomes very large. In other words, with a very large number of samples, the standard _____ of the mean will equal the standard _____ of the _____ divided by the square root of the number of observations in each _____ .

error
deviation — population
sample

For finite populations such as ours, the value of $\sigma_{\bar{x}}$ is only *approximately* equal to $\sigma/\sqrt{n}$. With such finite populations, $\sigma_{\bar{x}}$ approaches precisely the value $(\sigma/\sqrt{n})\sqrt{(N-n)/(N-1)}$ as the number of samples grows very large. We shall not include this finite correction factor in our discussion, since it would make the equation very cumbersome.

13-18 The value of $\sigma_{\bar{x}}$ for our example in Figure 13-2 is obtained when we divide the population standard deviation σ, which equals _____, by 4.47, which is the square root of 20. The result is _____ .

17.38
3.89

If we apply the finite correction factor, we obtain instead the value of 3.72.

13-19 The actual standard deviation of our sampling distribution is slightly _____ than the value which we just calculated from knowledge of σ. Why does this difference arise? Instead of a *very large* number of samples, we have only _____ samples in our sampling distribution. With a larger number, the value of the standard deviation of our sampling distribution should come closer to 3.89.

larger

50

13-20 Notice that the value of $\sigma_{\bar{x}}$ depends in part upon the size of σ. Increases in the value of σ would lead to _____ in the value of $\sigma_{\bar{x}}$.

increases

13-21 On the other hand, the value of $\sigma_{\bar{x}}$ also depends upon the size of the sample. Increases in the value of n would lead to _____ in the value of $\sigma_{\bar{x}}$.

decreases

13-22 If we wished to have a smaller standard deviation for our sampling distribution of means, we could take a set of samples for which n is _____ than 20. If n were equal to 100, the numerical value of $\sigma_{\bar{x}}$ would be _____ for our example.

greater
1.74

13-23 This relationship between the sample size and the amount of variability among sample means is reasonable. When samples are small, one expects to find that the amount of variability among the sample means is _____ than it would be with larger samples. Larger samples will resemble one another _____ than small samples do.

greater
more

13-24 It is also reasonable that greater variability in the population should produce _____ variability among samples. If the population is very homogeneous, the samples cannot differ much from one another.

more

13-25   *The symbol $\sigma_{\bar{X}}$ is called the* _____ *of the* _____ .
It is the value toward which the _____ *of the* _____
will tend as the number of _____ *becomes very large.*

13-26   *The value of $\sigma_{\bar{X}}$ increases with increases in* _____
and decreases with increases in _____ . *In the form of an*
equation, $\sigma_{\bar{X}} =$ _____ .

C.   Estimating the Standard Error of the Mean from a Single Sample

13-27   Before we go on, it will be well to recall our aim in this lesson. We are concerned with situations in which we know the mean of a sample $\bar{X}$ but we would like to be able to say something about the mean of the _____ from which the sample comes.

13-28   Let us use the Greek letter mu, written μ, to stand for the *population mean.* If we want to know μ and we only have the value of _____ to guide us, we shall certainly want to know how much the means of samples such as ours are likely to *vary* around the value of _____ .

13-29   But the mean of the sampling distribution of means is equal to μ when the number of samples is very large. Therefore, if we know how much the sample means vary around the mean of the sampling distribution, we shall also know how much they vary around the value of _____ .

13-30   For this reason, we shall be very eager to know the value of $\sigma_{\bar{X}}$, and we can begin to see also why this quantity is called the *standard* _____ *of the mean.* It is a quantity which helps us to judge *how far wrong we may be* if we assert that the population mean is like our sample mean.

13-31   It is important, therefore, to know the value of $\sigma_{\bar{X}}$. But its exact computation requires that we know the value of σ. Are we likely to know *this* value in practical circumstances? In order to know σ, the standard deviation of the _____ , we must already know the true value of μ. In that case, there would be no need to estimate μ from our sample mean $\bar{X}$ at all.

13-32   The only other way to determine $\sigma_{\bar{x}}$ *exactly* would be to take a large number of samples and determine the actual standard deviation of their _____. But this procedure would also require that we know about more than one sample. Ordinarily, we have only the one sample, with its n, $\bar{X}$, and s.

means

13-33   As a solution to this problem, we can obtain an *estimate* of σ from our sample statistics. We do this by going back to the quantity Σx_i^2, which is the sum of the squared _____ of the scores from _____. When we divide this quantity by n, we obtain the _____ of the sample; when we divide it by n and then take the square root, we obtain the _____ .

deviations
$\bar{X}$
variance
standard deviation

13-34   But if we divide Σx_i^2 by $n - 1$, we obtain *an estimate of the population variance* σ^2. The square root of $\Sigma x_i^2/(n - 1)$ will then be an *estimate* of the population _____ σ. We can use this estimate in determining the standard error of the mean when we do not know the actual σ.

standard deviation

13-35   We should compare carefully the two quantities, $\sqrt{\Sigma x_i^2/n}$ and $\sqrt{\Sigma x_i^2/(n - 1)}$. The first is the familiar sample _____ for which we have used the letter _____ . The second is the estimated _____ of the _____ for which there exists no generally accepted letter symbol. *Be careful not to use the letter σ for this quantity; σ is the symbol for the actual parameter, and this equation gives only an* _____ of the parameter.

standard deviation
s
standard deviation
— population

estimate

13-36   The two expressions defining the sample s and the estimated population standard deviation are different only in the *denominator* of the fraction under the radical. The denominator of the expression for the _____ is the larger of the two. Therefore, the value of the estimated population standard deviation will be somewhat _____ than the value of the sample s.

sample s

larger

13-37   Because of *sampling variability*, the standard deviation of a sample is in the majority of cases a little smaller than the standard deviation of the entire population. Dividing Σx_i^2 by $n - 1$ gives an estimate for the population standard deviation which is a little _____ than the value of s.

larger

This difference is in the right direction to correct for the most common kind of difference between s and σ, although it naturally cannot wholly wipe out the effects of sampling variability. If we use this estimate, we shall still be using only an *approximation* to the value of σ. But our approximation will sometimes be a little too large, and about equally often it will be a little too small. The division by $n - 1$ removes the *bias* which is present in the relationship between s and σ, that is, the tendency for the s to be too small *more often* than it is too large. For this reason, some books call $\sqrt{\Sigma x_i^2/(n - 1)}$ an "unbiased" estimate of the population σ and refer to $s = \sqrt{\Sigma x_i^2/n}$ as being also an estimate of the population σ but a "biased" one.

13-38   Sampling variability plays a greater or a lesser role, depending on the size of the sample. Sampling variability is likely to produce a _____ amount of variation among large samples than among small samples. The difference between $n - 1$ and n varies also in this way: n and $n - 1$ differ from each other relatively *less* for samples of _____ size than for samples of _____ size.

smaller

large — small

13-39   The difference between $\sqrt{\Sigma x_i^2/n}$ and $\sqrt{\Sigma x_i^2/(n - 1)}$ will be *smaller* for samples of _____ size than for samples of _____ size. This is appropriate because the effect of sampling variability is also smaller for _____ samples than it is for _____ ones.

large
small
large
small

13-40   If we now take the *estimated* standard deviation of the population $\sqrt{\Sigma x_i^2/(n - 1)}$ and use it instead of σ whenever we do not know the value of σ, we can determine an *estimated* standard error of the mean. For the actual $\sigma_{\bar{x}}$, we divide _____ by $\sqrt{n}$. For the *estimated* standard error, which is designated $s_{\bar{x}}$, we divide the estimated standard deviation of the population by $\sqrt{n}$, obtaining the expression, $s_{\bar{x}} = $ _____ .

σ

$\dfrac{\sqrt{\Sigma x_i^2/(n - 1)}}{\sqrt{n}}$

13-41   The expression $\dfrac{\sqrt{\Sigma x_1^2/(n - 1)}}{\sqrt{n}}$ can be simplified by multiplying $\sqrt{\Sigma x_1^2/(n - 1)}$ by $\sqrt{1/n}$ (or $1/\sqrt{n}$). The quantity then becomes

$$s_{\bar{x}} = \sqrt{\frac{\Sigma x_i^2}{n(n - 1)}}$$

The symbol $s_{\bar{x}}$ and its definition should be remembered as the _____ standard error of the _____ .

estimated — mean

13-42   *The quantity* $\sqrt{\Sigma x_i^2/(n - 1)}$ *is used as an estimate of the* _____ . *When n is very large, this quantity will not be very different from the sample* _____ .

population standard deviation

s

13-43 When σ is known, the standard error of the mean is determined by the equation $\sigma_{\bar{X}} =$ _____ . When σ is not known, an estimate of the standard error of the mean must be calculated. This estimate, symbolized by _____ , is equal to _____ .

$$\frac{\sigma}{\sqrt{n}}$$

$$s_{\bar{X}} = \sqrt{\frac{\Sigma x_i^2}{n(n-1)}}$$

○

D. The Interval Estimate and Confidence Limits

13-44 You are now able to visualize a sampling distribution of the means of samples, and you know how to determine an estimate of its standard deviation in cases where only the value of _____ for a single sample is known. There is one more important fact which is needed for our inference about the population mean: *When many large samples are drawn from the same population, the sampling distribution of means assumes approximately the form of a normal distribution.*

s

13-45 The approximation to the shape of a _____ is not very close for data such as ours in Figure 13-1 unless the sample size is large. The sampling distribution in Figure 13-2 does not come very close to such a shape because neither the _____ of the samples nor the _____ of samples drawn was very large.

normal distribution

size
number

> We should have obtained a more nearly normally distributed sampling distribution, even with such relatively small samples, if it had been the case that the *population* of aptitude scores itself were normally distributed. That is, the sampling distribution will be approximately normal if *either* (1) the variable X itself is normally distributed in the population *or* (2) the sample size is sufficiently large. Because the distribution of aptitude scores among Oberlin freshmen is markedly skewed to the left, neither of these conditions obtains for our example.

13-46 The approximation to a normal distribution is a very useful fact. We have already used the normal curve characteristics in Lesson 12 for making certain significance tests. The usefulness of the normal curve in the present case, also, rests upon the knowledge we have about the proportional _____ under the curve between certain pairs of z scores.

areas

13-47 Knowing that the shape of the sampling distribution of means of *large* samples is approximately normal, you are in a position to say what proportion of the means of such samples will lie within ±1 standard deviation of the _____ , how many will lie more than ±2 standard deviations away, and so on.

population mean

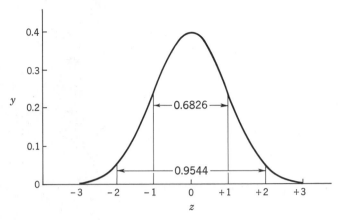

Figure 13-3. Areas under the normal probability curve.

13-48 Figure 13-3 will remind you of the proportions you have seen many times already. When the sampling distribution of means is approximately normal, you can be sure that about _____ per cent of all possible sample means will be found within ±1 standard error of the population mean and that about _____ per cent of all possible sample means will lie within ±2 standard errors of the population mean.

68

95

13-49 We can turn this last statement around and say that the probability is only about 0.05 that one would happen to obtain a sample whose mean is *more* than _____ standard errors away from the population mean. Notice that we are using the name "standard error" instead of "standard deviation" because the particular standard deviation which is relevant here is the standard deviation of the _____, called the _____ of the mean.

2

sampling distribution
— standard error

13-50 Since only about _____ per cent of all possible sample means will be found to lie more than ±2 standard errors away from the population mean, one can expect to get a sample whose mean lies within ±2 standard errors of the population mean in about _____ per cent of the experiments in which he uses such samples.

5

95

13-51 One of fifty samples in Figure 13-2, chosen at random, has a sample mean of 112.75. With a $\sigma_{\bar{x}}$ of 3.89, you can say that the probability is 0.95 that the sample mean is one of those which lie within $2\sigma_{\bar{x}}$ of the population mean. Hence there are 95 chances in 100 that the population mean lies somewhere between $112.75 + 2(3.89)$, or _____, and $112.75 - 2(3.89)$, or _____.

120.53 — 104.97

13-52 Notice the strategy here. You do not commit yourself to a precise *number* as your guess about μ. You do not say "The population mean *is* 112.75." Instead, you specify a *range of values* within which μ probably lies. This range is called a CONFIDENCE INTERVAL. You state that the probability is 0.95 that the population mean lies within this _____.

13-53 You can actually choose any level of probability (called LEVEL OF CONFIDENCE) which you wish in determining the limits of your _____ interval. You can make the probability 0.90 or 0.95 or 0.99 or any other value. In each case, the probability represents the likelihood that your statement about μ is _____. If you choose a probability of 0.95, your statement is made at the *95 per cent* level of _____.

13-54 The limits of the confidence interval are called CONFIDENCE LIMITS. In order to obtain a *higher* level of confidence, you must select your confidence interval so that the probability of your being *correct* is _____ than before. This change will require that the distance between the confidence _____ shall be larger.

13-55 If you were to specify a single number as your guess, we could call this a very *precise* estimate. When you state a confidence interval, your estimate is *less precise* because you are saying that the value may be *any one of a number of values* lying in a particular interval. The wider you make your confidence interval, the less precise your estimate becomes. So when you *increase* your level of confidence, you make your estimate _____ precise. If you are willing to take a greater risk of being *wrong,* you can make your estimate _____ precise.

13-56 Recall that our example in frame 13-51 makes use of the value of $\sigma_{\bar{X}}$, determined *exactly* because we happened to know the population standard deviation σ. If you do not know the value of σ—and usually, in practical circumstances, you do not—you have to use the estimate, _____, instead of $\sigma_{\bar{X}}$.

13-57 The estimated $\sigma_{\bar{X}}$, which we write as _____, may be a relatively good or a relatively poor estimate. If it is a very good estimate, then, of course, the reasoning about confidence limits can be applied just as well to $s_{\bar{X}}$ as to $\sigma_{\bar{X}}$ itself. If it is slightly different from $\sigma_{\bar{X}}$, then what we have said about the population mean lying within certain confidence limits will be only *approximately* true whenever you use _____ instead of _____ for establishing these limits.

13-58   The reasoning about confidence limits *is* customarily applied when $s_{\bar{x}}$ is used instead of $\sigma_{\bar{x}}$. But the reasoning can then be valid only if our estimate is fairly good. It is important to have a good estimate of $\sigma_{\bar{x}}$, and this is one of the reasons why an investigator tries to make his sample size as _____ as possible; large samples give _____ estimates of $\sigma_{\bar{x}}$ than small ones.

large
better

Review

13-59   *In making a guess about the population mean on the basis of a sample mean, you must first estimate the value of the* _____ *of the mean.*

standard error

13-60   *Then you must decide what level of* _____ *you wish to employ. This decision will enable you to determine the* _____ *within which the population mean should lie.*

confidence
confidence limits (or
  confidence interval)

13-61   *In order to achieve a high level of confidence, you will have to have a relatively* _____ *confidence interval. Thus, in achieving a high level of confidence, it is necessary to sacrifice precision in the estimate.*

wide

E.   Obtaining Multipliers from the Normal Curve Table

13-62   For the 95 per cent level of confidence, the lower confidence limit is found by multiplying the standard error by _____ and subtracting the product from the sample mean $\bar{X}$. The upper confidence limit is found by _____ the same quantity to $\bar{X}$.

2

adding

13-63   The factor by which the standard error $\sigma_{\bar{x}}$ (or its estimate $s_{\bar{x}}$) must be *multiplied* will be called a MULTIPLIER. For the 95 per cent level of confidence, the _____ is approximately 2 (it is *exactly* 1.96).

multiplier

13-64   For the 68 per cent level of confidence, the value of the multiplier is _____. The confidence limits are found by adding (and subtracting) _____ standard error(s) to (and from) the value of _____.

1
1
$\bar{X}$

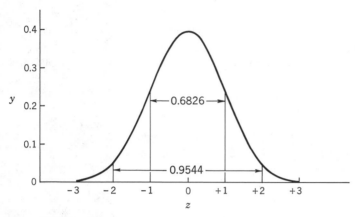

Figure 13-3 repeated

13-65 Notice, in Figure 13-3, that the confidence level 68 per cent corresponds to a proportional area of 0.6826 and that this proportional area is just *twice* the area between $z =$ _____ and $z = +1$. It is *twice* this area because 0.6826 is the proportional area within ± 1 standard error of the mean, that is, the area from $z =$ _____ to $z = +1$.

0

−1

13-66 The table of normal curve areas lists areas which lie between the _____, or $z =$ _____, and any particular value of z. The value 0.3413 is found in the normal curve table opposite a z of _____.

mean — 0

1

13-67 The confidence level 95.44 per cent corresponds to a proportional area of _____, which is the area lying between $z =$ _____ and $z = +2$. The area between $z = 0$ and $z = +2$ is _____, which is just *half* of _____.

0.9544

−2

0.4772 — 0.9544

13-68 The table of normal curve areas shows the number 0.4750 opposite $z =$ _____. The *exact* multiplier for the 95.00 per cent level of confidence is _____.

1.96

1.96

13-69 We see, then, that we can find the multiplier for any desired level of confidence if we first divide the confidence level (expressed as a decimal) by _____ and then look up the result in the normal curve table *in the column labeled "area from the mean to z."* The multiplier we are looking for will be the corresponding value of _____.

2

z

13-70 When we used the normal curve table in Lesson 12, we always looked up a certain z value in the table. But to find the multiplier for a certain level of confidence, we do the opposite thing: We look up in the table a certain _____ and find out from the table what value of _____ corresponds to it.

area

z

13-71 The area we look up is always just *half* the total proportional area within the confidence limits we want to establish. It is only *half* because the normal curve table treats areas under only _____ the normal curve. It treats only areas from the _____ to z.

half

mean

13-72 Suppose that you decided to set up confidence limits at the 98 per cent level and wanted to determine the proper multiplier. Your first step is to convert the 98 per cent to a decimal by dividing by 100; you obtain _____ . Then you divide this decimal by _____ and obtain the quotient _____ .

0.98 — 2

0.49

13-73 The number 0.49 is half the proportional area which should lie between your confidence limits; in other words, it is the area between the mean (of the sampling distribution) and the upper (or lower) confidence limit you are seeking. You take this number to the table of normal curve areas on the foldout and look for it in the column labeled _____ .

area (mean to z)

13-74 Your multiplier is the _____ value which corresponds to this area. It is _____ .

z

2.32

13-75 Therefore, for the 98 per cent level of confidence, you will multiply _____ by 2.32 and add this quantity to the value of your sample _____ ; you would thus obtain the _____ confidence limit. Subtracting the same value would give you the _____ confidence limit.

$s_{\bar{x}}$ (or $\sigma_{\bar{x}}$)

mean — upper

lower

Review

13-76 *When we make inferences about the population mean from a sample mean, we do not usually state that the population mean is a certain precise number. Instead, we state that the mean lies within a certain* _____ *at a certain level of* _____ .

confidence interval —
confidence

13-77 *The value of the level of confidence represents the probability that our statement is* _____ .

correct

13-78 *We are able to set up such confidence limits only because the* shape of the _____, for a very large number of samples, is approximately _____ around a mean equal to the _____ and with a standard deviation called the _____ of the mean.

sampling distribution
means — normal
— population mean
standard error

13-79 The standard error of the mean $\sigma_{\bar{X}}$ can be calculated precisely if σ is known by the equation _____. Otherwise, we estimate the standard error of the mean by the equation $s_{\bar{X}} =$ _____.

$$\frac{\sigma}{\sqrt{n}}$$

$$\sqrt{\frac{\Sigma x_i^2}{n(n-1)}}$$

13-80 A particular level of confidence corresponds to a certain proportional area under the normal curve centered around the _____ of the distribution. When the confidence limits are set up, the estimated standard error must be multiplied by a factor called a _____, which can be determined from a table of _____.

mean

multiplier
normal curve
  areas

13-81 Since the normal curve table includes only areas from _____, the proportional area between the desired confidence limits must be _____ before the table is consulted.

the mean to z
divided by 2

13-82 The number we look up in the table is the proportional _____ lying between the _____ and one of the desired confidence limits. The multiplier we are looking for is the corresponding value of _____.

area — mean

z

13-83 We choose a relatively wide confidence interval when we desire a _____ level of confidence and a relatively narrow one when we prefer a _____ degree of precision.

high
high

Problems for Lesson 13

13-1   The standard deviation of the population of Stanford-Binet IQ scores of a very large sample of white American-born U.S. citizens is 16. What is the standard error of the mean for samples with $n = 144$?

13-2   Suppose that we have determined the mean number of hours spent in sleep during a certain three-day period for each of a randomly selected group of 100 students at several different colleges. The mean is 7.15, and the standard deviation is 1.10. What is the value of Σx_i^2? What is the value of $s_{\bar{x}}$? What are the .95-level confidence limits for the value of μ estimated from this sample? What are the limits for the .99 level of confidence?

13-3   If the standard error is multiplied by 2 in setting up confidence limits, what confidence level will those limits represent? When the confidence limits are $\bar{X} \pm 2.5\sigma_{\bar{X}}$, what is the confidence level?

13-4   What multiplier of $\sigma_{\bar{x}}$ must be used to obtain the .90 level of confidence? To obtain the 98 per cent level of confidence?

13-5   (Optional problem, on the use of the "finite correction factor.") A particular student slept 6.6, 7.2, and 6.9 hours on March 18, 19, and 20, respectively. Take $s_{\bar{x}}$ as 0.17 and apply the "finite correction factor" $\sqrt{(N - n)/(N - 1)}$ to it, to compute and compare the .95 confidence limits for the following three estimates:

(a)   The mean number of hours of sleep for this student during the entire third week of March (of which these three days are a part).

(b)   The mean number of hours of sleep for this student during the 31 days of March.

(c)   The mean number of hours of sleep for this student during the 120 days of the spring semester.

How does the finite correction factor affect the confidence limits for these estimates? How does the *size* of its effect change, as the difference between n and N increases?

Actually, the chosen three-day period is not a proper random sample for *any* of the three populations in question. Why not?

Lesson 14.   Significance Tests Using the Normal Curve Table— II: Testing Hypotheses About the Means of Large Samples

In Lesson 13, we studied the procedure for making a guess about the value of the population mean when only a sample mean is available. Very often, though, it is less important to guess what the value of the population mean might be than to be able to assert something about the significance of obtaining a particular sample mean. If our sample mean is not quite what we might have anticipated on the basis of some hypothesis or other, is it different enough *from that expectation to signify that the hypothesis is wrong?*

This kind of question will be familiar to you from Lessons 5, 7, and 12, where we discussed ways of testing the null hypothesis with observations that could be classified into categories and treated as frequencies. We shall use the same line of reasoning in Lesson 14, but we shall be making significance tests which apply to means of frequency distributions. We shall make use of the concept of the sampling distribution of means which was presented in Lesson 13.

The normal curve table can be used in making these tests, whenever samples are sufficiently large. For smaller samples, a different kind of table must be used. Lessons 15 and 16 will be devoted to the tests which are appropriate for small samples as well as large ones.

A.   Testing Whether the Population Mean Differs from a Particular Value

14-1   The symbol $\bar{X}$ stands for the mean of a _____ . The symbol μ stands for the mean of a _____ .

sample
population

14-2   We shall let μ_0 represent *some particular value* that μ might assume according to a particular hypothesis. For example, if we have a large sample of IQ scores drawn randomly from a certain city, $\bar{X}$ would represent the _____ and μ would represent the _____ for that city. Suppose we wish to determine whether the value of μ for that city is likely to be 100. Our hypothesis will be that μ is *not significantly different from* 100, and we shall symbolize the value 100 as μ_0.

sample mean —
population mean

14-3 The null hypothesis in this example is the hypothesis that _____ is not significantly different from _____. To test this hypothesis, we shall have to determine whether a sample of the given size, with the observed value of $\bar{X}$, *could reasonably have been drawn randomly* from a population with _____ equal to _____.

$\mu - \mu_0$ *(or 100)*

μ
μ_0 *(or 100)*

14-4 In making this test, we shall first decide upon an acceptable level of significance. Then, if the probability of getting our observed value of _____ from a population with μ of 100 is *greater* than this level, we must be prepared to *accept* the null hypothesis. We shall be able to *reject* the null hypothesis only if the _____ of getting _____ from a population with _____ is *at least as low as* our level of significance.

$\bar{X}$

probability
$\bar{X} - \mu$ *of 100*

14-5 If the usual .05 level of _____ is chosen, we must be ready to reject the null hypothesis if the probability of getting $\bar{X}$ when $\mu = 100$ is _____.

significance

0.05 or less

14-6 In making the test, we must *imagine* a sampling distribution of the means of samples, all of which are exactly as large as our actual sample and all of which have been drawn in the same way from the same population (of IQs in that city). Since we are testing whether our sample could have come from a population with $\mu = 100$, we must assume that the mean of this sampling distribution of means is _____.

100

14-7 Since we have only a *sample* of the IQs from this city, we do not know the value of σ. Therefore, we cannot determine the exact value of the standard deviation of this sampling distribution of means; instead of $\sigma_{\bar{X}}$, we shall therefore have to use the estimate _____ given by the expression _____.

$s_{\bar{X}}$

$$\sqrt{\frac{\Sigma x_i^2}{n(n-1)}}$$

14-8 The value $s_{\bar{X}}$ is the _____ standard error of the _____, which is the standard deviation of the _____.

estimated
mean — sampling
distribution of means

14-9 The sampling distribution of means like our sample will have a mean of μ and a standard deviation of approximately _____.

$s_{\bar{X}}$

Since we are imagining a very large number of large samples, the sampling distribution of their means will have the shape of a _____.

14-10   If μ is *not* significantly different from 100, then the mean of the sampling distribution must, indeed, be about 100, and 68 per cent of all the sample means will lie within ± 1 _____ of this value.

14-11   Then, if μ is not significantly different from 100, the probability is 0.68 that one will obtain a sample whose mean does not deviate from 100 by more than _____ standard error.

Review

14-12   *In testing whether the mean of the population from which a sample has been drawn can be a particular value μ_0, we assume the null hypothesis that* _____ .

14-13   *According to such a null hypothesis, the sampling distribution of means of such samples should have a mean of* _____ *and an estimated standard deviation of* _____ *. With a very large number of large samples, the shape of the sampling distribution will be approximately* _____ *.*

B.   Rejection Regions for One- and Two-tailed Tests

14-14   When we assume a null hypothesis, we must also choose a particular *alternate* hypothesis which we intend to _____ if we can reject the null hypothesis. We have three possibilities to choose from: (1) that μ is *greater* than μ_0, (2) that μ is *less* than μ_0, and (3) that μ is simply *different* from μ_0.

14-15   Let us work first with the consequences of alternate hypothesis 1: that μ is greater than μ_0. To have evidence in favor of *this* alternate hypothesis, we would have to obtain a sample mean $\bar{X}$ which is _____ than μ_0 and by such a large amount that the null hypothesis is less reasonable than alternate hypothesis 1.

14-16   If we are going to reject the null hypothesis at the .05 level in favor of hypothesis 1, we shall have to find that the probability of getting $\overline{X}$ from a population with mean of μ_0 is less than _____ .

14-17 The probability will be less than 0.05 if it can be said that not more than _____ per cent of the means of samples from a population with mean of μ_0 will exceed μ_0 as much as $\overline{X}$ does.

14-18 This statement can be made if we find that our $\overline{X}$ lies *so far out* in the upper tail of the sampling distribution that no more than _____ per cent of the total area in the distribution would be found to lie _____ it when the distribution has a mean of μ_0.

14-19 Thus, we arrive at the idea that *there is a certain region of the sampling distribution* with mean of μ_0 which we can call a REJECTION REGION in the sense that, if we find $\overline{X}$ to lie in that region, we can _____ the null hypothesis at the .05 level. If we had chosen any other level of significance than .05, there would also be a _____ for that level different from the one for the .05 level.

14-20 The rejection region, with our alternate hypothesis 1, is the _____ of the area in the distribution for the .05 level. For the .10 level of significance, this region would have a _____ size than for the .05 level. For the .01 level, it would have a _____ size.

14-21 If we had taken alternate hypothesis 2, that μ is *less* than μ_0, then our rejection region would lie at the _____ extreme of the distribution. For the .05 level, it would include the _____ of the area in the distribution.

14-22 Both these alternate hypotheses 1 and 2 are of the sort which, as you learned in Lesson 12, require a _____-tailed test of significance because they specify the _____ of the expected difference.

14-23 When an alternate hypothesis requires a one-tailed test, its rejection region will always lie at _____ extreme of the distribution, that is, in _____ tail.

14-24 Our third alternate hypothesis was of a different sort: "μ is different from μ_0." This hypothesis does not specify the _____ of the expected _____ . It is the sort of hypothesis which requires a _____-tailed test of significance.

14-25 Since this hypothesis requires a two-tailed test, you should expect that its *rejection region* will be divided into two parts, one in each of the _____ .

tails

14-26 For the .05 level of significance, the rejection region for this hypothesis should be the _____ 2.5 per cent of the area in the distribution and the _____ 2.5 per cent of the area. If $\overline{X}$ lies in *either* of these parts of the rejection region, it will be among the *most extreme* 5 *per cent of the sample means.*

lower ↔
upper

Review

14-27 *The hypothesis that μ is not different from μ_0 can be rejected if we find that we have obtained an $\overline{X}$ which is very unlikely to occur when _____ equals _____ .*

$\mu - \mu_0$

14-28 *To test this hypothesis, we first imagine a sampling distribution around the assumed mean μ_0. Then we decide on a level of significance. On the basis of our _____ hypothesis, we can then determine a _____ region of the distribution. If $\overline{X}$ is found to lie in this region, we can _____ the null hypothesis.*

alternate
rejection
reject

14-29 *With an alternate hypothesis which specifies the direction of the expected difference, a _____-tailed test of significance is appropriate, and the rejection region will lie in _____ tail(s) of the distribution. With an alternate hypothesis which does not specify this direction, a _____-tailed test of significance is appropriate and the rejection region will occupy _____ tail(s) of the distribution.*

one
one

two
two (both)

14-30 *The amount of area lying in the rejection region is always equal to the number chosen as the _____ . If the rejection region lies in both tails, _____ of this area will be found in each tail of the distribution.*

level of significance
half

C.   The Ratio $(\overline{X} - \mu)/\sigma_{\overline{X}}$ as a z Score

14-31 Recall that we have used the normal curve table in two different ways. In Lesson 12, we first converted our observed result (e.g., a certain frequency of *alternations*) into a z score and then determined the *probability* of getting a z score *at least that large* by finding the _____ under the normal curve which lies beyond that z. In short, we went to the table with a value of _____ and obtained a *probability* in the form of an _____ under the curve.

14-32 In Lesson 13, however, as we tried to estimate μ from $\overline{X}$, we thought first in terms of the *probability* which would satisfy us and called that probability a level of _____ . Then we visualized the probability of being correct as an _____ under the normal curve and used the table of normal curve areas to find out the value of _____ which corresponded to that probability. In short, we went to the table with a probability in the form of an _____ and obtained from the table a value of _____ to use as a *multiplier*.

14-33 Setting up the boundaries of *rejection regions* is very much like setting up the boundaries of the _____ interval for estimating μ. In Section B of this lesson, we again used the normal curve table to find out the _____ value, or multiplier.

14-34 You will now begin to see that these *two ways* of using the *normal curve table* are equivalent and that any problem can be treated in *either* way. We can treat the question whether $\mu = \mu_0$ in the other way by proceeding as follows: Let us first treat our $\overline{X}$ as a *deviation score* and express it as a deviation from the mean of the sampling distribution. This mean is μ_0; the deviation score is therefore $\overline{X} -$ _____ .

14-35 When a deviation score is divided by the _____ of the distribution, it becomes a z score. We can turn our new deviation score $\overline{X} - \mu_0$ into a z score by dividing it by _____ .

14-36 If we divide $\overline{X} - \mu_0$ by $s_{\overline{X}}$, instead of by $\sigma_{\overline{X}}$, it will be a useful z score only if $s_{\overline{X}}$ is a good _____ of $\sigma_{\overline{X}}$. In general, this will be true when the sample size is very _____ .

14-37 The quantity $(\overline{X} - \mu_0)/\sigma_{\overline{X}}$ will behave like other z scores we have seen and will therefore have a *normal distribution* provided that the sampling distribution of means is a normal distribution. You can see this most clearly if you recognize that this quantity is analogous to the z score you already know, $(X_i - \overline{X})/s$. The quantity s is the standard deviation of a distribution of raw scores symbolized by

_____; the quantity $\sigma_{\bar{X}}$ is the standard deviation of a distribution of _____ symbolized by _____.

X_i

means — $\bar{X}$

14-38 The mean of a distribution of X_i is _____; the mean of our distribution of sample means is _____.

$\bar{X}$

μ_0

14-39 The quantity $X_i - \bar{X}$ is a _____ score; it is the _____ of a raw score from its _____. The quantity $\bar{X} - \mu_0$ is a _____ of a _____ from the sampling distribution _____.

deviation

deviation — _mean_

deviation — _sample mean_

mean

14-40 The z score $(X_i - \bar{X})/s$ is a member of a z-score distribution with a mean of 0 and a standard deviation of 1. Likewise, the mean of the distribution of $(\bar{X} - \mu_0)/\sigma_{\bar{X}}$ is _____ and the standard deviation is _____.

_0_

_1_

14-41 The distribution of $(X_i - \bar{X})/s$ is a distribution of the _deviations_ of scores around their mean, expressed in standard deviation units. The distribution of $(\bar{X} - \mu_0)/\sigma_{\bar{X}}$ is also a distribution of deviation scores, but the scores are the _____ of samples, and the mean from which they deviate is the mean of a _____. These deviation scores are again expressed in standard deviation units, and the standard deviation is the _____ of the mean.

means

sampling distribution

standard error

14-42 It is logical that the mean of the distribution of $(\bar{X} - \mu_0)/\sigma_{\bar{X}}$ should be 0, since some of the means will lie _above_ μ_0 and will have _positive_ deviation scores and some will lie _below_ μ_0 and have _____ deviation scores. Most of the scores lie relatively near the mean, and their _deviation_ scores will be _____ in size.

negative

small

14-43 Since we can expect $(\bar{X} - \mu_0)/\sigma_{\bar{X}}$ to behave like a z score, we can treat our question about the significance of $\bar{X}$ in just the same way we treated the question of significance in the alternation experiment (Lesson 12A). The result $\bar{X}$ is like a certain outcome in the alternation experiment, and each result can be converted into a certain _____ score.

z

14-44 Converting the alternation experiment result into a z score required assuming, on the null hypothesis, that the observed outcome belonged to a normal distribution with mean of Np and standard deviation of $\sqrt{Npq}$. Similarly, converting the $\bar{X}$ into a z score requires assuming that $\bar{X}$ belongs to a normal distribution with mean of _____ and standard deviation of _____.

μ_0 — $\sigma_{\bar{X}}$

14-45 Once the z score is found, it is easy to determine the probability of getting a z score *at least as extreme* as this one. We refer to a table of _____ , and find the _____ which lies under the _____ beyond this particular value of _____ .

normal curve areas
— area
normal curve — z

Review

14-46 *This section has shown that the question as to whether $\mu = \mu_0$ can be approached in either of two ways, both of which make a certain use of the normal curve table. One can reason "If $\mu = \mu_0$, then our observed value of* _____ *must be a member of a* _____ *distribution with a mean of* _____ *and a standard deviation of* _____ *. When this distribution is normal, the quantity* _____ *is a z score, and the probability of getting a z score at* least that extreme *can be determined from the normal curve table."*

$\bar{X}$ — sampling
μ_0
$\sigma_{\bar{X}}$
$\dfrac{\bar{X} - \mu_0}{\sigma_{\bar{X}}}$

14-47 *Or one can reason as in Section B, "If $\mu = \mu_0$, our observed value of $\bar{X}$ must belong to a sampling distribution with a mean of μ_0 and a standard deviation of $\sigma_{\bar{X}}$. When this distribution is normal, 95 per cent of the means will lie within a distance around μ_0 that is not greater than about 2* _____ *. If my $\bar{X}$ turns out to lie more than this distance away from the mean μ_0, it will lie in a* _____ *region (by a two-tailed test) and I can* _____ *the hypothesis that $\mu = \mu_0$."*

$\sigma_{\bar{X}}$
rejection
reject

14-48 *The first approach takes the exact result $\bar{X}$ and uses the normal curve table to determine its* _____ *under the null hypothesis. The second approach starts with an acceptable* _____ *(stated as a level of significance) and determines the* limits *within which $\bar{X}$ must lie if the* _____ *hypothesis is to be accepted as reasonable.*

probability
probability

null

D. Applying the Two Approaches to an Example

We shall now take an example and consider it in turn by each of the two approaches described in Section C. Suppose we are going to take a sample of 100 Stanford-Binet IQs from the population of a certain city and we want to determine whether the distribution of IQ in this city is typical of the distribution in the general population. If the distribution is not different from the general population, then our sample should turn out to have a mean similar to the means of other samples drawn from a population with a mean of 100 and a standard deviation of 16.

14-49 On the null hypothesis that μ is not significantly different from 100, we should find that our sample fits acceptably into a sampling distribution of means whose mean is _____ .

100

14-50 Because we know the value of σ in this case, we do not need to estimate it. We can compute the value of $\sigma_{\bar{X}}$ exactly by dividing _____ by _____ . We obtain $\sigma_{\bar{X}} =$ _____ .

$\sigma - \sqrt{n} - 1.6$ ·

14-51 Our null hypothesis, then, is the hypothesis that the μ of the population from which our sample will come (that is, all the IQs in this city) is not significantly different from 100. What about our alternate hypothesis? We must choose an alternate hypothesis *before we obtain our sample* in order not to be influenced by the results of the sample. Suppose we have no reason to expect either particularly high or particularly low IQs in this city; we shall therefore choose the alternate hypothesis μ is _____ μ_0.

different from

14-52 This alternate hypothesis will have its rejection region in the _____ tail(s) of the sampling distribution. If we choose the .05 level of significance, the region will include what area(s)? _____ .

upper and lower

The upper 2.5 per cent and the lower 2.5 per cent

14-53 We shall *accept* the null hypothesis if we find that our $\bar{X}$ is within the middle _____ per cent of the sampling distribution. Now we discover that determining the _____ region, when it is two-tailed, requires *exactly the same procedure* as setting up confidence limits for a statement about the population mean. In both cases, we are interested in specifying the *middle region* of the sampling distribution.

95

rejection

14-54 To find the limits of our confidence interval for the 95 per cent level of confidence, we first converted this percentage to a decimal, 0.95. Then we divided it by _____ to get that part of the area which lies between the _____ and one confidence limit. This area we then looked up in the table of _____ .

2

mean

normal curve areas

14-55 The limits of the confidence interval for the 95 per cent level of *confidence* are the same as the limits of the rejection region for the _____ level of *significance*. The confidence interval lies *inside* these limits, and the rejection region lies _____ them.

5 per cent (.05)

outside

14-56 Half of 0.95 is 0.475. In the table of normal curve areas, we find that this corresponds to a z of _____ . This z value is

1.96

our *multiplier,* which we use to multiply the value of _____ $\sigma_{\bar{X}}$
and thus to obtain the _____ of our rejection region. *limits*

14-57   If we now multiply $\sigma_{\bar{X}}$, which is 1.6, by our multiplier, 1.96, we
obtain _____. Since the mean of the sampling distribution *3.1*
is 100, the limits of our rejection region lie at 100 + _____ , *3.1*
or _____ , and 100 − _____ , or _____ . *103.1 — 3.1 — 96.9*

14-58   In arriving at this result, it was convenient to point out the
relation to the procedure for determining confidence limits. However,
we could have reasoned in a slightly different way. Knowing that the
upper part of our rejection region contains _____ per cent *2.5*
of the distribution, we could have reasoned, "50 per cent of the total
area is in the upper half, to which the normal curve table applies. If 2.5
per cent lies in the upper part of the rejection region, then there must
be _____ per cent between the mean and the limit of the *47.5*
rejection region." That line of reasoning would also have led us to look
in the normal curve table for the area _____ . *0.475*

14-59   When we take our sample of 100 IQs, then, and find that the
mean of the sample is 104, we shall know that this is a difference from
the general population mean which is _____ at the .05 *significant*
level. Although 4 IQ points does not seem to be a great deal, we know
from our calculations that only _____ per cent of all the *5*
samples of 100 IQs that might be drawn from a population with mean
of 100 and standard deviation of 16 would turn out to have means
greater than 103.1 or smaller than 96.9. We would have to *reject* the
null hypothesis.

14-60   Now let us suppose that we had initially *suspected* that the
population of this city would contain a large number of relatively high
IQs. We might then have taken the alternate hypothesis "μ is greater
than μ_0." This hypothesis takes a _____-tailed test, and *one*
its rejection region lies entirely at the _____ extreme of *upper*
the distribution.

14-61   To find the *limit* of this rejection region, we would reason
somewhat as in frame 14-58: "50 per cent of the total area in the distribution is in the upper half, to which the _____ table *normal curve*
applies. If the upper 5 per cent is the rejection region, then there must
be _____ per cent between the mean and the limit of the *45*
rejection region." We would then go to the table to look up the area
_____ . *0.45*

14-62 The area 0.45 corresponds to a z of _____ . This z is our _____ . The limit of our rejection region is 100 + _____ , which comes to the value _____ .

1.6
multiplier
2.6 (that is, 1.6 × 1.6) —
102.6

14-63 If we obtain an $\bar{X}$ of 104 with such an alternate hypothesis, we can again reject the null hypothesis. Notice particularly that the limit of the rejection region at the 0.05 level is *closer* to the mean when the rejection region lies in _____ tail(s) of the distribution. Remember that we noted in Lesson 12 that the required level of significance is reached _____ easily with a one-tailed test than with a two-tailed test. We find that to be true again in this example.

one

more

14-64 Let us turn now to the second approach by way of the z score $(\bar{X} - \mu_0)/\sigma_{\bar{x}}$. Using this approach, we shall calculate the probability of getting a sample mean at least as extreme as $\bar{X}$ if the _____ is valid.

null hypothesis

14-65 When $\bar{X} = 104$, the z score $(\bar{X} - \mu_0)/\sigma_{\bar{x}}$ can be evaluated for the hypothetical sampling distribution with $\mu_0 =$ _____ and $\sigma_{\bar{x}} = 1.6$. The z value is _____ .

100
2.5

14-66 We have therefore obtained a result which lies 2.5 standard errors above the mean of our sampling distribution. The probability on a one-tailed test of getting a z score at least as high as 2.5 can be determined by looking in the normal curve table for the _____ between the mean and $z = 2.5$ and subtracting this number from _____ . The probability is _____ .

area

0.5 — 0.0062

14-67 The probability of our result on a two-tailed test is equal to the probability of getting a z score at least as high as 2.5 or at least as _____ as _____ . This probability is exactly _____ as large as 0.0062, and it is therefore equal to _____ .

low — −2.5
twice
0.0124

Review

14-68 *Review this example by considering the problem of $\bar{X} = 104$ when a .01 level of significance is required. With the alternate hypothesis "μ is different from 100," we must accept the null hypothesis if $\bar{X}$ lies within the middle _____ per cent. The rejection region will include that _____ per cent of the area which lies in each tail of the distribution. Expressed as a decimal, this percentage is _____ . The area in one-half of the distribution, lying between*

99
0.5 (half of 1)

0.005

the mean and the limit of this rejection region, is _____. The multiplier of $\sigma_{\bar{x}}$ would be _____, and the upper and lower limits of the rejection region would be _____ and _____. Could we reject the null hypothesis at this level? _____.

0.495
2.6
104.2 — 95.8
No

14-69 *At the .01 level and with the alternate hypothesis "μ is greater than 100," the rejection region would be the _____. The area to be looked up in the table of normal curve areas is _____. The multiplier is _____, and the limit of the rejection region is _____. Could we reject the null hypothesis at this level with this alternate hypothesis? _____.*

upper 1 per cent
0.490
2.3
103.7
Yes

14-70 *Now compare these results with the probability calculated by the second approach in frames 14-64 to 14-67. The probability on the null hypothesis of a sample mean as extreme as 104 is 0.0062 on a one-tailed test and 0.0124 on a two-tailed test. We have just found that, by the first approach, the null hypothesis would be _____ at the .01 level on a one-tailed test and it would be _____ at the .01 level on a two-tailed test. The two approaches lead to equivalent conclusions.*

rejected
accepted

E. Review Section: Comparison of Tests Using the Normal Curve Table

This section contains no new material. It is written as a review, placing the significance tests of Lesson 12 alongside those of Lesson 14 for direct comparison.

14-71 Both Lessons 12 and 14 have been concerned with tests of the null hypothesis, using the _____ table to determine the probability of getting a certain result if the null hypothesis is valid.

normal curve

14-72 In Lesson 12, the observations to be tested consisted of *frequencies* which could be classified into exactly _____ categories. In Lesson 14, the observations consisted of *sets of scores* for which it was possible to calculate a _____ and a _____.

two

mean
standard deviation

14-73 In both lessons, we considered a distribution which had approximately the shape of the normal curve. In Lesson 12, this distribution was the _____ distribution, which becomes approxi-

probability

mately normal when the _____ in an experiment becomes very large.

number of observations

14-74 In Lesson 14, the distribution approximating normal shape was the _____ distribution of _____. Such distributions are approximately normal for a large number of samples when the size of the sample is very _____ .

sampling — means

large

14-75 In both these cases, it was necessary to calculate or to estimate the mean and standard deviation of this normal distribution. The mean of the probability distribution is _____ . Its standard deviation is _____ .

Np

$\sqrt{Npq}$

14-76 The mean of the sampling distribution of means is the same as the mean of the _____ from which the samples are drawn. Its standard deviation, called the _____ , is defined as $\sigma_{\bar{x}} =$ _____ .

population

standard error of

the mean — $\sigma/\sqrt{n}$

14-77 The value of $\sigma_{\bar{x}}$ can be determined exactly only when the value of _____ is known. If this value is not known, then σ_x is estimated by the equation $s_{\bar{x}} =$ _____ .

σ

$\sqrt{\dfrac{\Sigma x_i^2}{n(n-1)}}$

14-78 Once the mean and standard deviation of the normal distribution are known, the hypothesis-testing procedure is the same for the tests studied in both lessons. By examining the _____ hypothesis first, one determines whether the test to be applied must be a one- or a two-_____ test.

alternate

tailed

14-79 In Lesson 14, we showed that the idea of a one-tailed test is equivalent to the idea of a particular region *at one end* of a normal distribution, such that, if the observed result lies in that region, we shall _____ the null hypothesis.

reject

14-80 We called this special region a _____ region, and we also showed that a two-tailed test is equivalent to the idea of a _____ region which has _____ parts, one in each _____ of the distribution.

rejection

rejection — two

tail

14-81 A one-tailed test is used and the rejection region has _____ part(s) when the alternate hypothesis _____ . A two-tailed test is used and the rejection region has _____ part(s) when the alternate hypothesis _____ .

one — specifies the

direction of the

expected difference

two

does not specify the

direction of the

expected difference

14-82 From this point, the test can proceed according to either of two approaches. We can calculate the *probability* of getting a result at least as extreme as our observed result. In that case, we convert our observed result into a _____ score by using the mean and standard deviation of the normal distribution to which we consider that it belongs.

z

14-83 We then go to the normal curve table with this z score and find out the _____ which lies under the normal curve between the _____ and this value of _____. From this number, we can determine the _____ which lies beyond this value of _____ at one end (for a _____-tailed test) or both ends (for a _____-tailed test).

area
mean — z
area
z — one
two

14-84 If we use the other of the two approaches, we proceed to set up the limits of *rejection* regions. The *size* of the rejection region is determined by the _____ which is required. The proportion of the distribution contained in *each part* of a two-part rejection region is equal to exactly _____ of the number describing the _____.

level of significance

half
level of significance

14-85 In order to use the normal curve table, one must always determine what proportion of the rejection region will lie within _____ of the distribution only. The normal curve table gives areas for only _____ of the normal distribution, from the _____ to z.

half
half
mean

14-86 The normal curve table can be used to determine the number by which the standard deviation must be _____ in determining the limit of the _____ region at either end of the curve.

multiplied
rejection

14-87 These two approaches lead to equivalent conclusions. In using the first approach, we go to the normal curve table with a value of _____ and obtain an area which can be interpreted as a _____. In using the second approach, we go to the table with an area derived from a level of _____ which is stated as a probability, and we obtain a value of _____ to use as a multiplier.

z
probability
significance
z

14-88 It is important, finally, to remember that the whole line of argument just reviewed depends upon the existence of a distribution—either the probability distribution or the sampling distribution of means—which can be regarded as a close approximation to a _____ distribution.

normal

Problems for Lesson 14

14-1 A sample of 100 students from several colleges slept a mean number of 7.15 hours during a three-day period in March. A previous experiment had shown that 5,000 noncollege young people of college age slept an average of 7.90 hours during a comparable three-day period; the σ of that population was 1.35. Test whether the mean of the college sample is significantly different from the mean of the noncollege population.

14-2 A certain college recommends to its students that they study two hours outside of class for every hour spent in class. A dean wishes to determine whether the students do, in general, spend this amount of time in study. He plans to ask a randomly selected group of 100 students to report their study time over a period of two weeks. He will then determine the average number of hours of study per hour in class, for each student.

(a) The dean estimates that the standard deviation will be relatively large, in the neighborhood of 1. Assuming that $s = 1$, within what limits can the mean number of hours of study per hour in class lie, for the dean to be able to conclude at the .95 level of confidence that the true mean is 2?

(b) The dean obtains a mean of 1.83, with $s = 0.92$. What is the probability of a mean as extreme as this on the hypothesis that the students *do* really average two hours study per hour of class? Consider that the alternate hypothesis does not specify the direction of possible difference.

(c) Since the result approaches significance at the .05 level, the dean decides that the difference may be small but genuine. He thinks he can show it to be a significant difference by increasing the size of his sample. Assuming that the mean and standard deviation remain the same for a sample of $n = 200$, would the result be significant at the .05 level?

Lesson 15.   The *t* Distribution

Up to this point, we have restricted ourselves to the consideration of large samples when we have discussed the testing of sample means. This restriction is often inconvenient, since the study of large samples is so costly and time-consuming as to be prohibitive in many investigations. We shall therefore turn now to a consideration of methods which are suitable for small samples as well as large ones.

Lesson 15 introduces the *t* distribution, a new distribution which in many ways is analogous to the normal distribution but which is far more versatile. The nature of this distribution will be discussed in terms of the kind of problem treated in Lesson 14 for large samples: the problem of testing whether $\mu = \mu_0$. Lesson 16 will then apply this distribution to a slightly different sort of problem, testing the significance of the difference between the means of *two* distinct samples. Any significance test in which the *t* distribution is used is called *a* t test. Both Lessons 15 and 16, therefore, are concerned with the *t* test of significance.

It may be well at this point to remind you that our whole discussion, from Lesson 13 on through Lesson 16, rests upon the fundamental assumption that the variable *X* itself is approximately normally distributed. If the distribution of *X* is very different from normal, the sampling distribution of means will not be normal and the whole line of argument breaks down. In practice, the deviation of the *X* distribution from normal must be rather considerable before the normal curve tests and t tests have to be abandoned. Such cases do arise, however, and when they do, it is customary to make use of certain tests which are not based upon the assumption that *X* is normally distributed. These tests are called "nonparametric tests." We have studied only one nonparametric test, the chi-square test. There are many others, but they will not be considered in this book.

A.   The Effect of Small Samples on Normal Curve Tests

15-1   In Lesson 14, we made use of the quantity $(\overline{X} - \mu_0)/\sigma_{\overline{X}}$ as one approach to testing whether $\mu = \mu_0$. This quantity is a kind of z score, and the distribution of z scores has the shape of a _____   *normal* distribution.

15-2 The quantity $(\bar{X} - \mu_0)/\sigma_{\bar{X}}$ can be computed exactly only when the value of σ is known. If σ is not known, the value _____ must be substituted for $\sigma_{\bar{X}}$ and the substitution results in a new fraction, _____ .

$s_{\bar{X}}$

$\dfrac{\bar{X} - \mu_0}{s_{\bar{X}}}$

15-3 This new fraction can be regarded as a close approximation to the z score only if _____ is a close approximation to _____ .

$s_{\bar{X}}$

$\sigma_{\bar{X}}$

15-4 In general, $s_{\bar{X}}$ is a closer approximation to $\sigma_{\bar{X}}$ for large samples than for small samples. If the sample is large enough, $(\bar{X} - \mu_0)/s_{\bar{X}}$ can also be regarded as a _____ score, and the table of the normal distribution can be used.

z

15-5 The smaller the sample, the poorer $s_{\bar{X}}$ becomes as an estimate of $\sigma_{\bar{X}}$. It is known that for samples with n of 30 or less, the quantity $(\bar{X} - \mu_0)/s_{\bar{X}}$ does *not* have a normal distribution. Increasing the n above 30 makes this distribution approach more and more closely to the _____ shape.

normal

15-6 The quantity $(\bar{X} - \mu_0)/\sigma_{\bar{X}}$ has a normal distribution for small samples as well as for large samples. The quantity $(\bar{X} - \mu_0)/s_{\bar{X}}$ has a normal distribution only for _____ samples.

large

15-7 When a test of significance involves the quantity $(\bar{X} - \mu_0)/s_{\bar{X}}$, one can treat this quantity as if it were a z score and can use the normal curve table whenever n is _____ . When n is _____ , the quantity is not a z score because it does not have a _____ distribution.

large — small

normal

15-8 The quantity $(\bar{X} - \mu_0)/s_{\bar{X}}$ therefore has a special name. It is called the *t ratio* or more often simply t. The distribution of _____ is definitely not a normal distribution for n less than 30.

t

Review

15-9 *The difference between the t ratio and the quantity, $(\bar{X} - \mu_0)/\sigma_{\bar{X}}$, is in the term by which the deviation score, _____ , is divided. For the t ratio, this term is _____ .*

$\bar{X} - \mu_0$

$s_{\bar{X}}$

15-10 *Whenever $s_{\bar{X}}$ must be used instead of $\sigma_{\bar{X}}$, one must consider whether his sample has a value of _____ which is large enough*

n

to make the distribution of _____ take on normal shape. If
not, the table of _____ cannot be used.

t

normal curve areas

B. The Distribution of the *t* Ratio

15-11 The *t* ratio has a *different* distribution for each value of *n* until
n becomes large enough for the distribution to become approximately
like the _____ distribution. The distribution of *t* is therefore a whole *family* of distributions, one for each value of _____
up to 30 or more.

normal

n

15-12 Each of these different distributions had to be calculated
separately. The distributions were originally determined by an English
mathematician who wrote under the pseudonym "Student." Useful
tables of the *t* distributions are available, and they are used when *n* is
_____, much as the normal curve is used when *n* is
_____.

small

large

15-13 Each distribution of *t* has been calculated for a particular
number of *degrees of freedom* (d.f.). A sample of $n = 10$ has $n - 1 = 9$
degrees of freedom. A sample of $n = 30$ has $n - 1 = 29$ _____.
For any sample, the number of d.f. is always equal to $n - 1$.

d.f. (degrees of freedom)

> You have met the concept of d.f. already if you studied Lesson 7 on chi-
> square. We can apply it here in a quite similar way. If we have *n* observa-
> tions in a sample and all *n* have to make a particular sum, then $n - 1$ of
> the observations could take any arbitrary values ("freely") but the *n*th and
> last observation would be forced to take the value necessitated by the
> sum.

15-14 The choice of a proper distribution of *t* depends upon the
value of the sample _____. The distribution of *t* which
should be applied is the distribution with d.f. = _____.

n

n − 1

15-15 Figure 15-1 shows the *t* distributions for four representative
numbers of d.f. The dashed curve is for d.f. = 1, the solid curve for a
very large number of d.f. (d.f. = infinity). Under the curve for d.f. = 1,
the area within ± 1 standard deviation of the mean is _____
than the area under the corresponding part of the curve for d.f. =
infinity.

smaller (less)

15-16 Under the curve for d.f. = 1, the area *beyond* $z = +2$ is
_____ than the area under the corresponding part of the
curve for d.f. = infinity.

greater

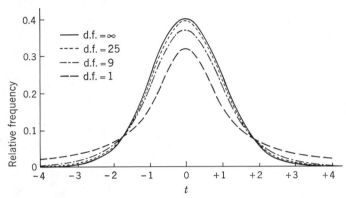

Figure 15-1. Distribution of t for various degrees of freedom. (*From D. Lewis, Quantitative Methods in Psychology, Iowa City, Iowa, published by the author, 1948.*)

15-17 If the t distributions for d.f. $= 1$ and d.f. $=$ infinity are compared, then, we find a relatively greater proportion of the area in the center, near the mean, under the curve for $n =$ _____ and   *infinity*
a relatively greater proportion of the area at the extremes, under the tails of the curve, for the distribution with $n =$ _____ .   *1*

15-18 The t distributions for d.f. $= 9$ and d.f. $= 25$ lie *between* the distributions we have just been discussing. Thus, as the number of degrees of freedom increases, the t distribution gradually comes to have a smaller and smaller proportion of its area under the _____ and the proportion of its area lying near the   *tails*
_____ increases.   *mean (center)*

15-19 *The t distribution for d.f. $=$ infinity is identical with the normal distribution.* But for d.f. less than 30, the t distribution contains a larger proportion of its area _____ than does the normal distribution.   *under the tails (at the extremes)*

15-20 Therefore, if we were to make the mistake of using the normal distribution table for a t ratio with d.f. less than 30, we would be led to suppose that the probability of getting a sample with $t = 3$ is rather _____ than it actually is. The probability of such extreme   *smaller*
t values is _____ for small samples than for very large   *greater*
samples.

Review

15-21 *There is a different t distribution for each number of degrees of freedom, but for more than 30 degrees of freedom, the t distributions are very similar to the* _____ *distribution. For a sample of size n,*   *normal*
the proper t distribution has _____ *d.f.*   *n − 1*

15-22 *When the sample size is small, the proportion of area in the tails of the t distribution is relatively* _____ *than the proportion of area in the tails of the normal distribution. Therefore, extreme values of t (such as t = 3) occur with* _____ *frequency in small samples than in large samples.*

C.   The *t* Table

Turn to the foldout between pages 336 and 337 and refer to the page containing the normal curve table. Below that table is a Table of Critical Values of t.

15-23   In the *t* table, there are _____ different rows, each for a different *t* distribution. These distributions differ from one another because there is a different *t* distribution for each number of

_____ .

15-24   The number of d.f. for a particular row is stated in the first column. The other columns in the table are labeled with six different probability levels. The numbers in these columns are values of _____ , which is the ratio $(\bar{X} - \mu_0)/s_{\bar{X}}$.

15-25   In order to use the *t* table, you must first look for the row with the appropriate number of degrees of freedom. For a sample of size n, the number of d.f. is _____ . For a sample of $n = 11$, you would use the row for which d.f. = _____ . You would use the row with 1 d.f. when the sample has $n =$ _____ .

15-26   Look at the first row, with d.f. = 1. In order to reach the 5 per cent level of significance ($p = .05$), the value of t must be at least 12.706. This means that the difference between $\bar{X}$ and the mean of the sampling distribution must be at least _____ times as large as $s_{\bar{X}}$ in order for the result to be significant at the .05 level.

15-27   In order to reach the .01 level of significance, the value of t for 1 d.f. must be at least _____ .

15-28   The *t* table is constructed for a two-tailed test. That is, the probability levels which head the columns represent areas in a rejection region which has _____ parts, one under each _____ of the distribution.

15-29   When we learn from the table that the t ratio $(\overline{X} - \mu_0)/s_{\overline{x}}$ must be at least 63.657 for 1 d.f. *in order to reach the* .01 *level of significance,* we know that 99 per cent of the area of this t distribution lies between the limits $t = -63.657$ and $t = +63.657$. Therefore, the percentage of total area which lies *beyond* $+63.657$ must be only _____ of 1 per cent.

half

15-30   If we wished to apply a one-tailed test, we would need to know the value of t *beyond which* _____ per cent of the area lies. In that case, since an equal area would be found beyond t at the *other* extreme, and since the probabilities in the t table are for a _____-tailed test, we would have to look up the t value in the column labeled with the probability _____ .

1

two
0.02

15-31   Suppose that we have a sample of $n = 21$. We shall find the t values for this sample size in the row for d.f. = _____ . At the .01 level of confidence, t for a two-tailed test is given in the table under the probability $p =$ _____ . The t value is _____ .

20

0.01 — 2.845

15-32   The t value for a *one*-tailed test at the .01 level of confidence, with $n = 21$, is found in the column with $p =$ _____ . The value is _____ . This value is _____ than the value of t for a two-tailed test under the same circumstances.

0.02
2.528 — smaller

15-33   When a two-tailed test is to be applied, the value of t is sought in the column whose probability is the *same* as the desired level of _____ . When a one-tailed test is to be applied, the value of t is sought in the column whose probability is just _____ as large as the desired _____ . The reason for this difference is that the t table is constructed for _____ tests.

significance
twice
level of significance
two-tailed

Review

15-34   *The t table contains a row for each* _____ *and a column for each* _____ . *The values entered in the rows and columns are the values of* _____ *beyond which the* _____ *region will be found.*

d.f.
probability
t
rejection

15-35   *The rejection region for which the table is appropriate is a* _____-*part rejection region. Therefore, the t values in a particular column are appropriate for a* two-tailed test *at the level of significance which is* _____ *the value of the probability for that column. The same t values are appropriate for a* one-tailed test *at a level of*

two

•

equal to

significance which is _____ the value of the probability for that column.

D. Comparison of the t Table and the Normal Curve Table

15-36 Look at the column for $p = 0.05$ in the t table. The value of t at this level of significance is _____ when d.f. $= 1$ and $n = $ _____. When $n = 3$, t has dropped to a value of _____; for $n = 4$, $t = $ _____.

15-37 The smallest value which t ever reaches, in the column $p = 0.05$, is the value _____. At d.f. $= 30$, the t value in this column has already reached _____.

15-38 As n increases, the value of t at any particular probability level _____. This change in t is rapid when the values of n are _____; it becomes less rapid as the values of n become _____.

15-39 Take the smallest t value, 1.960. Look at the normal curve table just above the t table, and find the area under the normal curve which corresponds to a z value of 1.960. The area is _____. Therefore, the area from the mean to 1.960, under the normal curve, is _____. The area *beyond* this value of z, under the upper tail of the curve, is _____.

15-40 From this information, you can say that the probability of getting a z score as large as 1.960 is _____ when a *one-tailed test* is used. The normal curve table considers only the areas from the mean out to z under one side of the curve.

15-41 If we wish to apply a two-tailed test and consider the like area at the *other* end of the curve, then we must multiply this probability by _____. The probability of a z score as large as 1.960 is _____ when a two-tailed test is applied.

15-42 We found that $t = 1.960$ when d.f. $= $ _____ and $p = $ _____. Therefore, the probability of a t ratio as large as 1.960 when a two-tailed test is applied *and when the sample is infinitely large* is _____.

15-43 The quantities t and z will *always* have the same value for a given level of significance when n is _____. The reason lies in the fact that the distribution of t is identical with the _____ distribution under these circumstances.

15-44 Compare one more pair of values from the two tables. This time, find the value of t for a *one-tailed test* when d.f. = infinity. Take a significance level of .05; you will find the t value in the column under $p =$ _____. It is _____ .

15-45 The value of t is 1.645 for a significance of 0.05 with a one-tailed test. Look up 1.645 in the normal curve table. The area from the mean to $z = 1.645$ is approximately _____. The area *beyond* $z = 1.645$ is _____. The probability, in a one-tailed test, of getting a $z = 1.645$ is _____. Such a large value of z is significant at the _____ level.

15-46 From these comparisons, we see that the information to be obtained from the normal curve table is the *same* as the information to be obtained from the _____ row of the t table because the t distribution is the same as the z distribution when n is _____ large.

15-47 Nevertheless, the two tables on the foldout *look* very different from each other. It may be helpful to point out the differences. The t values for d.f. = infinity are lined up in a *row* across the bottom of the table. The corresponding z values in the normal curve table are lined up in _____ up and down the table, and there are *many more* z values than t values given for the t distribution with d.f. = infinity.

15-48 More z values can be given because the normal curve table gives information about only *one* distribution. The t table must give information about many different distributions, one for each different value of _____ .

15-49 The areas under the normal curve correspond to *probabilities*. These probabilities appear in the normal curve table in columns opposite their z values. The probabilities appear in the t table in a _____ across the _____ of the table as labels for the various _____ .

15-50 The probabilities stated in the t table refer to the areas under the two *tails* of the distribution. The probabilities in the normal curve table refer to the areas between the _____ and z. In order to find the area under a *tail*, it is necessary to subtract the area given in the table from the total area under half the distribution, which is _____ .

mean

0.5

15-51   These differences in the tables are merely differences in *form*, which arise because the t table has to give information about a _____ number of distributions than the normal curve table.

greater

15-52   The only difference between the tables which affects their use in an *essential* way is the fact that the normal curve table, referring to only *one-half* of the normal distribution, has values which can be applied directly in a _____-tailed test. The t table, on the other hand, contains values which are to be applied directly to a _____-tailed test. The rejection region indicated in the normal curve table is a _____-part rejection region; that indicated in the t table has _____ part(s).

one

two
one
two

Review

15-53   *From a comparison of normal curve and t tables, we have found the following differences: The normal curve table gives proportional areas from only one distribution; the t table gives proportional areas for several different distributions, each one appropriate for a different value of* _____ .

d.f.

15-54   *To get areas under the* tails *of the distribution, you take the probabilities as they are stated in the* _____ *table, but you must subtract the areas given in the* _____ *table from 0.5.*

t
normal curve

15-55   *If you wish the area under only one tail of the curve, you take the area given in the normal curve table and* _____ *it from 0.5. If you wish the area under only one tail of a t distribution, you look up the t value in the column whose probability is exactly* _____ *times as large as your level of significance.*

subtract

two

15-56   *The* _____ *can be used for a sample of any size provided that the distribution with the correct number of* _____ *is selected. The normal curve table can be used only when* _____ *is very large, or when* _____ *is known exactly, because the ratio* _____ *does not have a normal distribution for samples of a* _____ *size.*

t table
d.f.
n
σ
$\dfrac{\bar{X} - \mu_0}{s_{\bar{X}}}$
small

Problems for Lesson 15

15-1 With $n = 10$, $\bar{X} = 50$, $\mu_0 = 47$, and $s_{\bar{X}} = 1.05$, what is the value of t? Between what values does the probability of such a large difference $\bar{X} - \mu_0$ lie with a two-tailed test? With a one-tailed test?

15-2 For significance at the .05 level by a two-tailed test, how large must t be when $n = 10$? When $n = 20$? When $n = 31$?

15-3 For significance at the .01 level by a one-tailed test, how large must t be if $n = 12$? By a two-tailed test?

15-4 For significance at the .02 level by a two-tailed test, how large must t be if $n = 18$? At the .01 level?

Lesson 16.   **Applying the *t* Test**

In Lesson 1, when we first pointed out the problem of deciding whether or not a difference is "significant," we raised the question of significance with regard to the ¼-inch difference in average height between samples from two fictitious colleges, Alpha and Omega. At that time, we could only point out that the problem existed; we could not show how to decide whether the difference is significant because we had no way as yet to estimate how much difference can be expected between samples drawn from the same population.

Now we are in a position to solve this problem. It is the problem of testing the significance of the difference between two sample means. The t test is the most commonly used method of making this kind of test, and it may be that testing the difference between two means is the most common kind of problem met with in psychology and social science. We are therefore completing our discussion of statistical inference with the significance test which you are most likely to read about and perhaps to use.

The lesson begins with a short example, showing how the t test may be applied to the sort of problem discussed in Lesson 14, testing whether $\mu = \mu_0$, when there is only one sample. In Section B we shall begin to consider cases in which there are two samples to be compared.

A.   Testing Whether $\mu = \mu_0$ on the Basis of a Small Sample

16-1   The *t* test must be used instead of a normal curve test whenever the ratio $(\bar{X} - \mu_0)/\sigma_{\bar{X}}$ must be replaced by the ratio _____ and the sample *n* is smaller than approximately 30.

$\dfrac{\bar{X} - \mu_0}{s_{\bar{X}}}$

16-2   The *t* ratio must be substituted for the *z* ratio whenever _____ is unknown. For *n* less than 30, the *t* ratio does not have a _____ distribution; it has a variety of distributions, depending upon the number of _____ .

σ

normal

d.f.

16-3   In the example we studied in Lesson 14, we determined whether an $\bar{X}$ of 104 in a sample with $n = 100$ could reasonably be considered to have come from a population of IQ scores whose mean is 100 and whose σ is 16. We were able to use a normal curve test. Could we have used a normal curve test with a much smaller sample, such as a sample of $n = 20$? _____, because the value of _____ was known and therefore the _____ ratio could still be used.

Yes

$\sigma - z$

16-4 The result of our test would have been somewhat different with $n = 20$ because the standard error of the mean of such samples is larger. Since $\sigma_{\bar{X}} = \sigma/\sqrt{n}$, $\sigma_{\bar{X}}$ for the distribution of samples of $n = 20$ would be $16/4.47 =$ _____ .

3.6

16-5 The deviation of $\bar{X}$ from $\mu_0 = 100$ is equal to _____ . The z ratio is therefore _____ . Even by a one-tailed test, the probability of obtaining a z at least as large as this value is _____ . The probability would be _____ than this in a two-tailed test.

4
1.1

0.14 — greater

16-6 A decrease in the size of the sample, therefore, means that a given value of $\bar{X}$ becomes _____ likely to reach significance. But as long as σ is known, the _____ table can still be used.

less
normal curve

16-7 Now, let us merely suppose that we do *not* know the value of σ and that we have a sample of $n = 20$. Suppose again that the value of $\bar{X}$ is 104, and let $\Sigma x_i^2 = 1,839.2$. Then the *estimate* of $\sigma_{\bar{X}}$ will be found through dividing _____ by _____ and taking the square root.

1,839.2 — 380 (that is, 20 × 19)

16-8 In this way, we find that $s_{\bar{X}} = 2.2$, rather larger than the value of $\sigma_{\bar{X}}$ which we worked with in Lesson 14. The value of t, on the assumption that $\mu_0 = 100$, will be _____ .

1.8

16-9 The appropriate row in the t table is the row with d.f. = _____ . Look across this row, and find the first value which is *greater* than 1.8. This value lies in the column with $p =$ _____ .

19
0.05

16-10 Since the t-table probabilities are stated for a two-tailed test, we know that our t value is not _____ enough to reach significance at the .05 level by a two-tailed test. It would have to be at least as large as _____ .

large

2.093

16-11 The t value is *larger* than the value in the column with $p = 0.10$. If we apply a one-tailed test, this column gives the t values

needed to reach significance at the _____ level. Since our
t value is larger than 1.729, the result reaches significance at the
_____ level when a one-tailed test is used.

Review

16-12   *In testing whether $\mu = \mu_0$, the t test must be used when both of
two conditions are true: when _____ and when _____.*

16-13   *The t test in such cases is applied in just the same way as the normal curve test. But the deviation $\bar{X} - \mu_0$ must be divided by _____
instead of by _____, and the resulting value of _____
must be looked up in a _____, with d.f. = _____.*

B.   Testing the Difference between Means of Two Correlated Samples

*Suppose that we have two samples of observations and wish to test whether
they could have been drawn from the same population. In certain cases,
both samples consist of observations made on the same group of persons at
different times. Such cases are met whenever an experimenter compares
scores (or other observations) taken* before *some experimental variable is
changed and* after *the change has had a chance to operate. For example, a
college might compare the same students' scores on a test of knowledge
about social science taken* before *and* after *the required courses in social
science have been completed.*

*When both samples come from the same group or from two groups which
have been explicitly matched person for person, we say that the samples
are* correlated. *Section B is concerned with the method for testing the significance of the difference between means of* correlated *samples.*

16-14   Consider two sets of social science test scores, both from the
same group of students. Let us designate as X_1 the mean of that set of
scores obtained first, before the students took their college social
science courses. We shall call the other mean $\bar{X}_2$, from the set obtained
after the courses have been taken. We are interested in determining
whether _____ is significantly different from _____.

16-15   Our null hypothesis is that $\bar{X}_1$ and $\bar{X}_2$ are not significantly different from each other. In other words, it is the hypothesis that the difference $\bar{X}_2 - \bar{X}_1$ is not significantly different from _____.

0

16-16   The most plausible alternate hypothesis in this case, where we are concerned with the expected effect of college instruction, is that $\bar{X}_2$ is _____ than $\bar{X}_1$ and that $\bar{X}_2 - \bar{X}_1$ will have a _____ sign.

greater — positive

16-17   Each of the students tested has two scores. If we subtract his first score from his second score, we shall obtain a *difference* score, that is, a new score representing the _____ between his performance on the two occasions when he took the test.

difference

16-18   If we determine this difference score for each student, we reduce our *two* sets of raw scores to *one* set of _____ scores. We can set up a frequency distribution of these _____ scores, with its mean and standard deviation.

difference
difference

16-19   Let us designate the mean of a sample of difference scores as $\bar{D}$. We can imagine a large number of such means, each of them obtained in just the same way: by obtaining the set of the difference scores for a group of persons and taking the arithmetic mean of these scores. The distribution of values of $\bar{D}$ from samples, all drawn in the same way from the same population, will constitute a new kind of _____ distribution of means. *It is a* _____ *distribution of means of difference scores.*

sampling — sampling

16-20   In this way, we have made our problem much like the problem of testing whether the mean of a single sample is significantly different from the value μ_0 which is expected under the null hypothesis. We have a mean $\bar{D}$ of a single sample of _____ scores. We can compare it with a sampling distribution of _____ .

difference
means of difference scores

16-21   The null hypothesis is that $\bar{D}$ is not significantly different from 0. According to the null hypothesis, we would expect the mean μ_0 of the sampling distribution of $\bar{D}$ to be equal to _____ .

0

16-22   The null hypothesis enables us to visualize what this sampling distribution of $\bar{D}$ should be like. In such a distribution with mean = 0, some values of $\bar{D}$ which occur should have a _____ sign and some should have a _____ sign. A few values would be relatively large, but most of them would be relatively small and close to zero.

positive ↔
negative

16-23 In order to determine the probability of getting a particular observed value of $\bar{D}$ when $\mu_0 = 0$, we shall need to know the _____ of the sampling distribution of the means of difference scores. We shall call this quantity simply $\sigma_{\bar{D}}$.

16-24 There is ordinarily no way in which $\sigma_{\bar{D}}$ can be determined exactly. Therefore, we shall have to be content with an estimate, $s_{\bar{D}}$. You can anticipate that it will rarely be possible to use the _____ table for this test; we shall have to use the _____ instead.

16-25 The estimate of $\sigma_{\bar{D}}$ is found by the equation

$$s_{\bar{D}} = \sqrt{\frac{\Sigma x_D^2}{n(n-1)}}$$

where the term Σx_D^2 is the sum of the squares of the deviations of the *difference scores* around their mean $\bar{D}$. This equation is exactly analogous to the definition of $s_{\bar{X}}$ as equal to $\sqrt{\Sigma x_i^2/[n(n-1)]}$, where we were not dealing with difference scores but with raw scores and where the term Σx_i^2 was the sum of the squares of the _____ of the _____ scores around their mean _____.

16-26 The t ratio is a deviation score divided by the estimated standard deviation of a sampling distribution. In this case, the deviation score will be the _____ of the mean $\bar{D}$ from the mean of the _____, which has the value _____ under the null hypothesis.

16-27 The t ratio will therefore be $\bar{D} - 0$, or simply $\bar{D}$, divided by _____.

16-28 This t value, for a sample of size n, would be looked up in a t table in the row with _____ degrees of freedom.

Review

16-29 *Suppose a distribution of 15 difference scores derived from the two occasions on which 15 students took the social science test. If $\bar{D} = 50$ and $s_{\bar{D}} = 20$, the value of the t ratio will be* _____. *In this case, d.f. =* _____.

16-30   *For d.f. = 14, a t ratio of 2.5 would be significant beyond the* _____ *level for a two-tailed test and significant beyond the* _____ *level for a one-tailed test.*

.05
.025

C.   Testing the Difference between Means of Uncorrelated Samples

16-31   We now return to consider the Alpha-Omega heights, where the groups are different and *unmatched.* According to the null hypothesis, these samples are just two slightly varying samples drawn from the same population. Let the mean of the Alpha sample be $\overline{X}_A$ and the mean of the Omega sample be $\overline{X}_O$. Under the null hypothesis, the difference $\overline{X}_A - \overline{X}_O$ is not significantly different from _____ .

0

16-32   Since both samples are assumed to come from the same population, their means belong to the same *sampling* distribution of _____ .

means

16-33   Imagine that we were to draw, at random, *pairs of means* from that sampling distribution and calculate the *difference* between the members of each pair. What would the distribution of these *differences* look like? Since the greatest number of means lie in the center of the distribution, we would often happen to draw pairs which lie *close* to each other. If $\overline{X}_1$ is the member drawn first and $\overline{X}_2$ the other member, the difference $\overline{X}_1 - \overline{X}_2$ would have a relatively _____ size in such cases.

small

16-34   Sometimes we would draw pairs with $\overline{X}_1$ larger than $\overline{X}_2$, and the value of $\overline{X}_1 - \overline{X}_2$ will have a _____ sign. In other cases, $\overline{X}_2$ will be larger and $\overline{X}_1 - \overline{X}_2$ will have a _____ sign.

positive
negative

16-35   The distribution of a large number of values of $\overline{X}_1 - \overline{X}_2$ would be a _____ distribution of *differences between means* of samples, all of which belong to the same population. Its mean should equal _____ , since random selection of the pairs should mean that those with negative sign will equal those with positive sign.

sampling

0

16-36   We now have a familiar problem: an observed value and a sampling distribution of such values. In this case, the observed value is a _____ , $\overline{X}_A - \overline{X}_O$; the sampling distribution is a sampling distribution of _____ .

16-37 We can treat the value $\overline{X}_A - \overline{X}_O$ as a *deviation* from the mean of its sampling distribution, which is equal to _____ . If we find the estimated standard deviation of that sampling distribution $s_{\overline{x}_1 - \overline{x}_2}$, we shall be able to calculate a _____ ratio $(\overline{X}_A - \overline{X}_O)/s_{\overline{x}_1 - \overline{x}_2}$.

16-38 Estimating the standard deviation of the sampling distribution requires two steps. We must first estimate the value of σ, the standard deviation of the _____ to which the samples are supposed to belong. Then we shall use that estimate to arrive at an estimate for $s_{\overline{x}_1 - \overline{x}_2}$.

16-39 We could estimate σ from *either* sample. But since both are supposed to come from the same population, we can "pool" the two, treat them as a single larger sample, and estimate σ from the pooled combination. Because the combined samples make a single sample with a larger n, an estimate made from the combination should be _____ accurate than an estimate from either sample alone.

16-40 Let $\Sigma x_A{}^2$ be the sum of squared deviations from $\overline{X}_A$ for the Alpha sample, and let $\Sigma x_O{}^2$ be the sum of squared deviations from $\overline{X}_O$ for the Omega sample. The estimate of σ from the combined samples s_P is given by

$$s_P = \sqrt{\frac{\Sigma x_A{}^2 + \Sigma x_O{}^2}{n_A + n_O - 2}}$$

The denominator of the term under the radical is 2 less than the n for the _____ samples. *This term also represents the number of degrees of freedom for this kind of test.*

> The number of degrees of freedom with a single sample whose deviations are taken around a single mean is $n - 1$. When we combine two samples and take some of the deviations around each of *two* different means, another degree of freedom is lost and d.f. $= n - 2$ for the combined sample.

16-41 Therefore, the estimated population *variance* $s_P{}^2$ is obtained by adding the two _____ for the samples and dividing this total by the number of _____ .

16-42 We now use the value of $s_P{}^2$, the estimated _____ , to get an estimate of the standard deviation of the sampling distribu-

---

difference between means
differences be-
   tween means

0

t

population

more

combined

sums of squared deviations
degrees of freedom

population variance

---

tion of differences between means. The estimate is given by

$$s_{\bar{X}_1 - X_2} = \sqrt{\frac{s_P^2}{n_A} + \frac{s_P^2}{n_O}}$$

Remember that the two quantities under the radical sign must be added *before* the square root can be taken.

16-43   With this estimated standard deviation of the sampling distribution, we can determine a t ratio for the obtained difference $\bar{X}_A - \bar{X}_O$. We must divide this difference by the value of _____ to obtain t. This value of t can then be compared with the distribution of t with d.f. = _____ .

> Most people do not memorize the equations in frames 16-40 and 16-42 unless they have to do a great deal of statistical computation. You can always return to look them up if you should need them. The important thing to remember from this section is the line of reasoning, which is reviewed in the frames below.

Review

16-44   *When you must test the significance of the difference between the means of two samples, you must first determine whether the two samples are* correlated. *If the two samples are each made up of observations from* _____ *or from* _____ , *then they are* correlated samples.

16-45   *With correlated samples, you can directly determine the* _____ *scores and imagine a sampling distribution of* _____ . *According to the null hypothesis, such a sampling distribution should have a mean of* _____ . *The t ratio is obtained by dividing* $\bar{D}$, *the mean of the* _____ *scores, by* _____ , *the* _____ . *It has* _____ *degrees of freedom.*

16-46   *With samples that are not correlated, you can regard the two samples as a single sample and determine an estimate of* _____ . *This estimate* s_P *is used to find an estimate of the standard deviation of a sampling distribution of* _____ . *The t ratio is the observed difference between the sample means* $\bar{X}_A - \bar{X}_O$ *divided by the standard deviation of the sampling distribution. It has* _____ *degrees of freedom.*

D. Applying the t Test for Differences between Means

Suppose that an investigator studies the effect of age upon speed of reaction. His subjects must respond to a flash of light by pressing a key; the experimenter records the time interval between light and key response. Group 1 is made up of 12 subjects between the ages of eighteen and twenty-one. Group 2 contains 10 subjects between ages sixty and sixty-five. The following statistics are obtained:

Group 1	Group 2
$n_1 = 12$	$n_2 = 10$
$\bar{X}_1 = 230$ *milliseconds*	$\bar{X}_2 = 240$ *milliseconds*
$\Sigma x_1^2 = 440$	$\Sigma x_2^2 = 460$

16-47 The null hypothesis, in this example, is that the difference $\bar{X}_1 - \bar{X}_2$ is not significantly different from _____ .

0

16-48 Without knowing the results of the experiment, you would select an alternate hypothesis of the form "$\bar{X}_1 - \bar{X}_2$ is *different* from 0," requiring a _____ test, or you would select the alternate hypothesis "$\bar{X}_1 - \bar{X}_2$ is _____ than 0," since you might well expect a faster reaction time from the younger subjects.

two-tailed

less

16-49 Regarding the two samples as coming from a single population, you can determine an estimate of σ for that population by the equation

$$s_P = \sqrt{\frac{\Sigma x_1^2 + \Sigma x_2^2}{n_1 + n_2 - 2}}$$

Since you want the value of s_P^2, it is not necessary to take the square root. The value of s_P^2 is _____ .

45

16-50 From $s_P^2 = 45$, you can now estimate the value of $s_{\bar{X}_1 - \bar{X}_2}$, the standard deviation of the sampling distribution of differences means of such samples. Using the equation

$$s_{\bar{X}_1 - \bar{X}_2} = \sqrt{\frac{s_P^2}{n_1} + \frac{s_P^2}{n_2}}$$

you find that $s_{\bar{X}_1 - \bar{X}_2}$ *squared* is equal to _____ .

8.25

16-51 The square root of 8.25 is 2.87. Therefore, the t ratio for the obtained difference $\bar{X}_1 - \bar{X}_2$ is equal to _____ .

−3.483

16-52 The value of t has a negative sign, since $\bar{X}_1$ is smaller than X_2; the sign must be disregarded when you look in the t table, since a deviation from the assumed mean of 0 has the same _____ no matter in which direction it occurs.

16-53 The proper row to consult in the t table is the row with d.f. = _____. With a two-tailed test, the obtained t ratio of 3.483 is significant beyond the _____ level.

16-54 Even though a one-tailed test could perhaps be justified in a case of this kind, the obtained difference is already clearly significant by the two-tailed test. By a one-tailed test, its significance would reach beyond the _____ level.

Review

16-55 *For a concluding example, test the significance of the ¼-inch difference in heights between Alpha and Omega Colleges when $n_A = 101$ and $n_O = 101$ and when $\Sigma x_A{}^2 = 1{,}225$ and $\Sigma x_O{}^2 = 1{,}300$.*

The estimated population variance is _____ .
The estimated value of $s_{\bar{X}_1 - \bar{X}_2}$ is _____ .
The observed difference $\bar{X}_A - \bar{X}_O$ is _____ .
The t ratio is _____ .
The t distribution for d.f. = _____ must be consulted.
The null hypothesis must be _____ .

Problems for Lesson 16

16-1 Five situations requiring a statistical test are described below and lettered **a** to **e**. With respect to this group of five situations, answer each of the following questions: (1) In which of the five situations would it be permissible to employ a *normal curve test?* Could a *t* test also be used? (2) In which of the five situations is there a question of the significance of a *difference between the means of two samples?* (3) Which of the situations listed in your answer to (2) involve *correlated* samples? Which involve *uncorrelated* samples?

(a) Testing whether a group of 20 students improved their grade averages between freshman and sophomore years.

(b) Testing whether the mean grade average of 20 freshmen is significantly different from the mean grade average for all 1,352 upperclassmen when the standard deviations of both groups are known.

(c) Testing whether the mean grade average of all 405 freshmen is significantly different from the mean grade average for all 1,352 upperclassmen when the standard deviations for both groups are known.

(d) Testing whether the mean grade average of all 405 freshmen is significantly different from the average required for graduation when the standard deviation of the freshman group is the only standard deviation known.

(e) Testing whether the mean grade average of 25 students who report studying less than three hours a day is significantly different from the mean grade average of 20 students who report studying four or more hours a day.

16-2 Determine whether the number of hours of study per day is significantly different for the two samples described below:

	Students with Grade Averages of B+ or Better	Students with Grade Averages of B— or Less
n	27	25
$\overline{X}$	4.15	4.38
s	0.95	1.30

16-3 Twenty-one students in a class of 32 made higher marks on the second of two examinations than they had made on the first. All students had taken a test of attitude toward the instructor at two times: between the first and second examinations and after the second examination was returned. A difference score $d = X_1 - X_2$ was computed for each student on the attitude test; a positive d indicated a more favorable attitude on the second testing.

The mean difference score for the 21 students who improved their marks on the second examination was 1.57. The standard deviation of the difference scores was 2.7. Was the change in attitude significant for this group? If so, could you conclude that getting a higher mark made the students have a more favorable attitude toward the instructor?

Lesson 17.   Linear Functions

Lesson 17 is a review of certain algebraic concepts needed in the subsequent lessons on correlation. You will not need to study Lesson 17 unless your knowledge of algebra and simple analytic geometry of a straight line is dormant. To determine whether you should study a particular section in Lesson 17, turn first to the review items in the box at the end of the section. If those items are easy for you, then go on to the next section; if not, then it may be worth your while to do the entire section before proceeding.

A.   Functions and Functional Relationships

17-1   A *variable* is a quantity which can assume different values. We shall not be concerned in this lesson with variables having *nominal* values but only with variables which assume *ordinal* or *interval* values. Unlike a variable, a *constant* is a quantity which always assumes _____ value.

the same (only one, a constant)

17-2   A group of rats was trained to follow a particular path through a maze to reach food. All were equally hungry before each training session, but some were trained for 5 and others for 10 sessions. The number of training sessions is a _____ in this experiment; the degree of hunger during training is a _____ .

variable
constant

17-3   The term FUNCTION is formally defined as follows: If the value of a variable Y *depends upon* the value of another variable X, so that for every value of X there is one and only one value of Y, then Y is said to be a FUNCTION OF X. In other words, if the value of Y can change *only if* the value of X changes, then Y is a _____ of X.

function

17-4   Let Y be a person's life expectancy (that is, the number of years the life insurance companies expect him to continue to live); let X be his age. As people grow older, their life expectancy grows shorter. Life expectancy and age are both _____ rather than constants. _____ is a function of _____ .

variables
life expectancy — age

17-5 When Y is a function of X, we say that a FUNCTIONAL RELATION-SHIP exists between X and Y. This relationship is symbolized by the equation $Y = f(X)$, which can be read "Y is a _____ ."

function of X

17-6 In the equation $Y = f(X)$, the letter f stands for the phrase _____ . It is a general term, and it does not specify precisely what the _____ relationship between Y and X is.

a function of
functional

17-7 When we write $Y = 2X$, we are specifying a *particular* functional relationship between Y and X. If $Y = 2X$, then for every value of X, there is a value of Y which is exactly _____ times as large as the value of X.

two

17-8 If $Y = 2X$ and $X = 1$, then $Y =$ _____ . The factor 2 multiplies every possible value of _____ . This equation specifies a particular _____ between _____ and _____ .

2
X
functional relationship
$-X \leftrightarrow Y$

17-9 If $Y = 0.5X$, then the _____ between Y and X is such that, for every value of X, there is one and only one value of Y, and this value is _____ the value of X.

functional relationship

one-half

17-10 "Y is some unspecified function of X." This statement can be written as $Y = f(X)$. "For each value of X, there is a value of Y which is ten times the value of X." This statement can be written _____ .

$Y = 10X$

17-11 In the equation $Y = 0.5X$, the value 0.5 is a _____ , since it does not assume different values. X and Y are _____ , since they may assume different values. However, Y must always have a value which is exactly _____ the value of X.

constant
variables

one-half

17-12 When $Y = f(X)$, the value of Y is *completely determined* as soon as X takes some particular value. This is the reason why we say that Y is a *function* of X: Its value is _____ by the value of X.

determined

Review

17-13 *The expression $Y = f(X)$ is read* "_____ ." *It means that the value of X* _____ *the value of Y.*

Y is a function of X
determines

17-14 $X = 0.5$, $Y = 2$, and $Y = mX$. *The value of m is* _____, *and the equation which describes this particular functional relationship is* _____ .

4

$Y = 4X$

B. Graphing Linear Functions

17-15 The *rectangular coordinate system* is the familiar pair of straight lines meeting at right angles to each other: a horizontal line designated as the X axis and a vertical line designated as the Y axis. To locate a point on such a coordinate system, we need a pair of values of which one is a value of the variable _____ and the other a value of the variable _____ .

$X \leftrightarrow$

Y

17-16 The pair of values which define a particular point are called the coordinates of that point; the X coordinate (value of the X variable) is always stated first, the Y coordinate second. Therefore, the coordinates of a point are an *ordered pair* of numbers. The point with the coordinates (2, 3) has the X coordinate _____ and the Y coordinate _____ . The point with $X = -1$ and $Y = 4$ is the point (_____ , _____).

2

3

(−1, 4)

17-17 The table below gives the X coordinates of five points, A through E.

	A	B	C	D	E
X	−2	−1	0	1	2
Y	___	___	___	___	___

If $Y = 2X$, the Y coordinates of the points are, from left to right, _____ , _____ , _____ , _____ , and _____ . Point A can be described as the point with the coordinates _____ .

−4, −2, 0, 2,

4

(−2, −4)

17-18 Figure 17-1 is a graph of the function $Y = 2X$ showing the location on rectangular coordinates of three of the five points discussed in frame 17-17. A *straight line* has been drawn through all

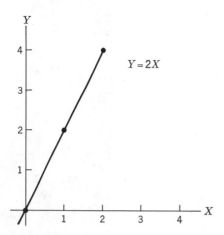

Figure 17-1. Graph of the function $Y = 2X$.

these points. All other points for which $Y = 2X$ will fall exactly on
_____. Relationships such as this, in which the graph of
the relationship between X and Y is some straight line, are called
LINEAR FUNCTIONS. The function $Y = 2X$ is a _____ .

17-19 Figure 17-2 is a graph of the function $Y = X$. Notice that the
function is a _____ function. Furthermore, when the value
of X is changed by a certain amount, Y changes by an _____
amount.

17-20 The simplest *general* expression for a linear function is the
expression $Y = mX$. In this expression, Y and X are variables and m is
a _____ . The graph of $Y = mX$ will always pass through
the *origin* of the coordinate system, which is the point $(0, 0)$. If $X = 0$,
Y must equal _____ for any value of m.

17-21 All linear functions of the form $Y = mX$ will yield a graph
which is a straight line passing through the origin. In such linear functions, the ratio Y/X is a constant. In Figure 17-1, for the point $(2, 4)$,
$Y/X = $ _____ . The value of Y/X for *any* point on the line
$Y = 2X$ will be _____ . [Since division by zero is prohibited,
the point $(0, 0)$ is the single exception.]

17-22 If both sides of the equation $Y = mX$ are divided by X, the
equation becomes $Y/X = m$. Since Y/X has the same value at all
points satisfying the equation, the value of m in any linear equation of
this simple form is a _____ .

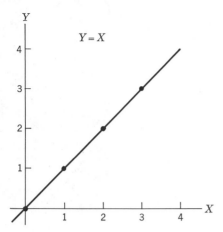

Figure 17-2. Graph of the function $Y = X$.

17-23 When you look at the graph of any linear function which passes through the origin, you can easily determine its equation. You know that the equation will be of the form _____ . To find the value of m, you may select *any* point on the line except the point $(0, 0)$ and determine its coordinates from the scales on the two axes. (Two useful points are indicated by dots in Figure 17-3.) If you now divide the _____ coordinate by the _____ coordinate, you find that $m =$ _____ . The equation of this function is _____ .

$Y = mX$

$\dfrac{Y - X}{3}$

$Y = 3X$

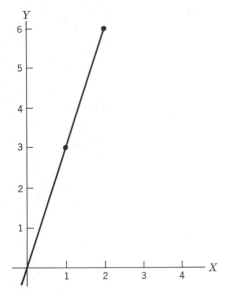

Figure 17-3. Graph of a simple linear function.

17-24 *All functions of the form $Y = mX$ are called* _____ *functions. When they are drawn as graphs on rectangular coordinates, such functions appear as* _____ *lines which pass through the point* _____ .

linear

straight
(0, 0)

17-25 *Given a linear function which passes through the origin and through point (2, 5), you can state that the equation for that function is* _____ .

$Y = 2.5X$

C. Slope of Linear Functions

17-26 If $Y = 2X$, then every time X increases by one unit, Y increases by _____ unit(s). The amount of change in Y for every unit change in X is indicated by the ratio Y/X. When $Y = 2X$, $Y/X =$ _____ .

two

2

17-27 The amount of change in Y for every unit change in X is the RATE OF CHANGE OF Y WITH RESPECT TO X. The ratio Y/X is a measure of the _____ of change of Y with _____ to X.

rate — respect

17-28 The rate of change of Y with respect to X is the SLOPE of a linear function. This term is a natural one, since in general, the graph of a linear function will climb more steeply when the value of the slope is _____ .

greater

17-29 Since the ratio Y/X describes the rate of _____, this ratio can be called the _____ of the linear function.

change of Y with respec to X — slope

17-30 If both sides of the equation are divided by X, the equation $Y = mX$ can also be written as $m =$ _____ . Therefore, m is equal to the _____ of the linear function.

$\dfrac{Y}{X}$

slope

17-31 Figure 17-4 is a graph of the function $Y = X$. Two points have been designated with coordinates (X_1, Y_1) and (X_2, Y_2). This figure will be used to develop the concept of the slope of a linear function mathematically. At (X_1, Y_1), the value of Y_1 is _____ . At (X_2, Y_2), the value of Y_2 is _____ . The *vertical* distance between these two points is equal to $Y_2 - Y_1$, which is _____ .

1

3

2

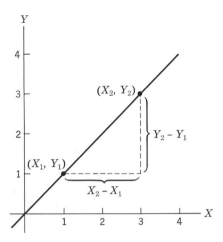

Figure 17-4. Slope of a linear function.

17-32 The value of X_1 is _____, and the value of X_2 is _____. The *horizontal* distance between the two points is $X_2 - X_1$, which is _____.

1

3

2

17-33 The *change of* Y between these two points is $Y_2 - Y_1$; the *change of* X between these two points is _____. The *rate* of change of Y with respect to the change of X is the ratio $(Y_2 - Y_1)/(X_2 - X_1)$, and *this ratio is the slope* of the linear function. Therefore, the constant m, which is also equal to the _____ of the linear function, is equal to the ratio _____.

$X_2 - X_1$

slope
$\dfrac{Y_2 - Y_1}{X_2 - X_1}$

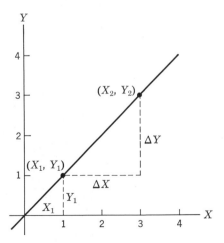

Figure 17-5. Slope of a linear function.

17-34 No matter which pair of points are selected from the points which fall on the line $Y = X$, the ratio of the distances $(Y_2 - Y_1)/(X_2 - X_1)$ will equal the value of m. In Figure 17-5, the same points from Figure 17-4 are shown, but the distance $Y_2 - Y_1$ has been labeled _____ and the distance $X_2 - X_1$ has been labeled _____.

ΔY

ΔX

The Greek capital delta, written Δ, commonly means an *increment* or increase (usually a small one). Using these symbols, the value of $m = $ _____.

$\dfrac{\Delta Y}{\Delta X}$

17-35 The same figure contains another pair of labeled increments. The distance $X_1 - 0$, which is the distance of the point (X_1, Y_1) from the Y axis, is labeled _____. The distance $Y_1 - 0$, which is the distance of the same point from the _____, is labeled _____. We can also say that $m = $ _____.

X_1

X *axis*

$\dfrac{Y_1 - Y_1}{X_1}$

17-36 As shown in Figure 17-5, $m = \Delta Y/\Delta X = Y_1/X_1$. The distances X_1 and ΔX, Y_1 and ΔY are the bases and the altitudes, respectively, of similar triangles. The ratio of the altitude to the base in one triangle is _____ this ratio for any other similar triangle. Therefore, the value of m will be a constant for *any* pair of points along the line. This constant will always equal the _____ of the linear function.

equal to (identical with

slope

Review

17-37 *The expression* $m = \Delta Y/\Delta X$ *states that the* _____ *of a linear function equals the ratio of the increment in Y, measured between any two points which fall on the line, to the* _____, *measured between the same two points.*

slope

increment in X

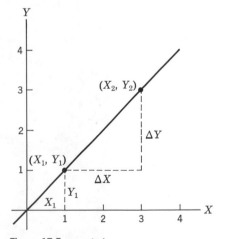

Figure 17-5 repeated

17-38 *The following table shows the coordinates of five points:*

	A	B	C	D	E
X	1	2	3	4	5
Y	0.5	1	1.5	2	____

The equation for this linear function is _____. The Y coordinate for the point E is _____. The slope of the function is _____.

17-39 *Given the following coordinates for three points (1, 2), (3, 6), (5, 10), what is the slope of the function? _____. What is the equation? _____.*

D. The Y Intercept

17-40 The linear functions in Figures 17-1 to 17-5 have all passed through the point (0, 0), which is the _____ of the rectangular coordinate system. For such functions, Y must equal _____ whenever $X = 0$.

17-41 Not all linear functions pass through the origin. In Figure 17-6, two linear functions are shown. The value of m, which is the same for both equations, is _____. The two functions have the same _____, and their lines are parallel to each other. But only one passes through the origin.

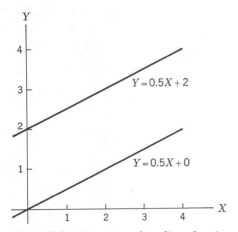

Figure 17-6. Comparison of two linear functions.

Margin answers:

$Y = 0.5X$
2.5
0.5

2
$Y = 2X$

origin
0

0.5
slope

17-42 The line $Y = 0.5X + 0$ *intercepts* (crosses) the Y axis at the point _____. The line $Y = 0.5X + 2$ _____ the Y axis at the point _____.

17-43 The general equation for a straight line is the equation $Y = mX + k$, where X and Y are variables and m and k are constants. Because the value of _____ determines the slope of the line, it is called the SLOPE CONSTANT.

17-44 The constant k determines the position of the line with respect to the Y axis. Since it determines the point at which the line will *intercept* the _____, it is called the Y INTERCEPT. In the equation $Y = 0.5X + 2$, the _____ is equal to 2.

17-45 For the equation $Y = 0.5X + 0$ in Figure 17-6, the Y intercept is _____. When $X = 0$, the line passes through the point where $Y = $ _____. For the equation $Y = 0.5X + 2$, $Y = $ _____ when $X = 0$.

17-46 Suppose that $Y = 2X + 1$. The line which is the graph of this function has a _____ of 2 and a _____ of 1.

17-47 Whatever the value of the Y intercept, the definition of the slope of the function does not change. For the equation $Y = X + 1$, Figure 17-7 shows that you can determine the slope exactly as you would for $Y = X$ by taking any pair of points and determining the ratio _____.

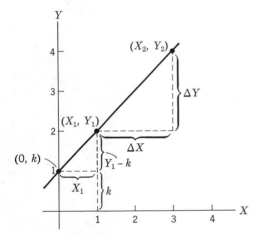

Figure 17-7. Slope of the linear function $Y = X + 1$.

17-48 $Y = 0.5X + 3$. When $X = 0$, $Y =$ _____. When $X = 2$, $Y =$ _____. When $X = 4$, $Y =$ _____. The slope of this function is _____. The Y intercept is _____.

3

$4 - 5$

0.5

3

17-49 The equation for the linear function which intercepts the Y axis at $Y = 3$ and which passes through the point (4, 7) is _____.

$Y = X + 3$

E. Positive and Negative Slopes

17-50 Figure 17-8 shows two functions. The equations for these lines are identical except for the _____ constant, which is positive in one equation and negative in the other.

slope

17-51 The equation $Y = 0.5X + 3$ has a slope constant which is a positive number. When X changes, Y changes *in the same direction*. If the value of X increases, the value of Y _____. All such functions with a positive slope constant are called INCREASING LINEAR FUNCTIONS. Whenever an increase in the value of X is accompanied by an increase in the value of Y, the linear function has a _____ slope constant and it is called an _____ linear function.

increases

positive
increasing

17-52 All linear functions with a positive slope constant are called

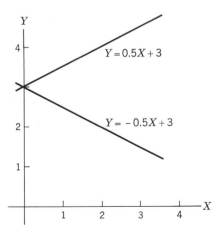

Figure 17-8. Linear functions with positive and negative slopes.

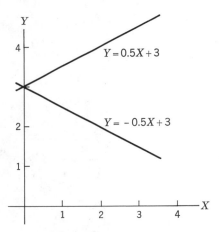

Figure 17-8 repeated

_____. We can also say, in such cases, that Y is an increasing function of X.

increasing linear functions

17-53 The other line in Figure 17-8 has the equation $Y = -0.5X + 3$. This equation has a _____ slope constant. When X changes, Y changes in the _____ direction.

negative
opposite

17-54 When the slope constant is negative, an increase in the value of X is accompanied by a(n) _____ in the value of Y. All such functions are called DECREASING LINEAR FUNCTIONS, and in such cases, Y is said to be a(n) _____ function of X.

decrease

decreasing

17-55 All linear functions with a negative slope constant are called _____. All linear functions with a positive slope constant are called _____.

decreasing linear functions
increasing linear functions
decreasing

17-56 The lower line in Figure 17-8 describes a _____ linear function, since increases in the value of X are accompanied by _____ in the value of Y. The value of the _____ is 3, and the slope of the function is _____.

decreases — Y intercept
−0.5

17-57 Consider a linear function with $k = 2$ and $m = 0$. The slope for this function is neither positive nor negative; therefore, it cannot be described as either an _____ or a _____ linear function.

increasing — decreasing

17-58 When $Y = 0X + 2$, every value which X assumes is multiplied by 0. Whatever the value of X, Y always equals _____. Changes in the value of X *do not affect the value* of Y.

2

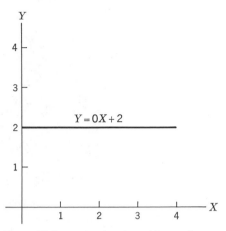

Figure 17-9. Linear function with zero slope.

17-59 When $m = 0$, we speak of a function whose slope is zero. The general equation $Y = mX + k$ reduces to the simpler form $Y = $ _____ . For every point on the line describing this equation, the value of Y is the same number, and Y is always equal to the value of the _____ .

k

Y intercept

17-60 Figure 17-9 shows the line $Y = 0X + 2$, or $Y = 2$. This line has a slope of _____ . For every value of X, the value of Y is _____ .

0
2

17-61 The graph of a linear function with zero slope is a straight line parallel to the _____ axis.

X

Review

17-62 *A decreasing linear function can be recognized as follows: It has a _____ slope constant, and every increase in the value of X is accompanied by a(n) _____ in the value of Y.*

negative
decrease

17-63 *When a linear function, graphed on rectangular coordinates, appears as a straight line parallel to the X axis, then the slope of that function is _____ .*

0

17-64 *The general equation for a linear function is _____ . There are two constants in this equation: One is called the _____ , and it is represented by the letter _____ ; the other is called the _____ , represented by the letter _____ .*

Y = mX + k
slope constant
m
Y intercept — k

Positive and Negative Slopes   **257**

17-65   *The general equation for a linear function is simpler in two special cases. When the function passes through the origin, the equation is* _____ *and the constant* _____ *is equal to zero. When the function has zero slope, the equation is* _____ *and the constant* _____ *is zero.*

$Y = mX - k$
$Y = k$
m

Problems for Lesson 17

17-1   What is the equation for each of the following lines?

    (a)   The line which passes through the origin and the point $(2, 5)$?

    (b)   The line which passes through the points $(0, 3)$ and $(4, 0)$?

    (c)   The line which passes through the points $(1, 2)$ and $(4, 5)$?

17-2   Which of the following functions pass through the origin?

    (a) $Y = -10X$?

    (b)   The line passing through the points $(2, 3)$ and $(5, 6)$?

    (c)   The line with a slope of -0.5 passing through the point $(2, 1.5)$?

    (d)   The line with a slope of 2.5 passing through the point $(10, 25)$?

17-3   **(a)**   What is the slope of the function which passes through the point $(5, 10)$ and has a Y intercept $= 3.0$?

    (b)   What is the slope of the function which passes through the point $(4, 7)$ and has a Y intercept of 3?

    (c)   What is the Y intercept of the function which has a slope $= -4.0$ and passes through the point $(3, 8)$? [Hint: $m = (Y - k)/X$].

17-4   What is the equation for the line passing through the points $(2, 10)$ and $(10, 10)$? What is the slope of this line? The Y intercept?

Lesson 18. Linear Regression and Correlation

One of the major topics in statistics is the topic of correlation, *the relationship between two (or more) variables. We shall consider in this book only the most elementary concepts of correlation, the concepts required in measuring the linear correlation between two variables. Unless you specialize in a field which makes extensive use of statistics, you will not be likely to hear any other kind of correlation discussed. However, linear correlation is the basis from which other kinds of correlation are generally taught; if you should later study other correlation methods, these lessons will provide a starting point.*

In Lesson 18, we shall first examine the nature of the problem we meet when we have to describe the degree of relationship, or "co-relation," between two variables. Then we shall show how a numerical measure of that degree of relationship, called the COEFFICIENT OF CORRELATION, *can be developed. Later lessons will explain the use and meaning of the correlation coefficient.*

A. The Scatter Diagram

Table 18-1 **Scores of 10 Students on Two Tests X and Y**

Score	*Students*									
	A	*B*	*C*	*D*	*E*	*F*	*G*	*H*	*I*	*J*
On X	2	3	6	7	8	10	11	14	16	17
On Y	4	5	8	9	10	12	13	16	18	19

18-1 Table 18-1 presents two sets of scores, one set on the test X and a second set on the test Y. Both sets were obtained from the same group of students, and each student has one score on each test. A brief examination of the table shows that the students who made high scores on X tended to make _____ scores on Y.

high

18-2   If we knew in advance about this tendency of high scores on X to accompany high scores on Y, then we would be able to say something about student J's score on Y from a knowledge of his score on X. We could say that, since his score on X is high, his score on Y is probably also _____. We could make a similar guess about the Y scores of other students.

18-3   Whenever there is some such orderly relationship between X and Y scores, information about the X score contains *some* amount of information about the _____. The orderly relationship is what we call *correlation*. When the degree of correlation is relatively great, then the X score contains a relatively large amount of information about the _____ .

18-4   We would like to be able to measure *just how much information* about the value of Y can be obtained from a knowledge of the corresponding value of X. In other words, we would like to be able to measure the degree of _____ between X and Y. This is the fundamental problem in correlation statistics.

Scores on test X

	1–2	3–4	5–6	7–8	9–10	11–12	13–14	15–16	17–18
19–20									/
17–18								/	
15–16							/		
13–14						/			
11–12					/				
9–10				//					
7–8			/						
5–6		/							
3–4	/								
1–2									

Scores on test Y

Figure 18-1.   Scatter diagram of test scores from Table 18-1.

Scores on test X

Scores on test Y	1–2	3–4	5–6	7–8	9–10	11–12	13–14	15–16	17–18
19–20									/
17–18								/	
15–16							/		
13–14						/			
11–12					/				
9–10				//					
7–8			/						
5–6		/							
3–4	/								
1–2									

Figure 18-1 repeated

18-5   We can treat the scores on X and the scores on Y as *two different frequency distributions*. But instead of tabulating the two sets of scores on separate graphs, we can tabulate them in a single graph called a SCATTER DIAGRAM. Figure 18-1 is a *scatter diagram* of scores from Table 18-1. Scores on X have been grouped into classes with a class interval of _____, and the labels appear at the _____ of the graph instead of at the bottom.

2

top

18-6   Scores on Y have also been grouped into classes with a class interval of 2. Their labels are arranged along the left margin in the position corresponding to the _____ axis in ordinary graphs.

Y

18-7   The vertical divisions of the diagram are called *columns*, and the horizontal divisions are called *rows*. There is a *column* in the _____ diagram for every class interval in the _____ distribution, and there is a *row* for every class interval in the _____ distribution.

scatter — X

Y

18-8 Every column in the diagram intersects with every row, creating a *cell* at each such intersection. Each cell represents a particular combination of one of the classes of X with one of the _____.
The cell in the upper right-hand corner represents scores of _____ and _____ on X and scores of _____ and _____ on _____.

classes of Y

17 ↔ 18
19 ↔ 20 — Y

18-9 If we were tallying the scores on Y alone, we would place our tally for a particular score alongside the _____ to which that score belongs. In the scatter diagram, we place our tally *simultaneously* alongside the proper Y class and *below the proper* _____. In other words, we place it in the _____ to which it belongs.

class

X class — cell

18-10 For example, Student A has a score of 2 on X and a score of 4 on Y. In Figure 18-1, we first locate along the top margin the class interval containing A's X score. This is the _____ column at the left. Then, moving down this column, we locate along the left margin the interval containing A's Y score. This is the _____ row from the bottom. We place our tally in the _____ formed by the intersection of this row and this column.

first

second
cell

18-11 Figure 18-1 shows the tallies for all 10 students. One cell has two tallies in it. These two tallies represent the pairs of scores made by students _____ and _____.

D ↔ E

18-12 You will perhaps notice that this procedure is very much like the procedure which you follow when you are plotting *points* on a graph with X and Y axes. Scores on test X are a kind of X axis here, and scores on test Y a kind of _____. We are treating the X and Y scores as X and Y coordinates would be treated in a commonplace graph. The figure looks a little different, but only because we have divided it up into separate cells.

Y axis

18-13 Notice that the tallies form a straight line, running diagonally from the lower left to the upper right corner. In a commonplace graph, points forming a straight line can be described by an equation in which Y is a *linear function* of X. The same is true for the scatter diagram in Figure 18-1. Because all the tallies fall along a single straight line, scores on Y are a _____ function of scores on X. Correlations approximating this general form are called LINEAR CORRELATIONS.

linear

Errors on maze X

	1	2	3	4	5	6	7	8	9	10	11	f_Y
10								1	1	1	1	4
9							1		1	2	1	5
8						1	1	2	4	1		9
7						4	5	3	2			14
6					1	6	4	4	1			16
5				1	5	3	5	1				15
4			2	2	4	4	2					14
3		1	3	3	2	1						10
2	1	2	1	1								5
1	1	1										2
f_X	2	4	6	7	12	19	18	11	9	4	2	94

(Errors on maze Y labels the left axis)

Figure 18-2. Scatter diagram of error scores made by a group of 94 rats in learning each of two mazes, X and Y.

18-14 Figure 18-2 is another _____. It is not so simple as Figure 18-1, but it contains nothing that is new in principle. A group of 94 rats learned two mazes, X and Y. Each rat made an "error score" on each maze, and the error scores have been tallied rat by rat just as the X and Y scores were tallied for students in Table 18-1. From the diagram, for example, you can tell that the number of rats which made six errors in learning Maze X *and* five errors in learning Maze Y is _____ .

18-15 Figure 18-2 is presented in order to give you an example of a scatter diagram in which the tallies do *not* fall nicely along a single straight line. There is a considerable amount of "scatter" in this scatter diagram. However, it is still true *in general* that high scores on Maze X are accompanied by _____ scores on Maze Y. The general *trend* of the tallies is again from the lower left to upper right along a rather straight path. Since the trend is along a straight line rather than along a curved line, we would still call this a _____ correlation.

18-16 Notice in this figure the *row* at the bottom labeled f_X and the *column* at the right labeled f_Y. The numbers in the column f_Y are the *row frequencies,* and the numbers in the row f_X are the *column frequencies.* For example, there are four tallies in the top row, and the number 4 appears in the top cell under f_Y. From the cells in the column f_Y, you can quickly tell the number of tallies falling into any particular class of the variable "errors on Maze _____."

Y

18-17 To find out how many tallies fall into any particular class of the variable "errors on Maze X," you will look at the cells in the _____ labeled _____ .

row — f_X

18-18 How many animals made seven errors on Maze X? _____ . How many made seven errors on Maze Y? _____ . How many made exactly seven errors on *both X and Y?* _____ .

18
14
5

18-19 The sum of the column frequencies f_X is 94, and the sum of the row frequencies f_Y is also 94. This number appears in the _____ corner of the diagram. It represents the total number of rats in this experiment. Since 94 is the total frequency for each distribution, we shall again represent it by the capital letter N.

bottom (lower) right

Review

18-20 *When there is some degree of correlation between X and Y, then information about an X value contains some _____ about the corresponding Y value. When we measure the amount of correlation, we are measuring the amount of _____ about _____ which is contained in _____ .*

information

information — Y
X

18-21 *In a scatter diagram, the frequency distributions for each of two _____ X and Y are tallied simultaneously. Classes of X are labeled along the top margin, and classes of Y along the _____ margin. There is a particular _____ for each class of X and a particular _____ for each class of Y.*

variables
left
column
row

18-22 *When the trend of the tallies in a scatter diagram follows a straight line rather than a curved line, the correlation is called a _____ correlation. When the tallies line up perfectly along such a straight line, scores on Y are a _____ function of scores on X.*

linear
linear

B. The Regression Line

18-23 When a scatter diagram contains only such tallies as lie perfectly along one straight line, Y is a linear function of X and the tallies can be described by an equation of the form $Y = mX + k$ (see Lesson 17 for a discussion of this type of equation). When the tallies do not all lie *on* such a line but the *trend* is nevertheless straight, we still call the correlation *linear* and the tallies can be *approximately* described by an equation of the same form, _____ .

$Y = mX + k$

18-24 In a linear correlation, Y is a linear function of X. When the correlation is perfect, all the tallies lie exactly on one _____ and Y is an *exact* linear function of X. When the correlation is not perfect, the tallies lie on or near one _____ line and Y is approximately a _____ of X.

straight line

straight

linear function

18-25 The equation which best describes Y as a linear function of X is called the REGRESSION EQUATION, and the straight line which is the graph of this equation is called the REGRESSION LINE OF Y ON X. When the correlation between X and Y is *perfect and linear,* all the tallies in the scatter diagram will lie exactly on the _____ line of _____ on _____ .

regression

$Y - X$

18-26 You should be careful not to forget to say "the regression line *of Y on X*." This phrase means that Y is being described as a _____ of X, that is, that we are measuring how much information about _____ we can get from knowing about _____. If we were, instead, to describe X as a _____ of Y, we would get a _____ line of _____ on _____ .

function

Y

$X - function$

regression — X

Y

18-27 Under certain circumstances, the two _____ lines —Y on X and X on Y—turn out to be the same line. But in most cases they are different lines. Anything which you learn about one regression equation can be applied without change to the other; therefore, for the sake of clarity, we shall discuss Y as a function of X. But remember always to use its complete name for the line: the _____ .

regression

regression line of Y on X

18-28 We now return to the maze example of Figure 18-2, which is repeated here for further discussion. It will provide us with our first example of a regression line of Y on X. Figure 18-2, as shown opposite, has an additional column and row at its margins. The bottom row,

	1	2	3	4	5	6	7	8	9	10	11	f_Y	M_x
10								1	1	1	1	4	9.5
9							1		1	2	1	5	9.4
8						1	1	2	4	1		9	8.3
7						4	5	3	2			14	7.2
6					1	6	4	4	1			16	6.9
5				1	5	3	5	1				15	6.0
4			2	2	4	4	2					14	5.1
3		1	3	3	2	1						10	3.9
2	1	2	1	1								5	2.4
1	1	1										2	1.5
f_X	2	4	6	7	12	19	18	11	9	4	2	94	
M_y	1.5	2.0	3.2	3.4	4.4	5.6	6.1	6.9	7.9	9.0	9.5		

(Left side vertical label: Errors on maze Y)

Figure 18-2. Repeated with M_x and M_y values.

labeled M_y, contains the *means* of the *columns*. For example, the first number at the bottom left is 1.5; that column has been treated *as a separate frequency distribution of Maze Y scores*, with $n =$ _____. The mean of 1.5 is the *mean number of errors on Maze* _____ *made by the two rats with tallies in that column.*

18-29 The second column from the left contains tallies pertaining to those animals who made _____ errors on Maze X. There are _____ such animals, and their Y scores can be treated as a separate frequency distribution with a mean of _____.

18-30 Each number in the row M_y therefore represents the _____ number of errors on Maze _____ made by the animals whose error score on Maze _____ appears at the top of the column.

18-31 The animals whose scores appear in a particular column are treated as a separate group, and their error scores on Maze _____ are regarded as a frequency distribution whose n is to be found in the row labeled _____.

2
Y

two
four
2.0

mean — Y
X

Y
f_X

Errors on maze X

	1	2	3	4	5	6	7	8	9	10	11	f_Y	M_x
10								1	1	1	1	4	9.5
9							1		1	2	1	5	9.4
8						1	1	2	4	1		9	8.3
7						4	5	3	2			14	7.2
6					1	6	4	4	1			16	6.9
5				1	5	3	5	1				15	6.0
4			2	2	4	4	2					14	5.1
3		1	3	3	2	1						10	3.9
2	1	2	1	1								5	2.4
1	1	1										2	1.5
f_X	2	4	6	7	12	19	18	11	9	4	2	94	
M_y	1.5	2.0	3.2	3.4	4.4	5.6	6.1	6.9	7.9	9.0	9.5		

(left axis label: Errors on maze Y)

Figure 18-2. Repeated with M_x and M_y values.

18-32 As we move across the row M_y from left to right, the numbers become progressively _____. What does this show? It shows that a group of animals which made a large number of errors on Maze X tends to have a _____ mean error score on Maze Y.

larger (greater)

high (large)

18-33 Now let us look at the column to the extreme right labeled M_x. It is quite analogous to the row M_y which we have just discussed. The column M_x contains the means of the _____. Each *row* has been treated as a separate frequency distribution of scores on Maze _____; the value of n for each row is contained in the column labeled _____.

rows

X

f_Y

18-34 Each number in the column M_x represents the _____ number of errors on Maze _____ made by the animals whose error score on Maze _____ appears at the left of the row.

mean

X

Y

18-35 These numbers grow larger as we move from the bottom to the top of the column M_x. Animals who made few errors on Maze Y tend to have relatively _____ mean error scores on Maze

low

X, and animals who made many errors on Maze Y tend to have relatively _____ mean error scores on Maze X.

high (large)

18-36 What is the *mean* error score on Maze X of animals making four errors on Maze Y? _____. What is the *mean* error score on Maze Y of animals making four errors on Maze X? _____.

5.1

3.4

18-37 Figure 18-3 is called a CORRELATION PLOT. The column means M_y from Figure 18-2 have been plotted as the Y coordinates of points whose X coordinates are the *midpoints of the class intervals on X*. Notice that the correlation plot does *not* use the means of the _____ from the scatter diagram (Figure 18-2). The lowest value of M_y, which is 1.5, is plotted above the value _____ on the scale of "errors on Maze X."

rows

1

18-38 The correlation plot in Figure 18-3 shows the mean number of errors on Maze _____ which were made by animals falling in each particular class of error scores on Maze _____.

Y

X

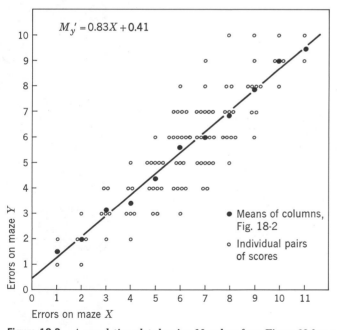

Figure 18-3. A correlation plot showing M_y values from Figure 18-2 as a linear function of errors on Maze X. The array of small circles around each of the M_y values represents the distribution of error scores on Maze Y from which the M_y values are computed. These small distributions can be compared with the *column* entries in Figure 18-2.

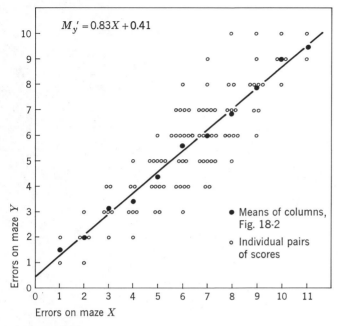

$M_y' = 0.83X + 0.41$

Figure 18-3 repeated

Each of these classes has therefore been treated as a separate frequency distribution of scores on Maze Y, and its _____ number of errors on that maze has been plotted as a function of the midpoint of the class.

18-39 The M_y values lie approximately along a straight line. Therefore, the relationship between errors on Maze X (which we shall call the variable X) and *mean number of errors on Maze Y* (which we shall call the variable M_y) is approximately a _____ relationship. M_y is approximately a _____ of _____ .

18-40 If M_y is approximately a linear function of X, then the points in the correlation plot can be described approximately by an equation of the form $Y = mX + k$, where instead of Y we have the variable M_y. Substituting M_y into the general equation for a straight line, we can say that the correlation plot is described approximately by a *regression equation* of the form _____ .

18-41 The line drawn on the correlation plot shown as Figure 18-3 is the graph of the equation $M_y' = 0.83X + 0.41$. This equation is the _____ equation of M_y on X, and the line is the _____ line of _____ on _____ .

mean

linear
linear function — X

$M_y = mX + k$

regression
regression — M_y — X

18-42   In the regression equation, you may have noticed that the term M_y' was used. Points which are described *exactly* by this equation and which fall *exactly* on the line are designated M_y' in order to distinguish them from the actual column means M_y. The values of M_y' lie _____ the regression line, but the values of M_y lie, in most cases, slightly _____ or _____ the line.

exactly on
above↔below

18-43   The variations from the regression line in the actual values of M_y are assumed to be the result of *sampling variability*, and the relationship between M_y and X is therefore considered to be a _____ relationship, since it can be described to a good approximation by a straight line.

linear

18-44   There are two constants which appear in this regression equation. The constant m, which is the *slope* constant, has a value of _____ and a _____ sign. The constant k, which is the Y intercept, has a value of _____. These numbers are called the REGRESSION CONSTANTS.

0.83 — positive
0.41

18-45   Before we leave this example, you should notice that *the regression line of M_y on X passes through that point which is both the mean for all the X scores and the mean for all the Y scores.* We have not mentioned these means $\bar{X}$ and $\bar{Y}$ before now; $\bar{X} = 6.2$ and $\bar{Y} = 5.6$. Observe that the line drawn in the correlation plot does, indeed, pass through the point which has 6.2 as its X coordinate and 5.6 as its Y coordinate. Since the two regression lines are similar in this respect, the regression line of X on Y must also pass through the point whose coordinates are (_____ , _____); the two _____ lines cross each other at this point.

(6.2, 5.6)
regression

Review

18-46   *In a scatter diagram, the individuals having the same score on the X variable fall in one particular column and can be treated as a group. Their scores on the _____ variable constitute a small frequency distribution of n cases, with a _____ and a standard deviation.*

Y
mean

18-47   *The column means can be designated M_y, since they represent the _____ score on the _____ variable; that is, any particular M_y value is the _____ of the scores on the _____ variable made by individuals falling into the same class on the _____ variable.*

mean — Y
mean — Y

X

18-48   *If M_y is plotted as a function of X, we obtain a* _____. *If M_y is approximately a linear function of X, a* _____ *equation of the form* _____ *can be set up, and the graph of this equation is a straight line called the* _____. *In this equation, the values of m and k are called the* _____.

C.   The Relation between the Regression Constants and the Correlation Coefficient

18-49   When two variables are linearly related, the amount of relationship between them can be expressed by a single number called the CORRELATION COEFFICIENT. When the relationship between the variables is strong, you might expect the correlation coefficient to be a relatively large number; when the relationship is weak, you might expect the _____ to be a relatively _____ number.

18-50   For example, one would expect that students with high college aptitude scores will tend to make _____ grades in college. But since there are other factors than aptitude which affect grades (motivation is one such factor), the _____ between the two variables will not be perfect and the _____ is not likely to be the highest possible number.

18-51   Suppose that we know the aptitude scores and college grades for four persons. A very simple way to deal with these scores is to convert them into *ordinal values, or ranks.* Each person will have a rank of first, second, third, or fourth on aptitude and a rank on _____ which might be the same as his rank on aptitude or might be different.

Although ranks on aptitude scores and grades are *ordinal* values, we shall make correlation plots of the ranks showing an *equal interval* on the X and Y axes between consecutive ranks. When equal distances are assigned to equal differences in rank, the implication is only that *rank differences* are considered to be equal, not that differences between scores or grades corresponding to rank differences are equal.

18-52   Each person thus has *two* ranks, and the idea of the correlation coefficient can be described simply if we compare the ranks held by the same persons. Figure 18-4 is a correlation plot for these ordinal values, with the X axis representing rank on _____ and the Y axis representing rank on _____ .

18-53   This correlation plot is much simpler than the plot in Figure 18-3, because the values in Figure 18-4 are *ordinal* values. There are few observations, and there are no means involved; means can only be computed for _____ values.

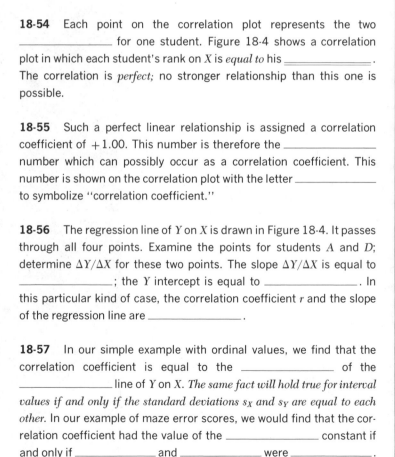

Figure 18-4. Correlation plot for $r = +1.00$.

18-54 Each point on the correlation plot represents the two _____ for one student. Figure 18-4 shows a correlation plot in which each student's rank on X is *equal to* his _____. The correlation is *perfect;* no stronger relationship than this one is possible.

18-55 Such a perfect linear relationship is assigned a correlation coefficient of $+1.00$. This number is therefore the _____ number which can possibly occur as a correlation coefficient. This number is shown on the correlation plot with the letter _____ to symbolize "correlation coefficient."

18-56 The regression line of Y on X is drawn in Figure 18-4. It passes through all four points. Examine the points for students A and D; determine $\Delta Y/\Delta X$ for these two points. The slope $\Delta Y/\Delta X$ is equal to _____; the Y intercept is equal to _____. In this particular kind of case, the correlation coefficient r and the slope of the regression line are _____.

18-57 In our simple example with ordinal values, we find that the correlation coefficient is equal to the _____ of the _____ line of Y on X. *The same fact will hold true for interval values if and only if the standard deviations s_X and s_Y are equal to each other.* In our example of maze error scores, we would find that the correlation coefficient had the value of the _____ constant if and only if _____ and _____ were _____.

18-58 The correlation coefficient r equals the slope constant m under two kinds of conditions: (1) whenever the values in the correlation plot are _____ rather than interval values and (2) whenever the two distributions of X and Y values, being interval values, have _____ .

18-59 Whenever variables with interval values are being correlated, then the slope m of the regression line of Y on X is equal to r *multiplied by the ratio* s_Y/s_X; that is, $m = r(s_Y/s_X)$. In a similar way, the slope of the *other* regression line, X on Y, is equal to _____ multiplied by the ratio s_X/s_Y.

18-60 Notice that in going from the slope of one regression line to the other, the fraction multiplying r has been "turned upside down," that is, converted into its reciprocal. For the regression of Y on X, the standard deviation of the _____ distribution is on top. For the regression of X on Y, the standard deviation of the _____ distribution is on top.

18-61 It follows from this rule that the slope of the regression line of Y on X will equal _____ × 1 whenever $s_Y = s_X$ and that the regression line of X on Y will also have a slope equal to _____ whenever $s_X = s_Y$.

18-62 The two regression lines must *both* pass through the point whose coordinates are $\bar{X}$ and $\bar{Y}$; that is, the lines must always pass through the point whose coordinates are the _____ of the two distributions. Any pair of straight lines having the same slope and having at least one point in common must be identically the same line. Therefore, when $s_X = s_Y$, the regression line of Y on X is _____ the regression line of X on Y.

18-63 Since the slope m of the regression line of Y on X is equal to $r(s_Y/s_X)$, you could find m if you knew the values of r, _____ , and _____ . Or if you knew both standard deviations and knew m, you could find _____ .

These relationships among the correlation coefficient, the slopes of the regression lines, and the standard deviations are presented here in order to make the *concept* of correlation clear to you. These relationships *could* be used for computing the correlation coefficient, but you will find simpler and more efficient methods of computation in the standard textbooks of elementary statistics. If you should ever have statistical computations to carry out, look up the appropriate *computing formulas* designed to make computation convenient. The equations in this book are intended not for computation but for explanation.

18-64   When scores on variables X and Y are converted into ranks and each individual has the same rank on X and on Y, the correlation is perfect and r has the value _____. The value of the correlation coefficient can never be _____ this value.

+1.00
greater (larger) than

18-65   Suppose two distributions of scores X_i and Y_i. Let every X score be converted to a z score z_x and every Y score to a z score z_y. We now have two distributions of standard scores, each with a mean of _____ and a standard deviation of _____. If we draw a correlation plot for the regression of the standard scores z_y on the standard scores z_x, the slope of the regression line will equal _____ because _____.

0
1
r
the standard deviations
 of the distributions
 are equal

D.   Correlations Other than +1.00

18-66   In Figure 18-4, each student's rank on Y was the same as his rank on X. The slope $\Delta Y/\Delta X$ of the regression line was equal to _____, and the correlation coefficient had a value of _____ with a _____ sign.

1.0
+1.0 — positive

18-67   Now suppose a case in which some students have a rank on Y different from their rank on X. Figure 18-5 shows one such case. For persons _____ and _____, the Y rank equals

$A \leftrightarrow D$

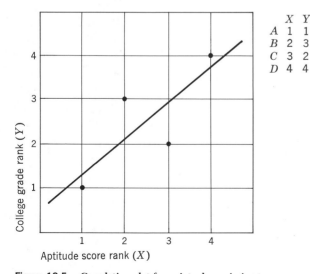

	X	Y
A	1	1
B	2	3
C	3	2
D	4	4

Figure 18-5.   Correlation plot for points shown in inset.

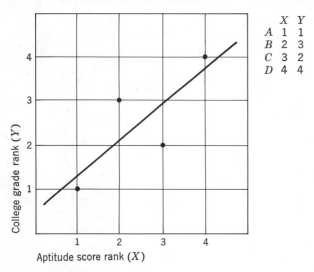

	X	Y
A	1	1
B	2	3
C	3	2
D	4	4

Figure 18-5 repeated

the X rank. For persons _____ and _____ , the   *B ↔ C*
two ranks are different.

18-68 In Figure 18-5, the regression line of Y on X passes through
the middle rank on both variables, that is, the point (2.5, 2.5). The line
also passes through the point (0, 0.5), which is the _____   *Y intercept*
of the line. Determine ΔX and ΔY between these two points. The slope

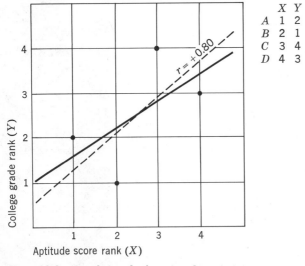

	X	Y
A	1	2
B	2	1
C	3	4
D	4	3

r = +0.80

Figure 18-6. Correlation plot for points shown in inset.

$\Delta Y/\Delta X$ is equal to a value of _____. Since these are ordinal values, r also equals _____.

0.80
.80

18-69   In Figure 18-6, no person has the same rank on both X and Y. For each person, there is _____ unit(s) difference between his two ranks. The solid line in Figure 18-6 is the regression line of Y on X for these ranks; it passes through the midpoint of both sets of ranks (2.5, 2.5) and has a Y intercept equal to 1.0. The slope of the line is equal to _____, and $r =$ _____. (The regression line from Figure 18-5 is shown as a dashed line for comparison.)

one

0.60 — .60

18-70   Compare Figures 18-5 and 18-6. There is more "scatter" of the points around the regression line in Figure 18-_____, and the slope of the regression line of Y on X has a _____ value. As the amount of scatter increases, the value of r _____.

6
lower
decreases

18-71   Figure 18-7 compares the correlation of $+.60$ (dashed line) with the correlation calculated for the ranks shown in the inset. Person _____ has the same rank on both X and Y, persons _____ and _____ have pairs of ranks which differ by one unit, and person _____ has a pair of ranks which differ by two units. The solid line is the regression line of Y on X for these ranks, and it passes through the points (2.5, 2.5) and (0, 1.5). The slope of this line is _____, and $r =$ _____.

A
B $\leftrightarrow$ C
D

0.40 — .40

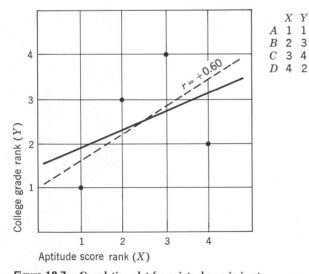

	X	Y
A	1	1
B	2	3
C	3	4
D	4	2

Figure 18-7.   Correlation plot for points shown in inset.

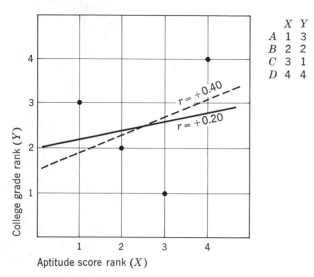

	X	Y
A	1	3
B	2	2
C	3	1
D	4	4

Figure 18-8. Correlation plot for points shown in inset.

18-72 Figure 18-8 compares the correlation of .40 (dashed line) with one of .20 (solid line). The inset shows the ranks whose correlation is .20. The effect of the greater rank difference in this inset is to _____ the value of r.

decrease

18-73 Figure 18-9 shows a set of ranks whose correlation coefficient

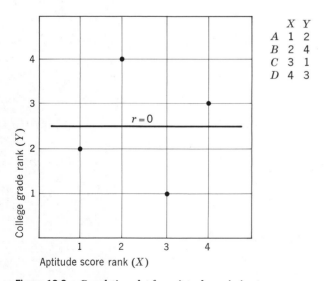

	X	Y
A	1	2
B	2	4
C	3	1
D	4	3

Figure 18-9. Correlation plot for points shown in inset.

is _____. The regression line of Y on X is now parallel to the _____ axis. In such a case X and Y are described as UNCORRELATED variables. The regression equation takes the form $Y' = k$.

Since it may be evident from these examples that *rank differences* determine the value of r for observations which consist of ranks, we can point out here that the correlation coefficient for ranked values is defined as

$$\rho = 1 - \frac{6\Sigma D^2}{N(N^2 - 1)}$$

where the Greek letter rho, written ρ, represents the correlation coefficient for ranked values; D is the difference between the two ranks for any particular person; and N is the number of persons (or pairs of ranks). The term ΣD^2 is the sum of the squared rank differences for all N persons. If you substitute the values from any of the examples (Figures 18-5 to 18-9) in this equation, you will discover that the equation yields the expected value for the correlation coefficient. Notice that an *increase* in the size of the rank differences will produce an *increase* in the size of the fraction to be subtracted from 1 and therefore will produce a *decrease* in the value of the correlation coefficient.

18-74 If the rank differences for the four students are made even larger than they were in Figure 18-9, the correlation coefficient becomes *negative* in sign. Figure 18-10 shows the correlation plot for the ranks given in the inset. The regression line of Y on X passes through the points (2.5, 2.5) and (0, 3). The slope of this line has a _____ sign and a value of _____; $r =$ _____ .

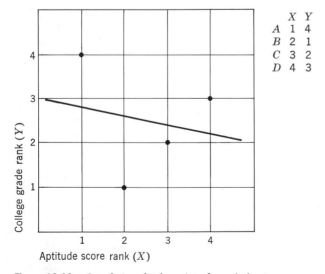

	X	Y
A	1	4
B	2	1
C	3	2
D	4	3

Figure 18-10. Correlation plot for points shown in inset.

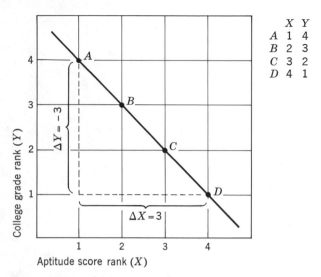

	X	Y
A	1	4
B	2	3
C	3	2
D	4	1

Figure 18-11. Correlation plot for inset points. A perfect negative correlation.

18-75   Now let us take a rather unlikely supposition: Suppose that persons with the *highest* aptitude scores (X) make the *lowest* grades in college. Figure 18-11 shows the correlation plot which results when the person ranking lowest on aptitude ranks highest on grades, and vice versa. The regression line of Y on X passes through *all* four plotted points, and the correlation is perfect. The slope is equal to _____. This is a PERFECT NEGATIVE correlation, and $r =$ _____.

−1.00
−1.00

18-76   When we considered several positive correlations, we found two kinds of changes as r decreased from $+1.00$ to 0: The slope of the regression line of Y on X took on values which were closer and closer to _____, and the degree of scatter of the points around the line became progressively _____.

zero
greater

18-77   Similar things are true of a series of negative correlations in which r is changing from -1.00 toward 0. The slope of the line takes on values which are closer and closer to _____, and the degree of scatter becomes _____.

zero
greater

Review

18-78   *Any correlation that is perfect has a correlation coefficient whose numerical value (regardless of its sign) is _____. A perfect positive correlation has a coefficient of _____; a perfect negative correlation has a coefficient of _____.*

1.00
+1.00
−1.00

18-79 When a correlation is positive, *low scores on the X variable tend to be associated with* _____ *scores on the Y variable. When a correlation is* negative, *low scores on the X variable tend to be associated with* _____ *scores on the Y variable.*

low

high

18-80 *When X and Y are uncorrelated, the value of* r = _____. *The regression line of Y on X will be a* _____ *line parallel to the* _____.

0

straight

X axis

E. The Least-squares Principle

18-81 The regression line of Y on X does not pass through all the points in the correlation plot unless the correlation is _____. When the correlation is _____, the points will show some degree of "scatter" around the regression line. *Many different straight lines could be drawn;* the amount of scatter around some would be greater than that around others. *The regression line is that line around which the amount of* _____ *is smallest.*

perfect

not (less than) perfect

scatter

18-82 The amount of scatter is most often defined in terms of the *sum* of *squares* of the *vertical* deviations of the points from the line. In Figure 18-12, the vertical deviations of the points are drawn as straight lines between the four points of the correlation plot and the regression

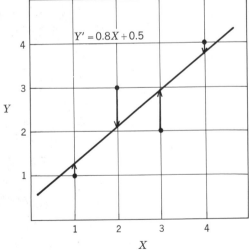

X	Y	Y'	$Y - Y'$ (D)	D^2
1	1	1.3	-0.3	0.09
2	3	2.1	0.9	0.81
3	2	2.9	-0.9	0.81
4	4	3.7	0.3	0.09
			ΣD^2	$= 1.80$

$Y' = 0.8X + 0.5$

Figure 18-12. Correlation plot illustrating vertical deviations, with table for computing sum of squared deviations.

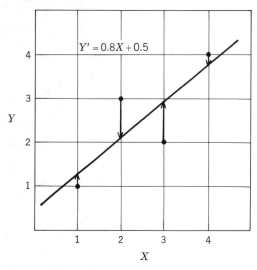

X	Y	Y'	Y − Y' (D)	D²
1	1	1.3	−0.3	0.09
2	3	2.1	0.9	0.81
3	2	2.9	−0.9	0.81
4	4	3.7	0.3	0.09

$$\Sigma D^2 = 1.80$$

Figure 18-12 repeated

line. The slope of the regression line is _____, and its Y intercept is _____. The equation for the regression line is therefore _____.

0.8
0.5
$Y' = 0.8X + 0.5$

18-83 For each four values of X, a value of _____ can be computed from the regression equation. These values are shown in the table beside Figure 18-12. The vertical deviation of any actual Y rank from the regression line is given in the table by the difference, $Y −$ _____. These deviations are shown in the table in the column labeled _____, standing for "deviation."

Y'

Y'
D

18-84 *The regression line of Y on X is defined as that straight line from which the* SUM *of the* SQUARED DEVIATIONS $\Sigma(Y − Y')^2$ *is smallest.* This sum (ΣD^2), for the regression line in Figure 18-12, is _____.

1.80

18-85 The regression line is selected, therefore, according to the principle of LEAST SQUARES. It is the straight line around which the amount of scatter is _____ when scatter is defined in terms of the _____ of the _____ of the _____ of the points from the line.

least
sum — squares
deviations

18-86 The regression line of Y on X in Figure 18-12 was selected according to the principle of _____. We shall not actually prove it in a mathematical way (such a proof is available in any elemen-

least squares

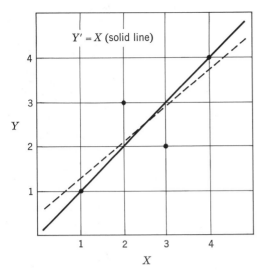

Figure 18-13. Correlation plot showing vertical deviations from solid line, $Y = X$.

tary statistics text), but the sum of the squared _____ of *deviations*

the plotted points from *any other line* would be greater than 1.80.

18-87 Suppose that we select another possible line—one that might reasonably be said to "fit" the points in Figure 18-12—for comparison. Figure 18-13 shows this comparison. The dashed line is the least-squares line from Figure 18-12; the points are the same as those in Figure 18-12. The solid line $Y' = X$ is a "reasonable" alternative regression line, since it actually passes *through* two of the four points. The value of D^2 for those two points is therefore _____ . *0*

18-88 The deviations of the other two points from the solid line (points at $X = 2$ and $X = 3$) are each equal to _____ unit(s), *one*
as you can easily tell from the graph. The *sum* of the squared deviations from this line would therefore be _____; this sum is *2*
_____ than the sum of squared deviations from the regres- *greater*
sion line $Y' = 0.8X + 0.5$ selected according to the least-squares principle.

Review

18-89 *The regression line is that line from which the* _____ *sum*
of the _____ *is least. Therefore, the regression line is said to be* *squared deviations*
selected according to the principle of _____ . *least squares*

18-90 *Whenever a regression line is selected according to the principle of least squares and the value of s_X is equal to the value of s_Y, then the correlation coefficient will have a value equal to the* _____ *of the* _____ .

slope
regression line

Problems for Lesson 18

18-1 **(a)** On the coordinates given in Fig. P18-1, draw the regression line of Y on X for a correlation of $+.75$ between the ranks of nine persons on two variables X and Y. What is the regression equation describing this line? Label this line A.

(b) On the same coordinates, draw the regression line of Y on X for a correlation of $-.50$ between the ranks of nine persons on the same two variables. What is the regression equation for this line? Label this line B.

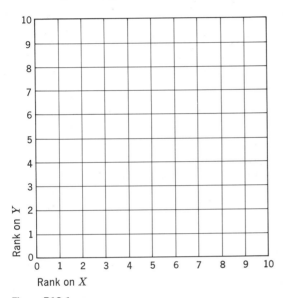

Figure P18-1

18-2 Under what circumstances will r equal the slope of the regression line of Y on X?

18-3 The correlation between two variables X and Y is $r = +.60$. $s_X = 4.0$ and $s_Y = 3.6$. What is the slope of the regression line of Y on X? What is the slope of the regression line of X on Y?

18-4 The correlation plot in Fig. P18-4 shows the points determined by the pairs of ranks on two variables X and Y for nine individuals. Two regression lines of Y on X have been drawn through these data, only one of which is correct according to the criterion of least squares. Below the correlation plot are the ranks on X and Y for the nine individuals together with the Y' values computed from the regression equation for each of the two lines.

(a) Using the least-squares principle, decide which of the two lines, the solid or the dashed line, is the correct regression line for this set of ranks.

(b) Write the regression equation for each line.

(c) What is the correct value of r for this set of ranks?

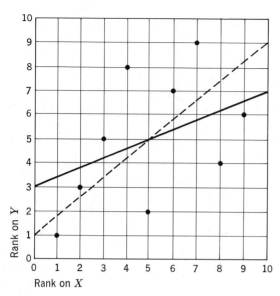

Figure P18-4

Solid Line			Dashed Line		
X	Y	Y'	X	Y	Y'
1	1	3.4	1	1	1.8
2	3	3.8	2	3	2.6
3	5	4.2	3	5	3.4
4	8	4.6	4	8	4.2
5	2	5.0	5	2	5.0
6	7	5.4	6	7	5.8
7	9	5.8	7	9	6.6
8	4	6.2	8	4	7.4
9	6	6.6	9	6	8.2

Lesson 19. Uses of the Correlation Coefficient

One of the major uses of the correlation concept is found in scientific investigation. By determining whether two variables are closely related to each other, an investigator can test his conjectures about the factors which control these variables. The discovery of unexpected correlations may raise further questions for investigation.

Correlation coefficients are also useful in connection with psychological tests. This lesson will focus upon three important practical uses of correlation coefficients: in determining the reliability of a psychological test (Section A), in determining the validity of such a test (Section B), and in formulating a prediction about someone's future performance (Sections C, D, and E).

To most people, a "psychological test" means an entire series of problems or tasks, such as an intelligence test or the College Entrance Examination Board aptitude test. Technically, though, any one problem or "item" of such a series can be called a "test." The important fact is that a test is something on which each individual taking it makes a score. A person makes a score on each item (although the score may be only pass or fail) as well as a total score on the entire series. Psychologists who construct and employ tests work with the scores of large numbers of individuals on every particular test.

A. Determining Reliability

19-1 A test is designed to be a *measuring instrument*. A classroom test is intended to _____ how much a student knows about the content that has been covered in the class.

measure

19-2 An intelligence test is an instrument for measuring intelligence. The number of points earned on an intelligence test is analogous to the number of _____ per hour recorded on a speedometer. Both the intelligence test and the speedometer are _____ instruments.

miles
measuring

19-3   A measuring instrument is good only if it will reliably give the same result each time the same thing is measured. A yardstick which repeatedly gives the same measurement of a particular object is a *reliable* measuring instrument. A rubber yardstick would have _____ reliability.

low (no, little)

19-4   With a reliable yardstick, repeated measurements of the same object will give the _____ result. If one is in doubt about the reliability of a yardstick, he can check its reliability by measuring the _____ object several times and comparing the results.

same

same

19-5   If he finds that these measurements differ considerably from one another, he does not conclude that the object has changed its length from moment to moment; he concludes instead that the _____ has changed from time to time and that it is not a _____ measuring instrument.

yardstick

reliable

19-6   There are some psychological tests which can be given more than once to the same individual. To determine the reliability of such a test, one could administer it two or more times to the _____ persons and compare the results.

same

19-7   However, since any test is only a *sample* of the person's test-taking behavior, there will be some _____ variability affecting the scores, and some amount of difference between the first and second scores will be expected by chance even when the test is reliable. Such a problem does not arise in measurements of length; repeated measurements of length can be directly compared with one another.

sampling

19-8   Because of this chance variation in the two scores made by any one individual at different times, it is wise to consider the scores of a *group* of individuals. Each person's scores will be affected by sampling variability, but it is unlikely that all scores will be affected in the same way. Therefore, to determine the reliability of a test, it is best to administer the test at _____ different times to the same _____ of individuals.

two

group

19-9   Repeated psychological measurements on the same group of persons cannot be simply compared and expected to correspond exactly. Instead, a coefficient of correlation is computed between the first set of scores and the second set of scores. The test will be considered *reliable* only if the correlation coefficient between the two sets of scores is _____ .

high

19-10   The correlation coefficient between the two sets of scores will be high if, in general, the persons scoring highest on the test during the first administration also score _____ on the test during the second administration— if, that is, the rank of each person within the group tends to remain the _____ on each administration of the test.

high (or highest)

same

19-11   When the correlation coefficient is used in this way, it is called a RELIABILITY COEFFICIENT. The reliability coefficient expresses the amount of correlation between two sets of scores made on the same test by the _____ group of persons.

same

19-12   There are certain kinds of tests which, if they were presented a second time in exactly the same form, would be certain to give differ- ent results. Intelligence tests are of this sort. Since a person may *remember* some of the answers to intelligence test problems, his score on the *second* administration of the test ought to be _____ than his score on the *first* administration.

higher

19-13   But different individuals may improve by different amounts between the two administrations, depending on their memory ability. If we are interested in measuring intelligence, we want to avoid this effect of memory. In cases like this one, the _____ coefficient cannot be simply the correlation between two sets of scores made by a group on the *same test.*

reliability

19-14   For cases of this sort, the psychologist makes up a large num- ber of problems of the same general kind and divides them randomly into two sets. These two sets ought then to be *equivalent forms* of the same test, and a reliability coefficient can be defined as the _____ between scores made by the _____ group of persons on the two _____ of the test.

correlation — same
equivalent forms

Review

19-15   *The reliability of psychological tests is determined by computing the correlation between two sets of* _____ *made by the same persons on the* _____ *test or on* _____ *of the test.*

scores
same — equivalent forms

19-16   *When a correlation coefficient is used to measure reliability, it is* *called a* _____. *Reliability cannot be measured from scores made by only one individual; scores from a* _____ *of individuals must be obtained.*

reliability coefficient
group

B. Determining Validity

19-17   A reliable test will give very nearly the same scores every time it is used to measure the same persons. But it is not always clear what these scores represent. In the case of a yardstick, we know that we are measuring *length;* a yardstick is therefore a *valid* measure of _____ .

length

19-18   When a psychological test is labeled a "college aptitude test," the question should be raised "Does it really measure aptitude for college?" This question concerns the VALIDITY of the test. It is important to know whether the test is a _____ measure of college aptitude.

valid

19-19   True-false classroom tests are objectively scored, and they tend to have high reliability coefficients. Sometimes, however, true-false items are written in such a way that the answers can be guessed without knowledge of the content. For such items, the test will not be a valid measure of the student's _____ of the course material. It may instead be a valid measure only of his ability to _____ the answers from the way the item is written.

knowledge
guess

19-20   A test can therefore be *reliable* without being a _____ measure of what it is intended to measure. But a test is never a valid measure unless it is _____ .

valid

reliable

19-21   If a psychological test is offered as a measure of mechanical aptitude, scores on the test ought to be highly correlated with performance on jobs which require _____. Performance on such jobs can serve as a CRITERION, or standard, for determining the validity of the test.

mechanical aptitude

19-22   The validity of a test is measured in terms of the correlation coefficient between scores on the test and scores on the _____ of validity. Such a correlation coefficient is called a VALIDITY COEFFICIENT.

criterion

19-23 In order to determine the validity of a college aptitude test, it is necessary to find a criterion with which to compare the scores made on the test. The criterion for mechanical aptitude tests is usually mechanical performance; the criterion for college aptitude tests is usually _____ .

college performance (grades in college)

19-24 If scores made on a college aptitude test correlate highly with grades earned in college, the test is considered to have a _____ degree of validity. The validity of medical school aptitude tests is measured by correlating the test scores with _____ .

high

grades in medical school

19-25 It is not always easy to find a good criterion for measuring validity, for there is often no objective way besides the test itself to measure the quantity being considered. For example, to measure the validity of an intelligence test, one needs a good, independent criterion of _____ .

intelligence

19-26 Early in the history of intelligence testing, teachers were asked to give ratings of their pupils' intelligence, and these ratings were taken as the _____ for calculating the _____ of intelligence tests.

criterion — validity coefficients

19-27 Now that a few good measures of intelligence (such as the Stanford-Binet test) have been worked out from careful theoretical considerations, scores on such widely accepted tests provide the best criterion for determining whether a new test is a _____ of intelligence.

valid measure

19-28 A validity coefficient is a coefficient of correlation between the scores made by a group of individuals on the _____ and the scores made by the same individuals on a _____ of validity.

test
criterion

19-29 Both the validity coefficient and the reliability coefficient require _____ sets of scores from a single group of individuals. For the reliability coefficient, these are scores on the _____ test or on _____ of the test. For the validity coefficient, one set of scores is on the _____ and one set is on the _____ .

two

same — equivalent forms
test ↔
criterion

19-30 A test that is not _____ cannot be _____ . But a test that is not a _____ measure of what it claims to measure may nevertheless be _____ .

reliable — valid
valid
reliable

C. Formulating Predictions Based on Correlation

19-31 Predictions about changes in the weather are made partly from changes in the barometer reading. Barometer changes occur *first*, and they are correlated with changes in the weather which *follow* them. Similarly, a good college aptitude test is correlated with grades in college. The test can be given before a student enters college, and his score can be used to _____ his average grade in college.

predict

19-32 The procedure in making such predictions can be described most simply if we continue with the example from Lesson 18C. In that section, the *ranks* of four students (*A*, *B*, *C*, and *D*) on aptitude and on college grades were presented as the *X* and *Y* variables. Recall that, in the special case of ordinal values, the slope of the regression line is equal to the _____ .

correlation coefficient

19-33 In Lesson 18, the *Y* axis represented rank on grades in college and the *X* axis represented aptitude score. It is conventional to label the axes in this way so that the variable which is to be predicted is on the _____ axis and the variable from which prediction is being made is on the _____ axis.

Y

X

19-34 The basis for prediction is always the straight line best fitting the points, called the _____ . For ordinal values, this line has a _____ equal to the correlation coefficient. For interval values, the _____ of the line is equal to $r(s_Y/s_X)$, where s_Y is the standard deviation of the *Y* scores, S_X is the standard deviation of the *X* scores, and *r* is the _____ .

regression line

slope

slope

correlation coefficient

19-35 The general way in which *Y* tends to vary as *X* varies is described by the regression line. When we take the aptitude and grade scores of students whose grades are already known and plot them on a graph, the resulting points tend to lie on or near the _____ .

regression line

19-36 In general, we shall expect the same kind of relationship to hold for future groups of students whose grades are not yet known. The points (which we do not yet know) representing *their* aptitude and grade scores ought to turn out to lie on or near the _____ .

regression line

19-37 This expectation will hold no matter whether we are working with raw scores or with *ranks*. We shall talk hereafter, in this lesson, in terms of ranks (rather than raw scores) because the relationship between the _____ and the _____ is simpler for ordinal values.

regression line

↔ correlation coefficient

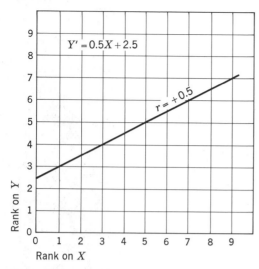

$Y' = 0.5X + 2.5$

$r = +0.5$

Rank on Y

0 1 2 3 4 5 6 7 8 9
Rank on X

Figure 19-1. Correlation of $r = +.5$ between ranks on X and Y.

19-38 If we know the individual's rank on X, our best guess about the point representing his ranks on X and Y (as yet unknown) is that the point will lie on the regression line. Since we know the X coordinate of that point already, and since there is only one point having that X value *and* lying on the regression line, we can determine the Y coordinate. It is the value of Y at the point on the regression line directly above the _____ rank for that individual.

X

19-39 Suppose we know that a person ranked third of nine persons on variable X (aptitude) and that the correlation coefficient between X and Y is $+.5$. The predicted Y rank (grades) for this person can be determined from Figure 19-1. It is the value of Y at the point where the regression line is directly above the X value of _____. The predicted Y rank is _____.

3

4

19-40 Using Figure 19-1 again, determine the predicted Y rank for a person whose rank on X is 7. The predicted Y rank is _____.

6

19-41 A person whose X rank is 5 will have a predicted Y rank of _____. This rank is peculiar, since it is the _____ rank on both X and Y.

5 — middle

19-42 A person who has the middle rank on one variable will always be predicted to achieve the _____ rank on the other variable because *the regression line always passes through the point that is*

middle

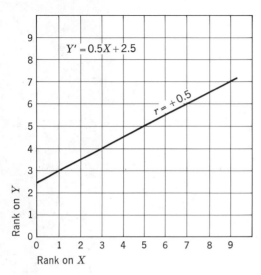

Figure 19-1 repeated

the middle for both variables. The point that is the middle point for both X and Y in Figure 19-1 is the point with coordinates _____ .

(5, 5)

19-43 Suppose there were 11, instead of 9, persons in the group and therefore 11 rank positions. The middle rank for such a group is _____ . A person with the rank of _____ on the X variable would be predicted to have the *same* rank on the Y variable.

6 — 6

19-44 This fact can be used in order to *construct* the regression line when only the correlation coefficient is known. The regression line is that line whose slope is equal to the _____ and which passes through the point which is the _____ point for both variables.

correlation coefficient
middle

19-45 Consider a group of 11 persons when the correlation coefficient between X and Y is $+.50$. Which of the three lines drawn on the graph in Figure 19-2 is the regression line? _____ . What is its slope? _____ . What is the middle point of both variables? _____ .

b
+0.50
(6, 6)

Review

19-46 *When the correlation between X and Y is known, a prediction about a person's probable Y rank can be made on the basis of his*

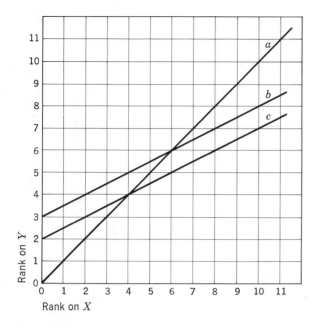

Figure 19-2. Regression line for ordinal values with $r = +.5$ and two other lines.

X rank

regression line

X rank

_____. *The prediction will be that his Y rank is the value of Y at that point on the _____ whose X coordinate is equal to his _____.*

19-47 *Since the regression line always passes through the point that is the _____ point for both X and Y, a person whose X rank is at the middle point for X will always be predicted to achieve a Y rank which is at the _____ point for Y.*

middle

middle

D. The Effect of Different Values of r on the Predicted Y Rank

19-48 Predictions based on correlation coefficients have some unexpected characteristics, which can be discovered through examining Table 19-1. This table compares the Y ranks which would be predicted

Table 19-1

Person	X Rank	r = +1.00	r = +0.75	r = +0.50	r = 0
A	1	1	2	3	5
B	2	2	2.75	3.5	5
C	3	3	3.5	4	5
D	4	4	4.25	4.5	5
E	5	5	5	5	5
F	6	6	5.75	5.5	5
G	7	7	6.5	6	5
H	8	8	7.25	6.5	5
J	9	9	8	7	5

for nine persons, designated by the letters A through J, when the value of _____ is +1.0, +.75, +.50, or 0.

r

19-49   For one person in the group, the predicted Y rank stays the same regardless of the value of r. This person is designated by the letter _____ , and he holds the rank _____ on X. In every case, no matter what the value of r, he will be predicted to achieve a rank of _____ on Y, since this is the _____ rank.

$E - 5$

$5 - middle$

19-50   Notice, in the table, that the *range* of predicted Y ranks varies with changes in r. Although there are nine persons and nine rank

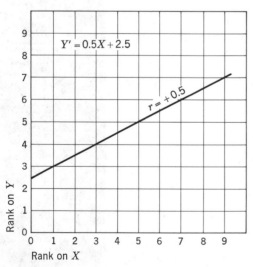

Figure 19-1 repeated

positions on X, the predicted Y rank values range from 1 to 9 only when $r =$ _____ .

19-51   As r diminishes toward zero, the range of predicted Y ranks grows _____ ; when $r = 0$, all the predicted Y ranks equal _____ . This variation is unexpected, and it may not seem reasonable at first. It would probably seem more natural, when we have nine persons to make predictions for, to assign the numbers 1 through 9 as predicted Y ranks no matter what the value of r.

19-52   Yet according to Table 19-1, for a correlation coefficient of $+.50$, the predicted Y ranks are confined to the numbers between _____ and _____ . There are therefore a number of decimal or fractional ranks in the series. You may find it hard to imagine what a rank of "3.5 out of 9" could mean; this meaning will become clear in a moment.

19-53   The peculiar restriction in the range of predicted Y ranks arises because the procedure is designed to make the prediction as accurate as possible. When the correlation between X and Y is known to be perfect, it is safe to predict extreme ranks on Y for persons who hold _____ ranks on X. In this case of a perfect correlation, and only in this case, the persons at the extremes on X will be *certain* to be at the extremes on Y.

19-54   With a correlation that is less than perfect, you will recall that the regression line does not fit the points perfectly. Persons holding extreme ranks on X are very likely *not* to hold such ranks on Y but will more likely hold ranks which are somewhat nearer to the _____ rank. (Look back at Figures 18-3 to 18-8, which show these differences.)

19-55   If one predicts that such a person will have a Y rank somewhat nearer the middle, there will probably be a smaller difference between his prediction and the outcome to be known later. There will almost certainly be some degree of error in the prediction, but the size of the error will be _____ if he sticks closer to the middle in his predictions.

19-56   The Y rank predicted for a person will therefore be a kind of compromise between his X rank and the middle rank. The necessity for this compromise is least when the correlation is almost perfect. With a high positive correlation coefficient, the predicted Y rank will be nearer to the _____ than to the middle. But with a low positive correlation, the prediction will be nearer to the _____ .

X rank
middle

19-57   Now a word about ranks such as 3.5. Such numbers are assigned in the ranking procedure whenever two persons are *tied* for the same rank. Thus, if a set of *scores* for nine people were to be 130, 124, 119, 119, 116, 115, 109, 109, 99, the third and fourth persons are *tied* for rank 3; both would be assigned a rank of 3.5. The seventh and eighth persons are also tied for rank _____ , and both would be assigned a rank of _____ .

7
7.5

19-58   But in Table 19-1, the presence of these numbers indicating tied ranks simply indicates that *we are predicting a narrow range of variation* in the Y scores. Tied ranks occur more frequently when the differences in scores within a group are slight. Many tied ranks means many pairs of identical scores and a _____ range of variation in scores. Few tied ranks means few pairs of identical scores and a _____ range of variation in scores.

narrow (small)

wide (large)

19-59   The presence of the tied ranks, with low positive correlations, indicates then that we are predicting a narrow range of variation in the expected Y scores. We do this, not because we really expect the variability of actual Y scores to be small, but as a matter of *strategy*, to make the amount of _____ between predicted and actual Y ranks as small as possible when the correlation does not give us a chance to be very exact.

difference

Review

19-60   *When the correlation is perfect and positive, the best prediction we can make for any individual is that his Y rank will equal* _____ . *When the correlation is zero, the best prediction is that his Y rank will equal* _____ .

his X rank
the middle rank

19-61   *The value of the correlation coefficient does not affect the predicted Y rank for the person who holds the* _____ *rank on X. No matter what the correlation, this person will always be predicted to achieve the* _____ *rank on Y. This fact is related to the fact that the regression line always passes through the point that is the* _____ *for both variables.*

middle

middle

middle point

19-62   *With a low positive correlation, persons with extreme ranks on X will be likely to achieve Y ranks that are* _____ *extreme than*

less

their X ranks. Thus, the range of predicted Y ranks ought to be
_____ than the range of X ranks in order to minimize error.
With ranked scores, this change in the range of ranks results in some
_____ ranks.

narrower (smaller)

fractional (decimal, tied)

E. Reasons for Using the Correlation Coefficient in Prediction

19-63   In order to appreciate what a correlation coefficient can add to prediction, imagine that you are faced with the problem of making *some* sort of guess as to the grades a particular student is likely to receive in a particular college. Without using the correlation coefficient, you could make such a guess if you knew the grades which students with similar high school grades or similar aptitude scores had actually _____ at that college.

received

19-64   Knowledge of the correlation between aptitude scores and _____ at that college would enable you to make a numerical estimate about this student who went to that college. Such information about the _____ between grades and aptitude scores may be available many times when personal experience is not available.

grades

correlation

19-65   Unless the correlation is perfect, your numerical estimate is not likely to turn out to be precisely correct. It will almost surely be *in error* to some extent. About the best you can hope for, in making any such predictions, is to make the *least possible* amount of _____ .

error

19-66   The procedure for making predictions by correlation, as described in Section C, has been carefully designed by statisticians with this problem in mind; it has been devised, that is, so that the amount of error made will be as _____ as possible.

small

19-67   If you have a considerable number of such predictions to make, you will be more in error on some of the predictions than on others. But by following the specified procedure consistently, for every prediction, you will make a _____ amount of error in the long run than if you used any other procedure, including an "intuitive" procedure.

lesser

19-68 The procedure dictates that, if the correlation between aptitude and grades is known to be zero, or if there is no known correlation, your best move is to predict the _____ rank, or average grades, for every person, no matter what his aptitude score. If you do this consistently, you will be less in error, on the average, than if you attempted other predictions.

middle

19-69 On the other hand, the procedure dictates that, if the correlation is _____ than zero, you should predict ranks or grades which are more similar to the student's rank on aptitude scores, and your average error in the long run will be less.

greater

19-70 As Lesson 20 will point out in greater detail, the amount of error made in such predictions is decreased by the use of correlation coefficients, and as one would suppose, it is decreased *more* by _____ values of the correlation coefficient than by _____ values.

high
low

19-71 When we make any kind of informal prediction on the basis of prior experience, we are almost always basing our judgment on what we believe to be a _____ between certain variables, such as high school performance and college grades.

correlation

19-72 But when we do not know the precise value of this assumed correlation, we are likely to make mistakes about its size. We may underestimate the degree of correlation, and we sometimes overestimate it. When we do so, we shall make _____ mistakes than we would make if we followed the prediction procedure rigorously, using the numerical correlation coefficients which are available.

more

Concluding Comment. *This final section has presented the doctrine concerning consistent use of the correlation procedure in making predictions. Consistent use of the procedure is explicitly designed to make the amount of error as small as possible in the long run. Guessing at the size of correlations, explicitly or implicitly, is likely to lead to more error than a conservative use of the actual correlation coefficients that are available.*

Nevertheless, nearly everyone feels inclined at first to trust his "intuitive" judgment more than the mathematical procedures. You may leave this section not yet convinced or even annoyed. If so, you can find more detailed discussion of the issue of intuition versus correlation, in Paul Meehl's entertaining little monograph, Clinical versus Statistical Prediction *(University of Minnesota Press, 1954).*

Problems for Lesson 19

19-1 A person was given a color-preference test; he was shown a set of 20 color samples and asked to arrange them in an order from most preferred to least preferred. These ranks were correlated with the ranks he gave to the same samples when the test was repeated the next day. Was the correlation coefficient a reliability coefficient or a validity coefficient?

19-2 If you were a reader of essay examinations, how could you determine whether the marks you assigned to a set of papers were *reliable?* How could you determine whether they were *valid?*

19-3 In a large group of boys, the correlation between height and weight was found to be +0.8.

   (a) Predict the weight rank of a boy ranking third on height in a group of 25 boys.

   (b) Predict the weight rank of a boy ranking eighteenth on height in a group of 25.

19-4 A group of 21 took a language examination. The instructor recorded the amount of time each student spent on the examination and the number of errors the student made. He found a correlation of −.4 between the time spent and the number of errors. Predict the rank on amount of time spent (where 1 represents the shortest time) for the student who made the greatest number of errors (i.e., whose rank on errors was 21).

Lesson 20. Interpretation of the Correlation Coefficient in Terms of Error Reduction

When two variables X and Y are correlated, any information about X values contains some amount of information about the corresponding Y values. The correlation coefficient is a numerical description of the amount of this information. However, the correlation coefficient is not related to the amount of information in any very simple manner. A correlation of +.50 does not mean that we can get just "half" as much information from X as we might get if the correlation coefficient were +1.00 instead or just "twice" as much as we might get with r = +.25. Nor would it be proper to take the correlation coefficient for a percentage and to assume that a correlation of +.50 is a "50 per cent" relationship. These notions about the correlation coefficient are very natural, but they are misunderstandings.

This lesson and the following lessons will present carefully and in some detail two different ways of picturing the amount of relationship signified by the correlation coefficient. Both ways are simple to apply and very helpful in practice. Unless at least one of them is clearly understood, the correlation coefficient is likely to remain for you a rather meaningless numeral.

Lesson 20 begins with the outcome of Lesson 19: It is possible to use the correlation coefficient between two variables in making numerical predictions about one variable from knowledge of the other. When such predictions are made on the basis of a known correlation coefficient, some of the error of prediction can be eliminated; the amount of error eliminated is greater when the correlation coefficient has a larger numerical value. This lesson describes how to determine the amount of error of prediction which will be eliminated by the use of correlation coefficients of different sizes.

A. Error of Prediction When $r = 0$

20-1 Lesson 19 pointed out that anyone who has a large number of predictions to make (for example, about probable grades in college) will do well to follow some consistent numerical rules. He is bound to be in error some of the time, but he will make less _____, in   *error* the long run, if he uses the rules consistently than if he makes his predictions informally or "intuitively."

20-2   The rules of procedure apply to the case in which the value of r is *known* to be zero. When the predicter is dealing with ordinal values such as ranks, he ought always to predict the _____ rank when $r = 0$. If he does so, he will minimize his error in the long run.

middle

20-3   Thus, the case in which $r = 0$ is not different in practice from the case in which r is unknown. The predicter should predict the middle rank in any case in which he does *not* have information indicating that r is _____ zero.

different from (not equal to)

20-4   When the predicter is dealing with *interval* rather than ordinal values, the rule tells him to predict the *mean* value. In following this rule, he is again predicting the *middle* position, since the usual indicator of central tendency for interval values is the _____ .

mean

20-5   By following such rules, the predicter is not able to avoid error altogether. But he is able to judge *how much* error he is likely to make in the long run in making a _____ number of such predictions.

large

20-6   Suppose that we do not know a correlation different from 0 between college grades and any other variable. If we know the mean of the grades made by previous groups of students, we can make a prediction for each individual for whom a prediction is necessary. We shall predict that his grades will equal the _____ of the grades of previous students.

mean

20-7   Assuming that the grade distribution is approximately a normal distribution, we can say how frequently this prediction will be in error by certain amounts. When a variable is normally distributed, _____ per cent of the scores lie within ± 1 standard deviation of the mean. Therefore, we shall not be in error by *more* than 1 standard deviation for _____ per cent of our predictions.

68

68

20-8   We can say with confidence that 68 per cent of the group for which predictions are being made will actually receive grades which are within 1 standard deviation of the _____ of the distribution. We can put it another way and say that the probability is _____ that our prediction will be *correct within* 1 *standard deviation.*

mean

0.68

20-9   A more pessimistic person, however, would remind us that the probability is _____ that the grade actually received will be *further* than 1 standard deviation away from the grade we predicted. However, the probability is only 0.05 that it will be more than 2 standard deviations away from our prediction, since _____ per cent of the grades will be likely to lie within ±2 standard deviations of the mean.

20-10   If we want to make statements which will not be wrong more than 5 per cent of the time, in a large number of cases, we shall have to say, "The grade is going to lie somewhere between the mean and _____ standard deviations above or below the mean."

0.32

95

2

Review

20-11   *A predicter does not usually make predictions in the form "The grade will be the mean of last year's grades." Instead, he is likely to say, "The grade will lie near the _____, and the probability is 0.68 that it will not be further than _____ standard deviation away from this point."*

mean

1

20-12   *If the predicter says, "The grade will be within ±1 standard deviation of the predicted value," he has _____ chances in 100 of being wrong. If he sets wider limits, such as ±2 standard deviations, he has _____ in 100 of being wrong. He will be in error, in the latter case, in about _____ per cent of the cases for which he makes predictions in this way.*

32

5

5

B.   Confidence Limits

If you studied Lesson 13, you will have seen in Section A that the strategy of stating a range of values is precisely like the strategy followed in making statements about a population mean. Section B will now develop the procedure for establishing confidence limits when we are making predictions based on a correlation coefficient. Since some students may have omitted Lesson 13, Section B has been written so it does not depend upon knowledge of Lesson 13. Students who completed Lesson 13 should study

Section B for the application of confidence limits to this new situation; they may also wish to read the note at the end, in which the similarities and differences between these two situations are pointed out.

20-13 Turn to the foldout between pages 336 and 337 and refer to the scatter diagram of aptitude scores X and freshman grades Y for the 228 men who entered Oberlin College in 1956. The mean grade $\overline{Y}$ for the group is _____. The standard deviation of the grade distribution s_Y is _____.

These numbers may seem strange. Oberlin College uses a number system in which a grade of C is given the value 0, C+ the value of +1, B− the value of +2, and so on; C− has the value −1, D+ the value −2, and so on. (See the Table of Letter-grade Equivalents above the scatter diagram.) The mean grade for this group, 1.14, is a little better than C+.

20-14 The grade which is $1s_Y$ above the mean is _____. The grade which is $2s_Y$ above the mean is _____.

20-15 With no knowledge of any correlation greater than zero between X and Y, the best prediction that could be made about any entering freshman's probable grade average will have to be based on knowledge about the Y distribution for previous students. If we use the distribution given in the table, we can state that the probability is 0.68 that the grade average will lie between _____ and _____. We can also state that the probability is 0.95 that it will lie between _____ and _____.

20-16 When a prediction is made in this fashion, the boundaries mentioned are called "confidence limits." The statement "The grade average will lie between −0.81 and +3.09" sets the _____ limits for the .68 level of confidence. We may have confidence that the prediction will be right in _____ per cent of the cases.

20-17 The level of confidence indicates the probability of being correct. The higher the number stated as the level of confidence, the _____ the probability of being correct. When we say "The grade average will lie between −2.76 and +5.04," we set confidence limits for the _____ level of confidence, since the probability of being correct is _____.

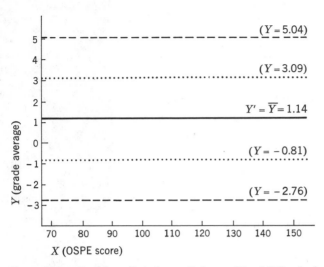

Figure 20-1. Confidence limits for predictions at .68 and .95 levels of confidence when $r = 0$.

20-18 Figure 20-1 shows the confidence limits for predictions that would be correct at the .68 and .95 levels of confidence when the correlation between X and Y is 0. The solid line in Figure 20-1 is the _____ of Y on X.

20-19 The confidence limits for the .68 level of confidence are represented by the dotted lines at $Y = 3.09$ and $Y = -0.81$. For any particular student, we shall predict a Y score Y', which lies on the _____ line directly above his _____. The probability is 0.68 that his actual Y score will not lie outside the region limited by the dotted lines.

regression — X score

20-20 The dashed lines lie at $Y = 5.04$ and $Y = -2.76$. These lines are the confidence _____ for the .95 _____. The probability is 0.95 that any actual Y score will not lie outside the region limited by the dashed lines.

limits — level of confidence

20-21 When we follow this line of argument, we are making two assumptions. We are assuming, first, that the grades of the incoming class of students (about which we are making predictions) will be like the grades in this scatter diagram (from which we have determined the correlation) and that both are samples drawn from the same larger population. This population should have parameters similar to the sample statistics. Our first assumption, then, is that the population mean is approximately equal to _____ and that the population standard deviation is approximately equal to _____.

$\bar{Y}$

s_Y

306   *The Correlation Coefficient in Terms of Error Reduction*

20-22 Our second assumption is that the shape of the *unknown Y* distribution will be very similar to the shape of a *normal* distribution. We make this assumption in order to be able to take the numbers by which we multiply s_Y (the number 1 for the .68 level, the number 2 for the .95 level) from our knowledge of the table of _____.

normal curve areas

20-23 We use three pieces of information in setting up our confidence limits. In order to pick a value Y' for the *center* of our confidence interval, we use our knowledge of the regression line of Y on X. In order to establish the *width* of the interval, we take the known value of _____ and multiply it by the number 1 or the number 2 taken from our knowledge of the table of _____ .

s_Y
normal curve areas

Review

20-24 *Instead of predicting a single Y value from the correlation between X and Y, it is customary to estimate that the unknown Y value will lie within certain* _____ *and to make this statement at a particular level of* _____ .

confidence limits
confidence

20-25 *This procedure assumes that the unknown Y distribution will turn out to be shaped like a* _____ *distribution and that its mean and standard deviation will be close to those of the known* _____ *distribution.*

normal
Y

Making a statement about Y' on the basis of Y is quite analogous to making a statement about μ on the basis of $\bar{X}$. In both cases, one decides upon a suitable level of confidence. Then one states that the value Y' (or μ) will probably lie within certain confidence limits around the value Y (or $\bar{X}$). The confidence limits are based upon the standard deviation of a distribution of Y values (or $\bar{X}$ values); since the multiplier is customarily taken from the normal curve table, it is necessary to be able to assume that this distribution of Y values (or of sample means) has approximately the shape of a normal distribution.

C. The Standard Error of Estimate

20-26 Setting confidence limits requires the use of a standard deviation. This standard deviation is called the STANDARD ERROR OF ESTIMATE s_E. When Y' is being predicted and $r = 0$, $s_E =$ _____ .

s_Y

20-27 The standard deviation used in setting confidence limits based on correlation is called the standard _____ of _____ . When $r = 0$, _____ $= s_Y$.

error
estimate — s_E

20-28   When r is different from 0, s_E is *smaller* than s_Y. Therefore, when r is different from 0, the distance between the confidence limits will be _____ than it is when $r = 0$.

20-29   When r is different from 0, s_E is _____ than s_Y. Sixty-eight per cent of the Y scores are expected to fall within $\pm 1 s_E$ of the value Y', and the number of scores falling within $\pm 1 s_Y$ of Y' will be _____ than 68 per cent.

20-30   The size of s_E is determined by the following relation:

$$s_E = s_Y \sqrt{1 - r^2}$$

If r is different from zero, $1 - r^2$ will be _____ than 1, $\sqrt{1 - r^2}$ will also be _____ than 1, and s_E will be _____ than s_Y.

   This equation should be memorized, because it is essential for you to be able to determine the relation of s_E to s_Y for any value of r. When you know how to determine this relation, you will be able to say how much an r of a particular size will improve the accuracy of prediction.

20-31   If $r = 0$, the expression $\sqrt{1 - r^2}$ will equal _____ and s_E will be equal to _____. For this reason, the standard error of estimate when $r = 0$ is the same as the standard deviation of the _____ distribution.

20-32   As r increases in numerical value (toward $+1$ or toward -1), the expression $1 - r^2$ will _____ in size and the quantity $\sqrt{1 - r^2}$ will _____ in size. The value of s_E will become _____ as r increases.

20-33   When $r = 1.00$, the expression $1 - r^2$ will equal _____ and the value of s_E will be equal to _____. In such a case, Y can be predicted from X precisely and with perfect confidence. The probability of being in error is 0.

20-34   If $r = .60$, the value of s_E will be _____ times s_Y. If $r = -0.60$, the value of s_E will still be _____ times s_Y.

20-35   The *sign* of the correlation coefficient does not affect the size of s_E, since only the _____ of the correlation coefficient enters into the equation.

20-36 *The standard deviation used in setting confidence limits when Y is to be predicted from X is called the* _____, *represented by the symbol* _____.

standard error of estimate

s_E

20-37 *The value of s_E is* _____ *than the value of s_Y when r is different from 0. The s_E becomes* _____ *as r increases toward $+1$ or toward -1, and when $r = +1$ or $r = -1$, the value of s_E is* _____.

smaller

smaller

0

D. Setting Confidence Limits by Means of the Standard Error of Estimate

20-38 There are three steps to follow in setting confidence limits. First, one must decide on an acceptable *level of confidence*. The conventional level of significance is the _____ level; at that level, one has a probability of _____ of being *wrong* when he rejects the null hypothesis. The corresponding level of *confidence* is the .95 level, at which the probability of being *correct* is _____ and therefore the probability of being *wrong* is _____.

.05

0.05

0.95

0.05

20-39 The second step is to determine the value Y', which will be the *center* of the confidence interval. The value of Y' for any individual is the Y value at that point at which the _____ line of Y on X crosses his _____ score. When the constants in the regression equation $Y' = mX + k$ are known, then Y' can be found by substituting the known value of _____ in the equation.

regression

X

X

20-40 For example, suppose $r = +.80$. For a person whose X score is $\bar{X}$, Y' will equal _____, since we know that a person scoring at the mean on X will always be predicted to score at the _____ on Y, whatever the correlation coefficient may be.

$\bar{Y}$

mean

20-41 The third step is to determine s_E and multiply it by the number appropriate to the level of confidence. For $r = +.80$, $s_E =$ _____ $\times s_Y$. The number appropriate to the .95 level of confidence is _____, since 95 per cent of the scores are expected to lie within $\pm$ _____ s_E of the value Y'.

0.6

2

2

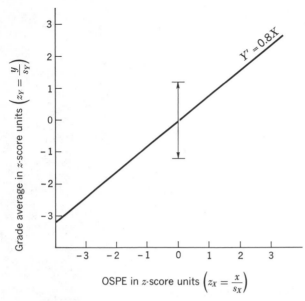

Figure 20-2. Regression line and confidence limits when $r = +0.80$ (both X and Y in z-score units.

20-42 Figure 20-2 illustrates this example. The correlation plot is drawn in *z-score units* for both X and Y, so that $s_Y = s_X$ and therefore $r = m$, the slope of the regression line. In z-score units, $\overline{X} = 0$. The regression line crosses the value $z_X = 0$ at the point where z_Y is equal to _____; therefore, Y' equals the _____ of the Y-distribution.

20-43 Since $s_E = 0.6s_Y$ in this example, the *upper* confidence limit for the .95 level lies at Y' plus _____ s_Y; the *lower* confidence limit lies at Y' _____. The vertical arrow shows the extent of this confidence interval in Figure 20-2.

20-44 Thus, the confidence interval can be described as $Y' \pm 1.2 s_Y$. If $r = 0$, the confidence interval for the same level of confidence would be described as $Y' \pm$ _____.

20-45 $1.2s_Y$ is $1.2/2 = 0.6 = 60$ per cent of $2s_Y$. The confidence interval when $r = +.80$ is _____ per cent as large as the interval when $r = 0$. By using this large a correlation coefficient, we have *reduced* the error by _____ per cent.

20-46 Suppose we are making a prediction for a person who scored 2.5 standard deviations *above the mean* on the X variable. With $r =$

$+.80$ and with both X and Y distributions converted to z-score units, the regression equation is $Y' = $ _____X. Y' for this person is _____ .

20-47 The confidence interval at the .95 level of confidence is described as _____ . Therefore, we shall estimate that that person's Y score will lie between a lower limit that is _____ s_Y above the mean of the Y distribution and an upper limit that is _____ s_Y above the mean.

Review

20-48 *The first step in setting confidence limits is to decide upon the* _____ . *The second step is to determine* _____ *from a knowledge of the regression equation.*

20-49 *The third step is to calculate* _____ *from a knowledge of r and s_Y. The equation which must be used is* _____ .

E. Amount of Error Reduction in Relation to the Value of r

20-50 Since $s_E = s_Y \sqrt{1 - r^2}$, we can write $s_E/s_Y = \sqrt{1 - r^2}$. We have already seen that, when $r = +.80$, $s_E/s_Y = $ _____ . Multiplying this number by 100, we can say that s_E is _____ per cent of s_Y.

20-51 When $r = 0$, s_E is _____ per cent of s_Y. If we compare $r = 0$ and $r = +.80$, we can say that when $r = +.80$, the size of s_E is only _____ per cent as large as it is when $r = 0$. Similarly, we can say that its size has been reduced by _____ per cent.

20-52 For any value of r, the quantity $\sqrt{1 - r^2} \times 100$ tells, in per cent, how large s_E is with respect to _____ . If we subtract this quantity from 100, we learn how much the size of _____ has been reduced when r differs from 0 by some particular amount.

20-53 Suppose that $r = +.60$. The quantity $\sqrt{1 - r^2} \times 100$ equals _____ ; therefore, _____ is _____ per cent of s_Y.

20-54 With $r = +.60$, the quantity $100 - (\sqrt{1 - r^2} \times 100)$ equals _____. An r of $+.60$ reduces the size of _____ by _____ per cent as compared with an r of 0.

20 — s_E

20

20-55 Table 20-1 gives the values of $\sqrt{1 - r^2}$ for six different values of r. Determine the error reduction percentages for the remaining blanks. Notice that *it takes relatively large values of r to get any apprecia-ble amount of reduction* in the size of s_E.

Table 20-1

r	$\sqrt{1 - r^2}$	Per Cent Reduction in s_E (Compared with $r = 0$)
1.0	0	100
0.8	0.6	40
0.6	0.8	_____
0.5	0.87	_____
0.4	0.92	_____
0.3	0.95	_____

20

13

8

5

20-56 In your reading, you may encounter correlation coefficients from time to time. You should remember one or two of the values in the table above so that you can quickly judge how much practical use can be made of particular values of r. It takes a correlation coefficient of _____ to reduce the size of s_E by 40 per cent. A correlation of .30 reduces s_E by only _____ per cent.

.8

5

20-57 Many of the correlation coefficients met with in psychology and social sciences are relatively low. Correlations of .30 are often mentioned. The correlation between grades and aptitude at Oberlin College is about $+.50$, not very different from the correlation between these variables at other institutions. A correlation of .50 will permit us to make predictions in which the s_E is _____ per cent *smaller* than it would be if $r = 0$.

13

Review

20-58 *The effectiveness of a particular value of r can be measured in terms of how much it reduces the size of* _____. *A reduction in this quantity means that the distance between the confidence limits for any* level of confidence will be somewhat _____. *The pre-cision of prediction is thereby somewhat* _____.

s_E

smaller

greater

20-59   *The size of s_E with respect to s_Y is given in per cent by the quantity* _____. *The amount of reduction in the size of s is given in per cent by the quantity* _____.

$\sqrt{1 - r^2} \times 100$

$100 - (\sqrt{1 - r^2} \times 100)$

20-60   *When r = .80, the per cent reduction in s_E is* _____.
When r = .30, the per cent reduction in s_E is _____.

40

5

Problems for Lesson 20

20-1 The standard deviation of a certain Y distribution is known to be 10. When the correlation between X and Y is unknown, what is the standard error of estimating Y from X? What is the standard error of estimating Y from X when the correlation is $+.714$? How much has the standard error been reduced through using the correlation between X and Y?

20-2 The correlation between grade point average (freshman first semester) and entrance examination scores ranges between $+.45$ and $+.55$ at Oberlin College, varying somewhat from class to class. When $r = +.55$, how much is the error of predicting grade average reduced by taking the correlation and the entrance examination score into account?

20-3 How large a correlation between X and Y would be required in order to reduce the error of predicting Y from X by 40 per cent (as compared with the error which would be made if $r = 0$)? Need the correlation be *positive*?

20-4 Suppose that the equation for the regression of students' monthly expenditure on entertainment Y on fathers' annual income X is $Y' = 0.00125X + 5$. What average monthly entertainment cost do you predict for a student whose father's income is $10,000 a year? If $s_Y = 5 and $r = +.75$, what are the 95 per cent confidence limits for this prediction?

Lesson 21. Interpretation of the Correlation Coefficient in Terms of Variance—I

In connection with any quantity which varies, such as college grade average, a question can be raised about sources of the variation. Does the variation in grade average arise solely because of differences among students in aptitude for college work? Probably it does not. The correlation coefficient can be understood as an indicator of the proportion of the variation in college grade average (or some other Y variable) which is related to aptitude score (or some other X variable). Lessons 21 and 22 will give careful consideration to the correlation coefficient as a way of measuring the contribution of one variable X to the variation in another variable Y.

The correlation coefficient will then be seen to provide a numerical answer to a question which can be stated in several different ways: How much information about Y is contained in X? How accurately can Y be predicted, when X is known? How much does the variation in X contribute to the variation which occurs in Y? To what extent can Y be described as a (linear) function of X? When the question is stated in one of the first two ways, it is best answered by the method discussed in Lesson 20. When it is stated in one of the other ways, it may be answered in terms of variance.

The variance concept is not difficult to understand, but its presentation will require the detailed study of a rather complete example. The example to be used has already been referred to in Lesson 20. Most of Lesson 21 is concerned with the details of this example; Lesson 22 will complete the task of drawing conclusions from the example. The observations contained in the example were obtained from the 228 men who entered Oberlin College as freshmen in 1956. All these students took the Ohio State Psychological Examination (OSPE), and the observations presented here show how their scores on this college aptitude test correlated with their grade averages at the end of their first freshman semester.

A. Description of the Scatter Diagram

21-1 In the scatter diagram on the foldout, the variable on the Y axis is _____. This is the variable which we would usually be

grade average

interested in predicting. The variable on the X axis is _____.

In the manner familiar from Lesson 8, we shall represent the raw scores of the X distribution by the capital letter X; correspondingly, the raw scores of the Y distribution will be represented by Y.

21-2 The class interval for the Y variable is _____ grade point(s). The class interval for the X variable is _____ score points. As in Figure 18-2, the labels for these distributions appear at the left and upper margins of the table.

21-3 The numbers in parentheses in the left column are the _____ of the Y classes. For the highest Y class, this number is _____; for the lowest Y class, it is _____ .

21-4 The numbers which appear in the first tally column under $X =$ 70 to 74 enumerate the students who scored from _____ to _____ on the OSPE. One of these students made a relatively high grade average of about (state the midpoint only) _____ . One made a low grade average of about _____ .

21-5 There are _____ students who scored 70 to 74 on the OSPE. The n for this column is found at the _____ of the column. The number of students who scored 75 to 79 is _____; the number who scored 110 to 114 is _____ .

21-6 The number of students who made grade averages from 4.51 to 5.0 is _____ . This n is found at the _____ end of the row for this class. Of the students in this row, how many scored from 135 to 139 points on the OSPE? _____ .

21-7 The number of students who made grade averages from 0 to −0.50 is _____ . The number of students who made grade averages from 2.01 through 2.50 *and* who scored from 115 through 119 on the OSPE is _____ .

21-8 The total number of students whose scores appear in the table is _____ . This number is at the lower right corner, and it can be obtained either by adding all the numbers in the column above it (that is, the n's for all the rows) or by adding all the numbers in the row to the left of it (that is, the n's for all the _____).

21-9 In the upper right corner of the page, outside the scatter diagram, the means and standard deviations for the two variables are shown. The mean grade average Y for these men students is _____, with a standard deviation s_Y equal to _____. We shall call $\overline{Y}$, which is the mean of all the Y values, the GRAND MEAN.

21-10 The numbers given at the upper right also indicate that the _____ for these two variables is $+0.49$. Notice that the trend of the tallies in the scatter diagram is from the lower _____ to the upper _____, as one would expect for a correlation that has a _____ sign.

21-11 As in the smaller scatter diagram of Figure 18-2, each row of this diagram can be considered as a small frequency distribution made up of the _____ scores of those students who made about the same _____. Each of these distributions has its own n, mean, and standard deviation. We shall refer to these means by the general symbol M_r for the "means of the rows."

21-12 Each column of the diagram can be considered as a small frequency distribution made up of the _____ of students who made about the same _____. The means of these distributions will be called M_c, for "means of the _____."

Review

21-13 *In this scatter diagram, following the customary procedure, the variable which is to be predicted is placed along the _____ axis while the variable from which predictions will be made is placed along the _____ axis.*

21-14 *The symbol $\overline{Y}$ stands for the mean of the _____ distribution, which will be called the _____ mean. The symbol M_c stands for the _____ of the _____; each of these is a mean of scores on the _____ variable made by students with approximately the same score on the _____ variable.*

B. The Variance as a Measure of Variability

Tables 21-1 and 21-2, which are to be used in Lessons 21 and 22, will be found on the foldout.

The Variance as a Measure of Variability   317

Right margin answers:

1.14 — 1.95

correlation coefficient

left — right
positive

aptitude
grade average

grade averages
aptitude score
columns

Y

X

Y
grand
means — columns
Y
X

21-15 In Table 21-1, the computation of s_Y is shown in detail. The second column shows the frequency n_r for each Y class; the numbers in this column are from the column at the right margin of the scatter diagram. The next column shows the _____ scores, which we shall designate as y scores. The _____ of the Y distribution (1.14) has been subtracted from the midpoint for each class.

deviation

mean

21-16 The fourth column in Table 21-1 shows the _____ of the _____ scores.

squares

deviation

21-17 The last column gives the product of _____ and _____ for each Y class. When this column is added, we obtain the _____ of the _____ deviation scores for the Y distribution. This number is at the bottom of the column; it is _____ .

n_r

y^2

sum — squared

868.64

21-18 The sum of the squared deviation scores is Σy^2. When this quantity is divided by $N = 228$, we obtain the _____ of the Y distribution, $s_Y{}^2$.

variance

21-19 The variance is the square of the _____ . By taking the square root of the variance, we obtain the value of _____ . Recall that this statistic can be called the _____-_____ _____ deviation; we have just traced the steps of computation which are contained, in _____ order, in this name.

standard deviation

s_Y

root — mean

square

reverse

21-20 The variance of this distribution has the value _____ . The value of s_Y is _____ . In Lessons 21 and 22, we shall make use primarily of the variance $s_Y{}^2$.

3.81

1.95

21-21 Arithmetical operations, such as addition and subtraction, are easier to interpret when they are applied to the *variance* than when they are applied to its square root, the _____ . After the operation of extracting the square root has been performed on a quantity, it is difficult to describe any sum to which it contributes in terms related to the original deviation scores.

standard deviation

21-22 We are interested in defining certain *component factors* which produce the variation in grades. We shall therefore need to be able to divide our measure of variability into components, which can be added together to produce the total amount of variation. Since the variance

can be divided into more useful additive components, we use the
_____ instead of the standard deviation as our measure of
variability.

Review

21-23 *The standard deviation is the _____ of the variance.*
Both standard deviation and variance are measures of _____,
but when a measure is to be broken up into additive components, the
_____ is the measure which can best be used.

21-24 *The standard deviation is the root-mean-square deviation. The*
variance could be called simply the _____ deviation. It is the
_____ of the _____ deviation scores.

C. The Means of the Columns

21-25 If there is a positive correlation between grades and aptitude
scores, then students who make low aptitude scores should tend to
make _____ grades than students who make high aptitude
scores.

21-26 Each column of the scatter diagram on the foldout contains
the tallies of students who scored within a particular class on the
_____ variable, which is _____. Since the
correlation is positive, we should find that the mean grade average for
the columns at the left of the diagram is _____ than that
for the columns at the right and that the size of the M_c values should
grow _____ as we move from left to right across the row.

21-27 Table 21-2 on the foldout will show how certain conclusions
can be drawn from the column means. The values of M_c for each X
class are shown in the third column of the table. The second column
contains the _____ for each of the classes, designated
_____.

21-28 For the class of scores 70 through 74, $M_c = -0.55$. For the
class 75 through 79, $M_c =$ _____. There are 16 classes
for the X variable, and therefore there are _____ column
means.

21-29 Figure 21-1, shown under the scatter diagram on the foldout, is a correlation plot for these observations. The column means have been plotted in the way already illustrated in Figure 18-3. The trend of the points is of the right sort for a positive linear correlation; they suggest a _____ line passing from lower _____ to upper _____ .

straight — left
right

21-30 The line best fitting these means, according to the principle of least squares, is the _____ line of Y on X. The slope of this line should equal $r(s_Y/s_X)$. Taking these values once more from the foldout, you will find that the slope should be equal to _____ .

regression

0.055

21-31 You now have the value of m for the regression equation $Y' = mX + k$. Since the line must pass through the _____ of the two distributions X and Y, you know that the equation must be valid when $X = 117$ and $Y' = 1.14$. Substituting for X, Y', and m, we find that $k = 1.14 - (0.055)117$. Therefore, the value of the Y intercept k must be _____ .

means

−5.3

21-32 With $m = 0.055$ and $k = -5.3$, the regression equation for Y on X is $Y' = $ _____ .

0.055X − 5.3

21-33 When $X = 100$, Y' should equal _____ according to the regression equation. Find this point on the correlation plot, and verify that it lies on the regression line.

+0.20

21-34 What would this plot look like if r were equal to $+1.00$? The slope of the regression line would equal $1(s_Y/s_X)$, or _____ , instead of 0.055. It would be approximately _____ times as great.

0.11
two

21-35 If r were equal to $+1$, the points representing the column means would lie exactly on the _____ . But in Figure 21-1, the means are slightly scattered around the line.

regression line

21-36 If r were to equal 0, on the other hand, the slope of the regression line would be _____ . The column means would all be the means of different samples drawn in the same way *from the same population,* since aptitude would make no significant difference in grades if r equaled 0. Therefore, the column means should scatter about the regression line _____ than they do in Figure 21-1. They would constitute a small sampling distribution of the means.

0

more

21-37 To study the regression line of Y on X, we plot the means of the various _____ classes against the values of _____. If the correlation is positive, there should be a tendency for these means to become _____ as the values of X grow larger.

$X - X$

larger

21-38 The regression equation of Y on X has the general form $Y' =$ _____. In order to determine the two constants _____ and _____, it is necessary to know five values (give the letter symbols only): _____.

$mX + k$

$m - k$

$r, s_Y, s_X, \bar{Y}, \text{ and } \bar{X}$

D. Applying the Rules for Prediction

In Lessons 19 and 20, you learned certain rules for predicting Y from X. These rules were intended for use whenever it is necessary to guess, in advance, what grades a prospective student is likely to make when his aptitude score is already known. It will help our explanation if we now apply these rules to the example we are working out.

21-39 Suppose that you asked someone to *guess* the grade averages of each of these 228 men and you gave him only two pieces of information: the grand mean $\bar{Y}$ and the set of aptitude scores (one for each man). Since he has no information about any correlation, his best guess for *each* student, regardless of aptitude score, will be _____.

$\bar{Y}(1.14)$

21-40 Consider one of the three students who scored from 140 through 144 on aptitude and whom *you* know (from the diagram) to have made a grade average of about 4.75. How far wrong will your guesser be on this student? The difference between his guess Y and the actual grade average is _____.

$3.61\ (4.75 - 1.14)$

21-41 The difference is the same as the _____ score for that individual student, since it is the difference between his actual grade and the _____ mean.

deviation

grand

21-42 Consider another individual student, one of the three who scored 135 to 139 on the aptitude test and whose grade average is about 0.75. The difference between the actual grade average and the guess will equal _____ in this case, and the deviation score is _____ in sign because the guessed grade is _____ than the grade actually obtained.

— 0.39

negative — higher

21-43 In Figure 21-1, the distances we have just discussed for these two students are marked by *solid arrows*. These differences correspond to the deviation scores $y = Y_i - \overline{Y}$ for these two students. The arrow pointing downward represents a deviation score which has a _____ sign, and the arrow pointing upward represents a deviation score which has a _____ sign. Such arrows could be drawn to represent the y scores of *each one* of the 228 men.

positive

negative

21-44 Now suppose that you were to give your guesser just a little more information. Suppose you tell him the mean M_c for each of the 16 columns. He will now be able to make his guesses come a little closer to the actual grades if, instead of guessing the grand mean $\overline{Y}$ for each student, he guesses the _____ for the class in which the student's aptitude score lies.

column mean

21-45 In effect, he is still guessing the mean score for each student, but he now knows *to which of the 16 different distributions* the student belongs. He guesses that the student will score at the _____ of his particular aptitude group.

mean

21-46 For the first student we took as an example above, who scores 140 to 144, the guesser's guess will now be _____ instead of 1.14. He will still miss the actual grade, but by a smaller amount; the difference between the actual grade and his new guess is _____. The difference $Y_i - M_c$ is positive because his guess is an *underestimation*.

3.15

1.60 (4.75 − 3.15)

21-47 For the other student taken as an example, the new guess will be _____. The value $Y_i - M_c$ equals _____, and the sign is _____, since the guess for this student is again an *overestimation*.

2.32 — −1.57

negative

21-48 The distances of these new guesses from the actual grade averages are shown in the figure by *dotted arrows*. Again, the arrow pointing downward represents a difference with a _____ sign, and the arrow pointing upward represents a _____ difference.

positive

negative

21-49 The dotted arrows can also be thought of as a kind of deviation score, different from the deviation scores shown by the solid arrows. The solid arrows represent the familiar deviation score $y =$ _____. The dotted arrows represent the deviation of the score Y_i from the _____, M_c.

$Y_i - \bar{Y}$
column mean

21-50 The deviation $Y_i - \bar{Y}$ is the *deviation of scores around the* _____ *mean.* The deviation $Y_i - M_c$ is the *deviation of scores around the* _____ *mean.*

grand
column

21-51 If the guesser were told the correlation coefficient, he would not use either the grand mean or the column means. He would predict Y', the grade average at that point where the _____ crosses the student's aptitude score. This procedure will be more satisfactory because the position of the column mean is determined in part by *sampling variability.* The correlation will vary less, from sample to sample, than will the sample means.

regression line of Y on X

Review

21-52 *If a guesser knows no correlation coefficient and no column means, he must predict the* _____ *for each student. The difference between his prediction and the actual grade for a particular student is the same as the deviation score* _____ *for that student.*

grand mean

$Y_i - \bar{Y}$

21-53 *If the guesser is told the column means, he can predict for each student the* _____ *for the class in which the student's* _____ *score falls. The difference between his prediction and the actual grade will be another sort of deviation score* _____ *which is the deviation of scores around the* _____.

mean
aptitude
$Y_i - M_c$
column mean

E. Measuring the Accuracy of Guesses Made from M_c and $\bar{Y}$

21-54 It is probably already obvious that your guesser will do *better* if he has information about the column means. However, to make this point quite clear, look at the column for scores 140 to 144 in the scatter diagram on the foldout. There are 15 grades in this column. Of these 15, there are _____ grade averages which are definitely closer to the grand mean (1.14) than to the column mean (3.15). For these grades, the grand mean prediction would be closer.

three

21-55 One grade average in the Y class 2.25 lies almost equally dis-
tant from the grand mean and the column mean. The remaining
_____ grades in this column are definitely nearer to the
column mean than to the grand mean. The column mean prediction
would be decidedly _____ for these grades.

21-56 We can measure the total amount of error which will be made
in all 228 cases in the same way in which we measured the deviation of
points around the regression line (Lesson 18E). For guesses made
from the grand mean, take the deviation $Y_i - \overline{Y}$ for each Y_i, square it,
and take the *sum of these squares*. For guesses made from the column
mean, we do the same thing, using the deviation $Y_i - M_c$. We take this
value for each _____ , square it, and take the _____
of these _____ .

21-57 A regression line is considered to fit its points most accurately
when the sum of the squared deviations is as _____ as
possible. Likewise, the guesses about the Y value made from the
column means will be considered better than the guesses made from
the grand mean if $\Sigma(Y_i - M_c)^2$ is _____ $\Sigma(Y_i - \overline{Y})^2$.

21-58 Table 21-1 contains the deviations $Y_i - \overline{Y}$ in its third column.
The _____ deviations are in the fourth column of the table,
and the sum of the _____ is at the bottom of the fifth
column. We examined this table in Section B, since it is essential in the
calculation of the two measures of variability in the Y distribution
_____ and _____ .

21-59 The sum of the squared deviation scores Σy_i^2 gives the variance of the Y distribution when it is divided by _____ . Its
square root gives the value of _____ , which you already
know to be equal to s_E when $r = 0$ or when no correlation is used for
prediction. This sum of squared deviation scores, or SUM OF SQUARES,
is very closely related to the total variance of the Y distribution.

21-60 To find the sum of the squared deviations $\Sigma(Y_i - M_c)^2$, look at
Table 21-2 on the foldout. In the last column, the sum of $(Y_i - M_c)^2$ is
given for each column in the scatter diagram. Each column contains
several values of Y, and $(Y_i - M_c)^2$ will be different for each of these
values. The individual squared deviations are not shown, and only the
sum for the column is given here. The first number at the top of the

column, 16.30, represents the _____ of the _____ of the five grade averages in the class 70 to 74 from their column mean, which is _____ for that class.

sum — squared deviations

−0.55

21-61 Regard that class for the moment as a separate small frequency distribution. The sum of the squared deviations $\Sigma(Y_i - M_c)^2$ which we are considering is the quantity we would use if we were to calculate the variance and standard deviation *for that separate distribution.* It is the sum of the squared deviations of these scores around the _____ of that separate distribution. To obtain the variance for that distribution, we would only have to divide the sum by _____ , which is the _____ for the distribution.

mean

$5 - n_c$

21-62 When all these sums in the last column of Table 21-2 are added, we have the total sum of squared deviations of all 228 grades *from their respective column means.* This sum measures the error made in guessing the grades from the column means. If the column mean is a better basis for guessing than the grand mean, this sum of squares should be _____ than the sum of squares from the grand mean.

smaller

21-63 The _____ obtained from the grand mean is 868.64. The _____ obtained from the column means is 660.07. The measure tells us that the better estimate is obtained when the _____ is used as the basis for guessing.

sum of squares
sum of squares

column mean

Review

21-64 *The relative accuracy of guesses based on the column mean or the grand mean can be measured by adding the _____ of the differences between the actual grade and the mean used to estimate it. This sum turns out to be smaller when the guesses are based on the _____ mean.*

squares

column

21-65 *Such a measure of accuracy is closely related to the variance and standard deviation. If the _____ from the grand mean is divided by total N, we obtain the value of _____ . If the _____ from any particular column mean is divided by n_c for that column, we obtain the _____ for that column, treated as a separate distribution.*

sum of squares
s_Y^2
sum of squares
variance

Problems for Lesson 21

21-1 Take the following values from the Oberlin data used in this lesson: $\overline{Y} = 1.14$; $s_Y = 1.95$; $\overline{X} = 117$; $s_X = 17.38$; $r = +.49$.

(a) Grade average Y can be predicted from OSPE score X by the regression equation of Y on X: $Y' = 0.055X - 5.3$. Predict Y' for a student whose aptitude score is 110. What is the standard error of this estimate with $r = +.49$? If r were equal to 0, what prediction would be made? What would be the standard error of the estimate with $r = 0$?

(b) Determine the regression equation of X on Y which could be used in determining the probable OSPE score from knowledge of the grade average.

21-2 Turn back to the scatter diagram of Figure 18-2 on page 267. From knowledge that $s_Y = 2.15$ and $N = 94$, you can determine the value of the sum of squares $\Sigma(Y_i - \overline{Y})^2$. What is the value? What is the value of the *variance* for this distribution of scores on Maze Y?

21-3 Again using Figure 18-2, determine the sum of squares $\Sigma(Y_i - M_c)^2$. This calculation is somewhat laborious; there is a different value of $(Y_i - M_c)^2$ for each *cell* in the diagram containing a number, and you must find each of these squared deviations, multiply it by its frequency (taken from the cell), and add the resulting products together. The calculation is precisely analogous to the calculation carried out for you in Lesson 21 with regard to the Oberlin College data. The means which are designated M_c in the Oberlin data are analogous to those designated M_y in Figure 18-2.

Lesson 22.   Interpretation of the Correlation Coefficient in Terms of Variance—II

Lesson 22 is a direct continuation of Lesson 21, in which the scatter diagram of grades and aptitude scores was discussed in detail. In Lesson 21,
we concluded by showing that the distances of scores from their column
means and from the grand mean can be compared by taking the sums of
squares of these distances. Lesson 22 explains why the sum of squared
deviations from the column means is smaller in this case than the sum of
squared deviations from the grand mean and how this fact is related to the
correlation between X and Y.

A.   Partitioning the Deviation Scores

22-1   For most of the grades in our distribution of 228 grades, the
deviation $Y_i - M_c$ is _____ than the deviation $Y_i - \bar{Y}$. We
know this both from our inspection of the scatter diagram and from
our comparison of the _____ of _____ of these
two deviations.

smaller

sums — squares

22-2   We can subtract $Y_i - M_c$ from $Y_i - \bar{Y}$ algebraically to find out
what makes $Y_i - \bar{Y}$ the larger of the two. If we take $(Y_i - \bar{Y}) -
(Y_i - M_c)$, we obtain the difference (put the quantity with the *positive
sign* first) _____ .

$M_c - \bar{Y}$

22-3   This algebraic subtraction shows that the *other* component,
besides $Y_i - M_c$, which makes up the deviation $Y_i - \bar{Y}$ is the deviation
of the _____ mean from the _____ mean. This
component will be called the MEAN-DEVIATION. Notice the hyphen, for
it is important.

column — grand

22-4   The dashed arrows in Figure 21-1 illustrate this mean-deviation
for the two students previously selected as examples. In both cases,
the arrow shows the mean-deviation to have a _____ sign.

positive

Both of these mean-deviations are at the right side of the table; those at the left of the table will have _____ signs, since they fall below the grand mean.

negative

22-5 Every deviation score $Y_i - \bar{Y}$ can therefore be divided or *analyzed* into two components: the deviation of the score from its _____ and the deviation of the _____ from the _____. The last is called the _____.

column mean
column mean — grand mean — mean-deviation

22-6 In Lesson 21, the deviation score $Y_i - M_c$ was compared and a sum of squares was computed for each. A sum of squares can also be computed for the other component _____.

$M_c - \bar{Y}$

22-7 The mean-deviation will always be the same for every grade that lies in a particular column. For all five grades in the class 70 to 74, the mean-deviation (shown in the fourth column of Table 21-2) has the value _____. This value has a negative sign because the column mean is _____ than the grand mean.

-1.69
smaller (less)

22-8 The squared mean-deviation for the class 70 to 74 is _____; this value appears in the fifth column of Table 21-2 under the heading $(M_c - \bar{Y})^2$. For that same class, the *sum* of the squared mean-deviations is given in the sixth column as _____. It is obtained by multiplying the value 2.86 by _____, the n_c for that class.

2.86

14.30
5

22-9 When this sum is obtained for all classes and all the sums are added, the total *sum of squared mean-deviations* for the 228 students is _____. Add this sum of squares to the sum of squared deviations from the column mean, which is 660.07. You obtain _____, which is practically the same as the sum of the squared deviations from the _____. (The small difference 0.15 is due to rounding off of decimals.)

208.42

868.49
grand mean

22-10 When we take the sums of squares for the two components of the deviation score, $\Sigma(Y_i - M_c)^2$ and $\Sigma(M_c - \bar{Y})^2$, and *add* these components, we find that their sum equals the value of $\Sigma($_____$)^2$.

$Y_i - \bar{Y}$

Review

22-11 *Any deviation score $Y_i - Y$ can be divided into two components symbolized as* _____ *and* _____. *The algebraic sum of the two components is always equal to* _____.

$Y_i - M_c \leftrightarrow M_c - \bar{Y}$
$Y_i - Y$

22-12 *This analysis of individual deviation scores holds also for the sums of squares of these components. The sum of all 228 values of (_____)² plus the sum of all 228 values of (_____)² is equal to the sum of all 228 values of (_____)².*

B. The Components of Variance

22-13 Each of the sums of squares we have arrived at can be divided by 228 to give a *mean squared deviation*. The sum of the squared deviation scores, $\Sigma(Y_i - \bar{Y})^2$, when it is divided by 228, will give a mean-squared deviation which is the value of the _____ for the entire Y distribution. We shall call this quantity the TOTAL VARIANCE, since it is derived from the whole deviation score before it has been divided into components.

variance

22-14 The sum of the squared mean-deviations gives another _____ if it is divided by 228. This quantity describes the variation of the column means around the _____ .

mean squared deviation
grand mean

22-15 The variation of the column means around the grand mean can be called the *variance of the column means*, or the VARIANCE BETWEEN COLUMNS. The name "variance" can thus be applied to any _____ deviation; the variance of the entire distribution, or _____ variance, is one *particular* _____ deviation.

mean squared
total — mean squared

22-16 Finally, the sum of the squared deviations of grades from the column mean can be divided by $N = 228$ to give a mean squared deviation representing the _____ of grades around their column means. This variation lies *within* the columns; it describes the variability of grades made by persons with the same _____ score.

variation

aptitude

22-17 If the variance within columns is *large*, any guesses about grades which are based on the column means will show _____ amounts of error. If the variance within columns is *small*, these guesses will show _____ amounts of error.

large

small

22-18 Recall the differences pointed out in Lesson 18, when graphs representing high and low positive correlation coefficients were compared. As r decreases from $+1$ toward 0, two changes occur: (1) The slope of the regression line becomes _____, and (2) the scatter of the points around the regression line becomes _____.

22-19 Each of our two variance components—the between-columns variance and the within-columns variance—gives us information about *one* of these two kinds of change. The scatter of the points around the regression line is closely related to the *within*-columns variance. The regression line is made to fit the _____ of the columns as closely as possible. The greater the amount of scatter of grades around their column means, the greater will be their scatter around the _____ and the _____ will be the value of the _____ variance.

22-20 The between-columns variance, on the other hand, gives some idea whether the slope of the regression line is near zero. If the between-columns variance is very _____, the means of the columns are very nearly equal.

22-21 Equal means of the columns will produce a horizontal regression line with a slope of zero. If the slope is to be greater than zero, indicating that r is greater than 0, the between-columns variance must be _____ than it would be when $r = 0$.

22-22 A high degree of correlation will therefore be associated with a _____ within-columns variance and a _____ between-columns variance. The *relative size* of these two variance components is closely related to the degree of correlation.

Review

22-23 *The quantity* $\Sigma(Y_i - \overline{Y})^2/N$ *is called the* _____ *variance. The quantity* $\Sigma(Y_i - M_c)^2/N$ *is called the* _____ *variance. The quantity* $\Sigma(M_c - \overline{Y})^2/N$ *is called the* _____ *variance.*

22-24 *If the correlation coefficient is high, the* _____ *variance is relatively high and the* _____ *variance is relatively low.*

less

greater

means

regression line — greater
within-columns

low

greater

low — high

total
within-columns
between-columns

between-columns
within-columns

C. The Correlation Coefficient and the Variance Components

22-25 From Tables 21-1 and 21-2 on the foldout, take the values of the variance components for the following blanks:

Total variance = _____

Between-columns variance = _____

Within-columns variance = _____

22-26 The sum of between-columns variance plus within-columns variance is _____, which is the same as the value of _____.

22-27 By dividing each of the 228 deviation scores into two components and determining the variance of each component separately, we have partitioned total variance into the variance of scores around their _____ and the variance of _____ around the _____.

22-28 We already know that the relative size of the two variance components is related to the degree of _____ between X and Y. Now take the *between-columns* variance and divide it by the *total* variance. This quotient is _____.

22-29 The square root of 0.24 is 0.49, which is the value of r for our example. *The correlation coefficient can be defined in all cases as the square root of the quotient* when _____ variance is divided by _____ variance.

22-30 Dividing the between-columns variance by total variance gives us between-columns variance as a *proportion* of total variance. This quotient tells us what proportion of total variance is made up of variance _____ columns. The remainder of total variance is made up of variance _____ columns.

22-31 The greater the proportion of total variance which comes from between-columns variance, the _____ the correlation coefficient. The greater the proportion coming from within-columns variance, the _____ the correlation coefficient.

22-32 The total variance is a measure of the variation of scores around the _____. We have been doing what amounts to an analysis of the sources of this variation. The between-columns variance represents the amount of variation which comes from the variation of _____ around the _____.

column means — grand mean

22-33 The extent to which the column means will differ from one another depends on the extent to which students with different *aptitude scores* actually have different _____. Therefore, the between-columns variance represents the *contribution to total variation in grades* which arises from differences in _____ among the students.

grades

aptitude

22-34 On the other hand, the within-columns variance represents the amount of total variance which comes from the variation of grades around their _____. It represents, therefore, the amount of variation in grades which is *still present among students who made the same* _____ scores. This amount of variation is *not* related to differences in aptitude; it arises from other sources not yet defined.

column means

aptitude

Review

22-35 *The correlation coefficient can be defined as the square root of the ratio of* _____ *variance to* _____ *variance.*

between-columns — total

22-36 *The between-columns variance represents the amount of variation which comes from the variation of* _____ *around the* _____. *When the between-columns variance is divided by total variance, we obtain the proportion of total variance in the Y distribution which is related to differences in the value of the* _____ *variable.*

column means
grand mean

X

22-37 *The within-columns variance represents the amount of variation which comes from the variation of the* _____ *values around their* _____. *This component of total variance is* _____ *to differences in the value of the X variable.*

Y
column means —
unrelated

D. Correlation as Proportion of "Variance Accounted for"

22-38 Because of the relation between the two variance components and correlation, it is possible to determine any one of these three numbers when the other two are known. The *square* of r gives the proportion of total variance which is made up of _____ variance. If $r = .5$, this proportion is equal to _____.

between-columns
0.25

22-39 The proportion of total variance made up of within-columns variance is equal to $1 - r^2$. If $r = .5$, this proportion is equal to _____.

0.75 (1.00 − 0.25)

22-40 The value of r in our example is approximately .5. We have just shown that about _____ per cent of the total amount of variation in grades could be attributed to variation in aptitude, and about _____ per cent must be attributed to other factors as yet undefined.

25

75

22-41 This observation brings us at last to the second of the two ways of picturing "amount of correlation" promised at the beginning of Lesson 20. We can picture the *square* of the _____ as indicating the proportion of variation in Y (grades) which is *accounted for* by differences in X (aptitude).

correlation coefficient

22-42 In order to find this proportion, we must take the correlation coefficient r and _____ it. If we then subtract the result from _____, we find the proportion of variance which still remains when the part accounted for by variation in X has been removed.

square
1

22-43 It is convenient, then, to designate the quantity _____ as the proportion of VARIANCE ACCOUNTED FOR. The quantity _____ is then the proportion of VARIANCE UNACCOUNTED FOR (by X).

r^2

$1 - r^2$

22-44 It is instructive to consider various values of r in this light. We have already seen that a correlation coefficient of .5 indicates that _____ per cent of the variance is accounted for by X and that _____ per cent remains _____ for.

25
75 — unaccounted

22-45 When $r = .3$, what per cent of the variance of Y is accounted for by X? _____. What per cent remains unaccounted for by X? _____.

$0.09 \times 100 = 9$ per cent
91 per cent

22-46 How large a value of r is required if at least 49 per cent of the variance is to be accounted for? The value of r must be at least _____.

.70 ($.70^2 = .49$)

22-47   In order to account for 81 per cent of the variance, a correlation coefficient of _____ would be required.

.90

Review

22-48   *There are now two ways in which you can interpret the meaning of a particular correlation coefficient between X and Y. You can square it and know that r^2 represents the* _____ *of* _____ *in Y that is* _____ *by X. Similarly, $1 - r^2$ will tell you the* _____ *of* _____ *in Y that is* _____ *by X.*

*proportion — variation accounted for
proportion — variation — unaccounted for*

22-49   *Or you can take the square root of $1 - r^2$, multiply it by s_Y, and obtain the standard* _____ *of* _____ *for predictions about Y made from knowledge of X. The quantity $1 - \sqrt{1 - r^2}$ indicates the proportion by which* _____ *has been reduced through the use of the correlation between X and Y to predict Y.*

error — estimate

s_E

22-50   *A correlation of .5, which is a typical degree of correlation between college grades and college aptitude scores, can be interpreted as follows: About* _____ *per cent of the variation in college grades can be* _____ *by differences in aptitude; if we must predict grades for incoming students for whom we have aptitude scores available, the confidence limits of our prediction will be about* _____ *smaller than they would be if $r = 0$.*

*25
accounted for*

13 per cent

Postscript to Lesson 22

In our example, we have analyzed the total variance of grade averages into only two components. The variance which remains unaccounted for, after taking the variation due to aptitude into account, is probably not due to any single source. A further analysis of this remaining variance might show a number of additional sources.

Techniques for separating total variance into two or more components are called analysis of variance *techniques. We have done a small analysis of variance in Lessons 21 and 22. When the analysis involves more than two components, it becomes slightly more complex but the principles remain unchanged. The development of analysis of variance techniques has been one of the important recent advances in statistics and experimental design. It has been particularly important for the biological and social sciences, in* which the explanation of most phenomena requires the simultaneous consideration of several factors.

Your completion of these final two lessons places you in a position of readiness to understand analysis of variance as well as more advanced kinds of correlation such as multiple correlation, partial correlation, and factor analysis. If you go on to study the more advanced analytic techniques of statistics, you will more than likely do so in a formal course of instruction. However, several references are provided on page 346, and these can be consulted if you wish to read independently on any of these techniques.

Problems for Lesson 22

22-1 When the correlation coefficient between X and Y is $+.4$, what is the proportion of total variance which is contributed by the between-columns variance? What proportion of total variance is contributed by the within-columns variance? How much of the variation in Y is accounted for by variation in X?

22-2 If the between-columns variance is 3.6 and the within-columns variance is 6.4, what is the value of total variance? What is the value of r^2? What is the value of r?

22-3 With a correlation coefficient of $+.37$, what proportion of variance in Y is accounted for by variation in X? What proportion remains unaccounted for? How much is the standard error of estimating Y from X *reduced* by a correlation of $+.37$?

22-4 Turn again to the scatter diagram of Figure 18-2. Determine the third sum of squares $\Sigma(M_c - \overline{Y})^2$. You now have the three sums of squares needed for determining total variance, between-columns variance, and within-columns variance. Show that $\Sigma(Y_i - M_c)^2 + \Sigma(M_c - \overline{Y})^2 = \Sigma(Y_i - \overline{Y})^2$ for the maze example. Show that the sum of between-columns variance and within-columns variance is equal to total variance. What is the value of r for the maze example? What *proportion of variance* on Maze Y can be accounted for by knowledge of performance on Maze X? With this correlation, what is the *standard error* of estimating the score on Y from knowledge of the score on X?

Scatter Diagram for Aptitude Score and Freshman Grade Average
(228 Men in Oberlin College Class of 1960)

Letter-grade Equivalents							
A+	7	B+	4	C+	1	D+	−2
A	6	B	3	C	0	D	−3
A−	5	B−	2	C−	−1	D−	−4

	N = 228	r = +0.49
	OSPE Scores	**Grade Averages**
Mean	$\bar{X} = 117$	$\bar{Y} = 1.14$
Standard Deviation	$s_X = 17.38$	$s_Y = 1.95$

Grade Averages \ OSPE Scores	70-74	75-79	80-84	85-89	90-94	95-99	100-104	105-109	110-114	115-119	120-124	125-129	130-134	135-139	140-144	145-149	Totals
4.51 to 5.0 (4.75)											1	2	3	4	3	1	14
4.01 to 4.5 (4.25)										1		1		2	1		5
3.51 to 4.0 (3.75)									1	1	2		1	5	2		12
3.01 to 3.5 (3.25)							2	1	2	1	2	1	1	4			14
2.51 to 3.0 (2.75)	1					1		1	2	1	4	2	1	1			14
2.01 to 2.5 (2.25)						1	1	3	3	3		1	2		1		15
1.51 to 2.0 (1.75)							2	1	4	3	5	2	1	1	2		21
1.01 to 1.5 (1.25)		1		1	1		3	2	3	3	3	2	6				25
0.51 to 1.0 (0.75)			1		2		2	1			2	1		2	3		14
0.01 to 0.5 (0.25)				2	5	2	1	2	5	4	2	3					26
−0.50 to 0 (−0.25)		2	2		1	2	2	2	4	1	5	2	3	1	1		28
−1.00 to −0.51 (−0.75)	2	1			3	1			1	1		1	2				12
−1.50 to −1.01 (−1.25)	1							2	3			1	1				8
−2.0 to −1.51 (−1.75)					1		2		1		2			1			7
−2.5 to −2.01 (−2.25)				1					1		1						3
−3.0 to −2.51 (−2.75)	1		1									1	2		2		7
−3.5 to −3.01 (−3.25)			1														1
−4.0 to −3.51 (−3.75)									1	1							2
Totals	5	3	6	4	13	7	13	17	28	25	25	21	24	21	15	1	228

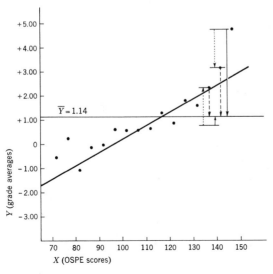

Figure 21-1. Correlation plot and regression line of Y on X.

Table of Areas under the Normal Curve

$z = \dfrac{x}{\sigma}$	Area (mean to z)	$z = \dfrac{x}{\sigma}$	Area (mean to z)	$z = \dfrac{x}{\sigma}$	Area (mean to z)	$z = \dfrac{x}{\sigma}$	Area (mean to z)
.00	0.0000	1.40	0.4192	1.96	0.4750	2.46	0.4931
.05	0.0199	1.45	0.4265	1.97	0.4756	2.48	0.4934
.10	0.0398	1.50	0.4332	1.98	0.4761	2.50	0.4938
.15	0.0596	1.52	0.4357	1.99	0.4767	2.52	0.4941
.20	0.0793	1.54	0.4382	2.00	0.4772	2.54	0.4945
.25	0.0987	1.56	0.4406	2.01	0.4778	2.56	0.4948
.30	0.1179	1.58	0.4429	2.02	0.4783	2.58	0.4951
.35	0.1368	1.60	0.4452	2.04	0.4793	2.60	0.4953
.40	0.1554	1.62	0.4474	2.06	0.4803	2.62	0.4956
.45	0.1736	1.64	0.4495	2.08	0.4812	2.64	0.4959
.50	0.1915	1.66	0.4515	2.10	0.4821	2.66	0.4961
.55	0.2088	1.68	0.4535	2.12	0.4830	2.68	0.4963
.60	0.2257	1.70	0.4554	2.14	0.4838	2.70	0.4965
.65	0.2422	1.72	0.4573	2.16	0.4846	2.72	0.4967
.70	0.2580	1.74	0.4591	2.18	0.4854	2.74	0.4969
.75	0.2734	1.76	0.4608	2.20	0.4861	2.76	0.4971
.80	0.2881	1.78	0.4625	2.22	0.4868	2.78	0.4973
.85	0.3023	1.80	0.4641	2.24	0.4875	2.80	0.4974
.90	0.3159	1.82	0.4656	2.26	0.4881	2.82	0.4976
.95	0.3289	1.84	0.4671	2.28	0.4887	2.84	0.4977
1.00	0.3413	1.86	0.4686	2.30	0.4893	2.86	0.4979
1.05	0.3531	1.88	0.4699	2.32	0.4898	2.88	0.4980
1.10	0.3643	1.90	0.4713	2.34	0.4904	2.90	0.4981
1.15	0.3749	1.91	0.4719	2.36	0.4909	2.92	0.4982
1.20	0.3849	1.92	0.4726	2.38	0.4913	2.94	0.4984
1.25	0.3944	1.93	0.4732	2.40	0.4918	2.96	0.4985
1.30	0.4032	1.94	0.4738	2.42	0.4922	2.98	0.4986
1.35	0.4115	1.95	0.4744	2.44	0.4927	3.00	0.4987

Appendix. Review of the Rectangular Coordinate System

Most readers will find it unnecessary to work through this lesson, which reviews the rectangular coordinate system. There are some technical terms used in the main part of the program with which the reader must be familiar; this lesson is intended for those readers who have initial or persistent difficulty with the terminology and system of notation relating to the designation of the axes of graphs, the location of points by coordinates, and the meaning of terms like "abscissa" and "ordinate." Therefore, a student might wish to study this lesson for either of two reasons: (1) He has been having difficulty in his study of other lessons which is traceable to lack of understanding of the coordinate system, or (2) he feels insecure in his retention of this information and wishes to review prior to study of the main lessons of the program.

A. Structure of the Coordinate System

A-1   Figure A-1 shows two straight lines which intersect one another at right angles. These lines are called the COORDINATE AXES. One of the _____ axes is horizontal, while the other coordinate _____ is vertical.

coordinate axis

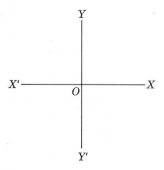

Figure A-1

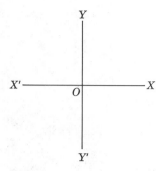

Figure A-1 repeated

A-2   The point of intersection of the _____ is called the ORIGIN. In Figure A-1, the _____ has been labeled *O*.

A-3   In order to differentiate clearly between the two coordinate axes, one is called the *X* axis and the other is called the *Y* axis. In Figure A-1, the horizontal line labeled *X'X* is the _____ and the vertical line labeled *YY'* is the _____ .

A-4   We shall wish to measure distances along each of the _____ . To do this, we can begin at the origin and mark off successive units of equal length in both directions from the _____ along each axis. This step is illustrated in Figure A-2.

A-5   All measurement requires some type of SCALE. If numbers are assigned in a particular way to the units of equal length which have been marked off along the axes, we shall create a particular type of numerical _____ along each axis.

A-6   Notice that in the construction of the scale along each axis, we begin counting from the origin; that is, on each of these scales, the origin has the value _____ . This is illustrated in Figure A-3.

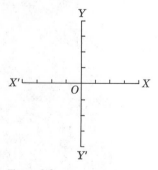

Figure A-2

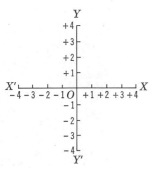

Figure A-3

A-7 Figure A-3 also indicates that, on the X axis, increasing positive numbers are assigned to the scale units to the _____ of the origin while increasing _____ numbers are assigned to the units to the left of the origin.

right
negative

A-8 In the numerical scale on the Y axis, increasing positive numbers are assigned to the units _____ the origin while increasing negative numbers are assigned to the units _____. Just as in the scale on the X axis, the zero point of the Y axis lies at

_____ .

above
below the origin

the origin

A-9 The origin divides each of the _____ into two segments, one of which is a positive segment and the other a _____ segment.

coordinate axes

negative

A-10 Notice that, in Figure A-3, all _____ numbers are located above and to the right of the origin and all _____ numbers are located below and to the left of the origin. The two coordinate axes and the numerical scales laid out along each comprise the RECTANGULAR SYSTEM OF COORDINATES.

positive
negative

A-11 We can describe any rectangle completely by measuring just two dimensions: its width and its height. The rectangular system of coordinates uses two coordinate axes, one of which corresponds to the dimension of width, is horizontal and is called the _____ , while the other, corresponding to the dimension of height, is _____ and is called the _____ .

X axis

vertical — Y axis

B. Location of Points

A-12 Let P represent any POINT on a plane surface. Using the rectangular system of coordinates, we can locate precisely any _____ which falls on a plane surface.

point

A-13 Actually, we have already located one point on a plane surface. This is the point of intersection of the _____, a point which we have called the _____ of the coordinate system.

A-14 In general, the intersection of any pair of lines, one of which is horizontal and parallel to the _____, the other of which is _____ and parallel to the _____, will locate a particular point in the rectangular coordinate system.

A-15 Figure A-4 illustrates the fact that a pair of lines, one horizontal and one vertical and which are parallel to the _____ and _____, respectively, can intersect each other at one and only one point in the plane. If either or both of the lines were located differently, they would intersect at a _____ point.

A-16 When a horizontal and a vertical line intersect each other at a point in the plane, they are said to DETERMINE that point. Because _____ pair of such lines can intersect at a given point, that pair of lines is said *uniquely* to _____ .

A-17 Notice again in Figure A-4 that the scales along the X and Y axes each have *positive* values to one side of the origin and *negative* values to the other. These numbers are used to indicate the SIGNED DIRECTION as well as the distance between the origin and the locations of the intersecting lines which determine a point. For example, in Figure A-4, the vertical line corresponding to the point is located in a *positive* direction from the origin, a distance of three units. The horizontal line is located in a _____ direction from the origin, a distance of _____ units. Therefore, the _____ direction of both intersecting lines is positive and is equal to three units on each scale.

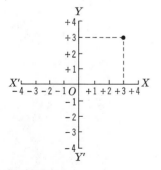

Figure A-4

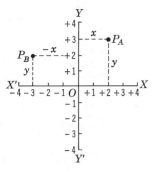

Figure A-5

A-18 The exact location of any point can be given by reference to the numerical scales along the coordinate axes. In terms of the units of these scales, we must determine (1) the _____ horizontal distance measured from the origin to the point along the _____-axis scale and (2) the _____ vertical distance measured from the origin to the point along the _____-axis scale.

signed

X — signed

Y

A-19 In Figure A-5 the point P_A has been located. The signed horizontal distance x is measured on the X-axis scale and is equal to _____ units from the origin. The signed vertical distance y is measured on the Y-axis scale and is equal to _____ units from the origin.

2

3

C.   The Coordinates of a Point

A-20 The signed horizontal distance x from the origin to any point is called the ABSCISSA of the point. The signed vertical distance y from the origin to any point is called the ORDINATE of the point. The _____ of a point is measured on the X axis, and the _____ is measured on the Y axis.

abscissa

ordinate

A-21 When we measure the signed distance x on the X-axis scale, we express this value as a number. Therefore, if the distance $x = 2$ units, the point has an _____ equal to 2. The value of the _____, measured in units of the Y-axis scale, can similarly be expressed numerically.

abscissa

ordinate

A-22 A particular point can have only one abscissa value and only one ordinate value. Therefore, every possible point in a plane is uniquely determined by just two numbers, one of which represents the

_____ of the point and the other of which represents the
_____ of the point.

abscissa ↔
ordinate

A-23 Together, the abscissa and the ordinate of a point are called the
COORDINATES of the point. We have used the symbols x to stand for the
abscissa and y to stand for the ordinate. We can use the combined
symbol (x, y) to represent a point whose _____ is x and
whose _____ is y. The _____ of a point are
represented by a symbol of the form (_____ , _____).

abscissa
ordinate — *coordinates*
x, y

A-24 When symbols of the form (x, y) are used to specify the
_____ , the value of the _____ is always given
first and the value of the _____ is always given second.

coordinates of a point -
abscissa
ordinate

A-25 Sometimes the symbol $P(x, y)$ is used and is read "the point
whose abscissa is x and whose ordinate is y." The same symbol can be
read more briefly "the point whose _____ are x and y."

coordinates

A-26 Notice that the coordinates of a point constitute an ORDERED
PAIR of numbers because the first number always refers to the value of
the _____ and the second to the value of the _____ .
If we have an _____ of numbers given as coordinates, such
as (3, 2), we can locate one and only one point which has _____
as its abscissa and _____ as its ordinate.

abscissa — *ordinate*
ordered pair
3
2

A-27 "The point having the coordinates 3 and 4" could be written as
the symbol _____ . In this example, the value of the abscissa
is _____ and the value of the ordinate is _____ .
A point located on a graph at the intersection of any abscissa and any
ordinate is said to be PLOTTED.

P(3, 4)
3 — 4

A-28 Suppose that you wished to plot the point whose coordinates
are (2, 3). You would first count _____ units along the
_____ axis to the right of the origin to determine the abscissa
of the point. Then, you would count _____ units along the
_____ axis above the origin to determine the ordinate of
the point. The point would then be plotted at the intersection of the
horizontal and vertical lines corresponding to these coordinates.

2
X
3
Y

A-29 In Figure A-5, a point labeled P_B is shown. Notice that this point
has a *negative* abscissa, and this signed distance is labeled $-x$. The
value of the abscissa of P_B is _____ .

−3 (minus 3)

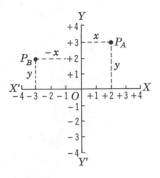

Figure A-5 repeated

A-30 The ordinate of P_B in Figure A-5 is labeled y. The value of the ordinate is _____ . The proper symbol denoting this point is written _____ .

> As long as it is clear that one is referring to the coordinates of a point when an ordered pair of numbers like (−3, 2) is given, the symbol P in front of the parentheses is superfluous. In all following examples, this part of the symbol is omitted.

A-31 In Figure A-6, the point P_C has been plotted. Its abscissa is _____ and its ordinate is _____ . The symbol denoting this point is _____ .

A-32 In Figure A-6, the point P_D is plotted. Its abscissa is _____ and its ordinate is _____ . The symbol for this point is written _____ .

A-33 For the point located at the origin, both the abscissa and the ordinate have the value _____ . The symbol denoting the origin is written _____ .

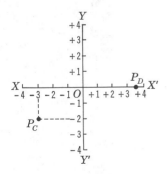

Figure A-6

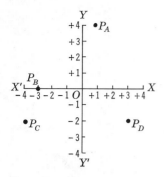

Figure A-7

A-34 In Figure A-7, the points P_A, P_B, P_C, and P_D have been plotted. The coordinates for these points, respectively, are _____;
_____ ; _____ ; and _____ .

(1, 4)
(−3, 0) — (−4, −2) —
(3, −2)

D. Quadrants

A-35 In Figure A-8, the area above the X axis and to the right of the Y axis is labeled with the Roman numeral I. This area is called the FIRST QUADRANT and is the area in which all points having positive values for both coordinates are plotted. The point with the coordinates (1, 4) is plotted in the _____ , since the _____ of the point both are _____ .

*first quadrant — coordi
   nates — positive*

A-36 Figure A-8 also indicates that points having _____ abscissas and _____ ordinates are plotted in the _____ , labeled II.

*negative
positive
second quadrant*

A-37 The point having the coordinates (−3, 2) is plotted in the _____ , since the _____ of the point is negative and the _____ is positive.

*second quadrant
   — abscissa
ordinate*

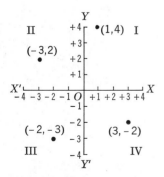

Figure A-8

A-38 Points having a _____ abscissa and a _____ ordinate are plotted in the first quadrant. Points having a _____ abscissa and a _____ ordinate are plotted in the second quadrant.

positive — positive

negative — positive

A-39 In Figure A-8, the area below the X axis and to the left of the Y axis is called the _____. It is the area in which points having _____ abscissas and ordinates are plotted. The point whose coordinates are $(-2, -3)$ is plotted in the _____.

third quadrant
negative
third quadrant

A-40 Figure A-8 also indicates that points having _____ abscissa values and _____ ordinate values are plotted in the fourth quadrant, labeled IV. $P(3, -2)$ is plotted in this quadrant as an example of such points.

positive
negative

A-41 You have probably noticed that beginning with the first quadrant, the four quadrants are numbered in a counterclockwise direction. Complete the following table:

	Quadrant			
	I	*II*	*III*	*IV*
Sign of abscissa	_____	_____	_____	_____
Sign of ordinate	_____	_____	_____	_____

I	*II*	*III*	*IV*
+	–	–	+
+	+	–	–

REFERENCES

For additional information and for convenient computational procedures, consult one of the standard textbooks on statistics. Some such books which the authors have found particularly useful and readable are listed below.

Ferguson, G. A.: "Statistical Analysis in Psychology and Education," McGraw-Hill Book Company, Inc., New York, 1959.

McNemar, Quinn: "Psychological Statistics," John Wiley & Sons, Inc., New York, 1962.

Edwards, A. L.: "Experimental Design in Psychological Research," rev. ed., Holt, Rinehart and Winston, Inc., 1960.

Rodger, R. S.: "Statistical Reasoning in Psychology: An Introduction and Guide," University Tutorial Press, London, 1961. (A compact and lucid treatment of the ideas involved in statistical reasoning, with no emphasis on computational procedures.)

McCarthy, Philip J.: "Introduction to Statistical Reasoning," McGraw-Hill Book Company, Inc., New York, 1957. (Especially Chapter 6 on random sampling.)

Siegel, Sidney: "Nonparametric Statistics," McGraw-Hill Book Company, Inc., New York, 1956.

ANSWERS TO PROBLEMS

Lesson 1

1-1 **(a)** The entire relevant March population consists of three numbers: the hours which that student spent in sleep on March 18, the hours spent on March 19, and the hours spent on March 20. **(b)** Yes, the entire population was actually collected. **(c)** No, there can be no question of "significance"; if the observations in the April population differ from those in the March population, then the two populations simply differ. All the relevant observations are available.

1-2 **(a)** 31 numbers: the hours spent in sleep by that student during each 24-hour period in March. **(b)** No, only a sample. **(c)** Yes, there is a question of significance because not all the relevant observations are available. These two three-day periods could differ because of sampling variability without there being any difference between the two populations from which they come.

1-3 **(a)** The number of hours of sleep for each of the 20 students for each of the three days March 18–20. **(b)** Yes. **(c)** No, since all the relevant observations are available.

1-4 **(a)** The number of hours of sleep for each of the 20 students for each day in March. **(b)** No, only a sample. **(c)** Yes, since not all the relevant observations are available.

1-5 **(a)** The numbers of hours of sleep for each student on campus for each of the three days March 18–20. **(b)** No, only a sample. **(c)** Yes.

1-6 **(a)** The number of hours of sleep for each student on campus for each day in the month of March. **(b)** No, only a sample. **(c)** Yes.

Lesson 2

2-1 No, the sample is biased; since the factors determining whether the questionnaire will be returned are not known, one cannot be sure that each student's response has an *equal chance* of being included. (It would be possible for *independence* to be violated as well; one roommate might bring both his own and his roommate's questionnaire to the box.)

2-2 No. Both conditions will be violated. Not all students are equally likely to be encountered in the course of a day's movement around campus. Some students will be encountered in groups, so that the inclusion of one group member's response is not independent of the inclusion of the response of another member of the same group.

2-3 **(a)** Seven alternations, three repetitions. **(b)** Expected frequency is 5; observed frequency is 7. **(c)** The 10 observations about the behavior of these 10 rats make up the entire population. All these observations are actually available, so the question of significance does not arise for this question. **(d)** The 100 possible observations about the behavior of all 100 rats in the colony on a first pair of runs in the T maze. The observations actually collected are only a sample, so the question of significance does arise. The difference between observed and expected frequency may be entirely due to sampling variability (one factor), or it may be due *also* to a tendency to alternate (i.e., to a real difference between this population and a nonsystematic population).

2-4 The probability that it is the name of a woman is ⅓. The probability that it is the name of a man is ⅔. The expected frequency of men's names in a random sample of 60 names is 40.

2-5 Statements (*b*) and (*e*) can be accepted on the existing evidence. Statement (*a*) is the crucial unknown element; most college classes are probably *not* random samples. Statement (*d*) could be accepted *if* one were sure that the class is a random sample. Statement (*c*) would be one's best *estimate* of the man-woman ratio in the college if the class were known to be a random sample.

Lesson 3

3-1 13/52, or 1/4.

3-2 1/4. The events are independent. The first drawing does not affect the probabilities of outcomes on the second provided the card is replaced.

3-3 12/51, since there are now only 12 spades in the deck and the deck now contains only 51 cards. The probability of a club is 13/51.

3-4 6. The probability that any one draw will yield a face card is 3/13; $3/13 \times 26$ gives 6.

3-5 $1/4 + 1/4 = 1/2$.

3-6 $1/13 \times 1/13 = 1/169$.

3-7 3/8. 1/4. *BBB, BBR, BRB, BRR, RBB, RBR, RRB, RRR.* Eight combinations, four kinds of outcome.

3-8 $(1/6)^3 = 1/216$.

3-9 $3 \times 1/216 = 1/72$. $1/6 \times 1/6 = 1/36$.

3-10 $6 \times 1/216 = 1/36$. $1/216$.

3-11 $0.1 \times 0.1 = 0.01$. $0.9 \times 0.9 = 0.81$. $2(0.1 \times 0.9) = 2(0.09) = 0.18$.

3-12 Because the two events are not independent. His call on the first toss may affect his choice of call on the second toss.

Lesson 4

4-1 $2^9 = 512$. 10. $1/512$. $9!/6!3! = 84$. $84/512$.

4-2 2,048 combinations; $1/2{,}048$. 165. $165/2{,}048$.

4-3 **(a)** $1/4$. **(b)** $3/8$. **(c)** $3/32$; $3/16$. **(d)** $56/256 = 7/32$. Not all 56 combinations can occur in the two-stage experiment; those 8 combinations which involve getting four alternations in one experiment and one alternation in the other would also give five alternations for the total of eight rats, but these combinations could not occur in the two-stage experiment described.

Lesson 5

5-1 **(a)** That this sample could have been drawn from a population of "zoology students over many years," in which men and women students are represented in the same proportions as in the college enrollment (i.e., $2:1$). **(b)** 30. **(c)** If the null hypothesis is true, any difference between observed and expected frequencies must be attributed to sampling variability. **(d)** That the population of "zoology students over many years" contains women in a *greater* proportion than does the college enrollment. **(e)** The probability of getting 50 or more women in a zoology class of 90 if the null hypothesis is true. **(f)** If the probability of obtaining this result under the null hypothesis is very slight, such as 0.05 or less.

5-2 **(a)** That the outcome will not differ significantly from the outcome of random guesses, in which the probability of a correct response is $1/2$. **(b)** That the outcome *will* differ significantly from the outcome of random guesses in one direction or the other, that there will be significantly more *correct* responses than would be expected in a series of random guesses, and that there will be significantly more *incorrect* responses than would be expected in a series of random guesses. **(c)** In order, the probabilities under each of the above alternate hypotheses would be $112/1{,}024$, $56/1{,}024$, and $1{,}013/1{,}024$. The *second* alternate hypothesis comes close to being acceptable at the .05 level. **(d)** If you had entertained the *second* of the three as your alternate hypothesis, you might worry about the Type I error, since it is almost significant at the .05 level.

5-3 **(a)** That the attitudes following the film do not differ significantly from attitudes before seeing the film. **(b)** The .02 level indicates the *greater* degree of significance. **(c)** Yes; no; risk of Type II error is increased at the .02 level.

Lesson 6

6-1 Nominal: **a, b**; ordinal: **d**; interval: **c, e.**

6-2 Discrete: **b, e**; continuous: **a, c, d.**

6-3 Lowest weight $= 80.5$; highest weight $= 90.49$; midpoint $= 85.5$. With the exact upper and lower limits as given above, one would classify this weight in the class 91–100, since it falls at the exact lower limit of this class.

6-4 Points to check: **(a)** Histogram. This figure should consist of vertical bars erected over each class interval having common boundaries between the bars. The boundaries should be erected over the exact lower limits of successive class intervals, and each bar should be at a height corresponding to the frequency of the class interval over which it is erected. Also, each bar should be exactly the same width; specifically, each should be 5 units wide, measured from the lower limit of one class interval to the lower limit of the next higher (or lower) class interval. **(b)** Frequency polygon. This figure should consist of points plotted over the midpoints of successive class intervals at a height corresponding to the frequency of the interval. Lines should be drawn between the points, and brought down to the X axis at each end of the figure.

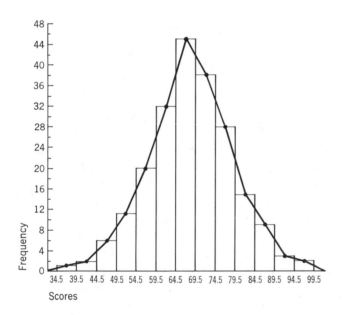

Lesson 7

7-1 $\chi^2 = 20^2/30 + 20^2/60 = 20$, d.f. $= 1$. Probability is less than 0.001 of getting such a large value of χ^2 if the null hypothesis is true.

7-2 For $N = 10$, $\chi^2 = 3.60$, d.f. $= 1$; probability is between 0.10 and 0.05. For $N = 100$, $\chi^2 = 36$, d.f. $= 1$; probability is less than 0.001. When the proportion of correct responses remains constant and N is increased, the value of χ^2 increases and the probability of the obtained result under the null hypothesis decreases.

7-3 The table of observed and expected frequencies is as follows:

Fathers' Incomes

	High	Middle	Low	Total
Class of 1953	450 500	750 800	400 300	1,600
Class of 1963	1,050 1,000	1,650 1,600	500 600	3,200
	1,500	2,400	900	4,800

$\chi^2 = 62.19$, d.f. $= 2$, probability is less than 0.001 under the null hypothesis.

Lesson 8

No, it cannot. When a variable is measured in terms of a nominal scale, the various categories forming the scale can be placed in any order without regard for concepts like "higher" and "lower." Also, a nominal scale lacks equality of scale units; any category may be broader or narrower than any other.

The mode, as a value in the distribution, can be computed only for interval values.

8-2 Two steps are necessary: **(a)** find the modal class interval, identifying its exact lower and upper limits, and **(b)** compute the midpoint of the modal class interval.

8-3 Nominal values: identification of modal class only.

Ordinal values: identification of modal class; computation of median.

Interval values: all four indicators can be used, although one would not ordinarily stop at identification of the modal class but would go on to state a value equal to the mode. Thus, computation of mean, median, and mode are permissible with interval values.

8-4 **(a)** The identification of the modal class only (nominal values). **(b)** All four, especially computation of mean, median, and mode (interval values). **(c)** Identification of the modal class (modal rank) and computation of median rank assigned by the 20 judges (ordinal values).

8-5 Mean $= 3,165/50 = 63.3$

Median $= 59.5 + (6/13)\,10 = 64.1$

Mode $= 64.5$

Among these three indicators of central tendency, the mean would be most strongly influenced by the occurrence of extreme scores and the mode least influenced.

Lesson 9

9-1   Range $= 10$.

AD $= 134/75 = 1.79$. This measure is computed as the sum of $f_i|x_i|$ divided by N, where $|x_i|$ is the absolute value of the deviation of the midpoint of a class from the mean and f_i is the frequency of that class.

$$s = \sqrt{\frac{\Sigma x_i^2}{N}} = 2.28$$

9-2   **(a)**   A single extreme score will greatly exaggerate the range. This measure is not sensitive to large "gaps" in the distribution.   **(b)**   The size of the range is likely to be greatly affected by the size of the sample, since as N increases, the probability of observing any extreme values in the population being sampled increases. Therefore, small samples are likely to produce smaller ranges than large samples drawn from the same population.

9-3 s^2, the variance, $= 5.20$. The variance can be defined as the square of the standard deviation, or you might call it the arithmetic mean of the squared deviations from the mean.

9-4   **(a)**   51.0.   **(b)**   71.2.   **(c)**   10.2.

In the ranges indicated, there are actually 53 scores in the area of the mean $\pm 1s$, 72 scores in the area of the mean $\pm 2s$, and 10 scores in the area between $+1s$ and $+2s$.

9-5   **(a)**   34 per cent, approximately.   **(b)**   84 per cent, approximately.   **(c)**   2 per cent, approximately.

Lesson 10

10-1

Cum. f_i	Cum. Proportions
75	1.000
74	0.987
70	0.933
64	0.853
55	0.733
45	0.600
29	0.387
19	0.253
11	0.147
6	0.080
2	0.027

10-2   **(a)**   60th percentile.   **(b)**   13.5.   **(c)**   In the construction of the graph, the only point likely to give difficulty is the location of the points with respect to the X axis. The points should be plotted as the exact upper limits of each class interval. If you have drawn your graph carefully, the score values corresponding to the 1st through 10th deciles should agree closely with the following computed values:

Decile	Value
1st	11.8
2nd	13.0
3rd	13.8
4th	14.6
5th	15.0
6th	15.5
7th	16.2
8th	17.1
9th	18.1
10th	20.5

To determine these points graphically, you should draw a horizontal line (parallel to the X axis) from the points on the Y axis corresponding to cumulative proportions of 0.100, 0.200, . . . , 1.000 to the right until the line intersects the curve of cumulative proportions. Then drop a vertical line from the point of intersection to the X axis. Read the value of the decile so determined from the X-axis scale.

10-3 The raw score 115 corresponds to a z score of -0.27. The raw score 134 corresponds to a z score of $+1.45$. The raw score of 99 corresponds to a z score of -1.73.

10-4 Mean $= 65$; $s = 8$; 98th percentile $= 81$.

10-5 In a normal distribution, 50th percentile $=$ a z score of 0. In a normal distribution, the 84th percentile corresponds to a z score of $+1.00$. In a normal distribution, a z score of $+2.0$ corresponds to the 98th percentile.

Lesson 11

11-1 Mean $= 450$; $s = 15$. Probability of 435 to 465 heads is 0.68. For 435 heads, $z = -1.0$, and for 465 heads, $z = +1.0$. The area from the mean to $z = +1.0$ is 0.3413, and twice this area is 0.6826. Probability of 465 to 480 heads is 0.136. The area between $z = +1$ and $z = +2$ is 0.1359 in Fig. 10-5. Probability of more than 495 heads is 0.0013; for 495 heads, $z = +3$.

11-2 Expected frequency of Republicans in 400 is 200; $s = 10$. The probability of a z as large as $+2$ or larger is 0.0228.

11-3 **(a)** $z = +1.5$.   **(b)** $z = -5$.   **(c)** $z = -1$.

Lesson 12

12-1 The null hypothesis can be rejected at the .05 level if *either* 480 or more heads occur or 420 or fewer heads occur, since the direction of the bias is not specified.

12-2 Hypotheses **(a)** and **(c)** require a two-tailed test; no direction of difference is specified.

12-3 $z = 1.67$ for the obtained result. Since no direction is specified, a two-tailed test is required, and the probability of such a large z in *either* direction is $2(0.0475) = 0.0950$. The null hypothesis cannot be rejected at the .05 level.

12-4 On the null hypothesis, there should be 32 positive and 32 negative signs in comparing the second grade with the first. There are actually 35 positive and 29 negative signs. Since $s = 4$, $z = 0.75$. A two-tailed test is required, and the probability of a deviation as great in either direction is 0.4532. The null hypothesis cannot be rejected.

12-5 The first hypothesis requires a one-tailed test; $p = 0.075$. The second hypothesis requires a two-tailed test; $p = 0.15$ by the normal curve test. Chi-square, which takes no account of the *direction* of differences between observed and expected frequencies, is always a two-tailed test; chi-square is 2.08 with 1 d.f., and the probability is between 0.20 and 0.10.

Lesson 13

13-1 Standard error of the mean $= \sigma/\sqrt{n} = 16/\sqrt{144} = 1.33$.

13-2 121; 0.110. For the .95 level, between 6.93 and 7.37. For the .99 level, between 6.87 and 7.43.

13-3 The .9544 (approximately .95) confidence level. The .9876 (approximately .99) confidence level.

13-4 For .90, the multiplier is 1.645. For the 98 per cent level, 2.327.

13-5 With the uncorrected $s_{\bar{x}}$, the confidence limits would lie at $6.9 \pm (0.17)(1.96)$, or 7.23 and 6.57. **(a)** With $N = 7$, the finite correction factor is the square root of 0.67, or 0.82. The confidence limits are $6.9 \pm (0.17)(1.96)(0.82)$, or 7.17 and 6.63. Thus, with n large relative to N, the correction factor makes the confidence limits lie closer together. **(b)** With $N = 31$, the finite correction factor is 0.96; confidence limits are 7.22 and 6.58. The increase in N relative to n has made the correction factor less important. **(c)** With $N = 120$, the correction factor is 0.99 and the confidence limits are very nearly as far apart as without the correction. To two decimal places, they are not different from what they would be were the correction factor not applied (7.23 and 6.57). These observations are not proper random samples because they were not selected randomly from the *entire* population of 7, 31, or 120 days, respectively.

Lesson 14

14-1 Taking σ as 1.35 and n as 100, the value of $\sigma_{\bar{X}}$ is $\sigma/\sqrt{n} = 0.135$. The difference $\bar{X} - \mu$ is $7.15 - 7.90 = 0.75$. Therefore, $(\bar{X} - \mu)/\sigma_{\bar{X}} = 5.6$, a result significant beyond the .001 level.

14-2 **(a)** With $n = 100$ and s assumed to be 1, an estimate of $\sigma_{\bar{X}}$ is given by $s/\sqrt{n} = 0.10$. If the true mean is 2.0, the .95 confidence limits will be 2 ± 0.2, or 1.8 to 2.2. Any mean which he obtains from his sample of 100 must lie within these limits if he is to conclude at the .95 level that the true mean is 2. **(b)** If $\bar{X} = 1.83$ and $s = 0.92$, $s_{\bar{X}} = 0.092$. The ratio $(\bar{X} - \mu)/s_{\bar{X}} = 0.17/0.092 = 1.85$. By a two-tailed test, the probability of z beyond $+1.85$ or beyond -1.85 is $2(0.03) = 0.06$. The difference is not large enough to reach the .05 level of significance. **(c)** With an n of 200, $s_{\bar{X}}$ would be 0.065. The value of z for a mean of 1.83 would be 2.61; the probability of such a large z at either extreme is $2(0.0045) = 0.009$. The result would easily reach significance beyond the .01 level.

Lesson 15

15-1 $t = 2.86$. With a two-tailed test, p is between 0.01 and 0.02. With a one-tailed test, p is between 0.005 and 0.01.

15-2 With $n = 10$, t must be at least 2.262; with $n = 20$, at least 2.093; with $n = 31$, at least 2.042.

15-3 With a one-tailed test, 2.718; two-tailed, 3.106.

15-4 At the .02 level, 2.567; at the .01 level, 2.898.

Lesson 16

16-1 (1) A normal curve test could be allowed in **(c)** and **(d)**; in the other cases, the samples are too small. A t test could be used for **(c)** and **(d)** equally well as a normal curve test. (2) Situations **(a)**, **(b)**, and **(e)** all involve testing the difference between means of two samples. (3) Only situation **(a)** involves correlated samples; **(b)** and **(e)** each involve a pair of uncorrelated samples.

16-2 These are uncorrelated samples; the population variance should be estimated by pooling the two samples, so the value of Σx_i^2 must be found for each of the two samples. For the B+ group, $\Sigma x_i^2 = 24.37$; for the B− group, 42.25. The estimated population variance s_P^2 equals 1.332, and the estimate of the standard deviation of the sampling distribution of the differences between means of paired samples $s_{X_1 - X_2}$ is 0.32. The value of t is -0.719; d.f. $= 50$. This value does not even approach significance at the .10 level.

16-3 $s_{\bar{D}} = 0.6$ for the standard deviation of a sampling distribution of means of difference scores. The t ratio is $1.57/0.6 = 2.6$; for 20 degrees of freedom, this value of t is significant beyond the .02 level by a two-tailed test. The change in attitude was significant, but it is not possible to conclude anything about the role that might have been played by getting a higher mark. The other 11 students who did *not* get higher marks may also have shown more favorable attitudes on the second testing, and it is even possible to imagine that getting a higher mark is the result, rather than the cause, of a favorable change in attitude.

Lesson 17

17-1   **(a)** $Y = 2.5X$.   **(b)** $Y = -0.75X + 3$.   **(c)** $Y = X + 1$.

17-2   **a** and **d**.

17-3   **(a)** $+1.4$.   **(b)** $+1.0$.   **(c)**   20.

17-4   Equation: $Y = 10$; slope $= 0$; Y intercept $= 10$.

Lesson 18

18-1   Line A should pass through the middle rank on both variables, which is the point with the coordinates $(5, 5)$, and the point $(9, 8)$. If your line passes through these two points, it is correct. The equation for this line is $Y' = 0.75X + 1.25$. Line B should pass through the points $(5, 5)$ and $(9, 3)$. The equation for this line is $Y' = -0.50X + 7.5$.

18-2   There are two sets of circumstances under which r equals the slope of the regression line of Y on X: **(a)**   If the two variables being correlated are in ordinal values (that is, ranked data), then $r = m$.   **(b)**   If the two variables being correlated are interval values, $r = m$ only if $s_X = s_Y$.

18-3   The slope of the regression line of Y on $X = 0.54$. The slope of the regression line of X on $Y = 0.67$.

18-4   **(a)**   The solid line passing through the points $(5, 5)$ and $(10, 7)$ is the correct regression line of Y on X for these ranked data.   **(b)**   Solid line: $Y' = 0.40X + 3$. Dashed line: $Y' = 0.80X + 1$.   **(c)** $r = +.40$ for the ranked data shown in the figure.

Lesson 19

19-1 A reliability coefficient.

19-2 You could determine reliability by grading the papers a second time and calculating a correlation coefficient between the two sets of grades. To determine validity, you would have to correlate the grades which you have assigned to the papers with a *criterion*, i.e., a set of marks representing what you could accept as the "true" value of these papers. The difficulty here is in finding a good criterion. Perhaps you could take the marks given to the papers by an expert, if one is available, or the averages of a panel of competent judges all of whom have read and marked the same set of papers.

19-3 You may proceed in several ways in making these predictions. You could graph the regression line, giving it a slope of r and making it pass through the middle rank on both X and Y. Then the predicted rank could be read from the graph, where the regression line crosses the X rank. Or you could set up a regression equation as follows: $Y' = +0.8X + k$, since these are *ordinal* (not interval) values. The line must pass through the point where $Y' = 13$ and $X = 13$, so k can be determined as $k = 13 - (0.8)13 = 2.6$. From the equation $Y' = 0.8X + 2.6$, you can find that **(a)** $Y' = 5$ when $X = 3$ and **(b)** $Y' = 17$ when $X = 18$. A third procedure is also possible: you can reason that a boy 10 ranks below the middle rank of 13 on X will be $(+.8)10$ ranks below the middle rank on Y and arrive at a rank of 5 on weight for the boy ranking third on height.

19-4 All three methods are again possible, but the regression equation will be least confusing. $Y' = -0.4X + k$. When $X = 11$, Y' must equal 11; therefore, $k = 15.4$. If $Y' = -0.4X + 15.4$, then $Y' = 7$ when $X = 21$.

Lesson 20

20-1 10; when the correlation is unknown, it is assumed to be 0, and the standard error is equal to s_Y. With $r = +.714$, the standard error is 7. The error has been reduced by 30 per cent.

20-2 About 17 per cent. The standard error is $0.83s_Y$.

20-3 To reduce the error by 40 per cent, the value of $\sqrt{1 - r^2}$ must be at least 0.6 and r must be at least $+.8$ or $-.8$. Since r is *squared* in computing the standard error of estimate, a negative correlation will do quite as well as a positive one.

20-4 The predicted cost is $17.50 a month. The standard error will be $3.30. Multiplied by 1.96 for the 95 per cent confidence limits, this standard error will give confidence limits of $11.03 and $23.97. Ninety-five out of every 100 students whose fathers' annual income is $10,000 are expected to spend not less than $11.03 and not more than $23.97 a month on entertainment according to these (fictitious) suppositions! (See the "Table of Areas under the Normal Curve" for the figure 1.96. In Lesson 9, the figure 2.00 was used as a close approximation to the 95 percent confidence limits.)

Lesson 21

21-1 **(a)** If $X = 110$, $Y' = +0.75$. With $r = +.49$, the standard error is 1.70. With $r = 0$, Y' would be $\overline{Y} = 1.14$ and the standard error would be $s_Y = 1.95$.

(b) $X' = 4.37Y - 112.02$.

21-2 434.5150.   4.622.

21-3 The sum of squares is found as follows:

Column Number	Y_i	M_c	$(Y_i - M_c)$	$(Y_i - M_c)^2$	f_i	$f_i(Y_i - M_c)^2$
1	1	1.5	−0.5	0.25	1	0.25
1	2	1.5	+0.5	0.25	1	0.25
2	1	2.0	−1.0	1.00	1	1.00
2	2	2.0	0	0	2	0
2	3	2.0	+1.0	1.00	1	1.00
3	2	3.2	−1.2	1.44	1	1.44
3	3	3.2	−0.2	0.04	3	0.12
3	4	3.2	+0.8	0.64	2	1.28
4	2	3.4	−1.4	1.96	1	1.96
4	3	3.4	−0.4	0.16	3	0.48
4	4	3.4	+0.6	0.36	2	0.72
4	5	3.4	+1.6	2.56	1	2.56
5	3	4.4	−1.4	1.96	2	3.92
5	4	4.4	−0.4	0.16	4	0.64
5	5	4.4	+0.6	0.36	5	1.80
5	6	4.4	+1.6	2.56	1	2.56
6	3	5.6	−2.6	6.76	1	6.76
6	4	5.6	−1.6	2.56	4	10.24
6	5	5.6	−0.6	0.36	3	1.08
6	6	5.6	+0.4	0.16	6	0.96
6	7	5.6	+1.4	1.96	4	7.84
6	8	5.6	+2.4	5.76	1	5.76
7	4	6.1	−2.1	4.41	2	8.82
7	5	6.1	−1.1	1.21	5	6.05
7	6	6.1	−0.1	0.01	4	0.04
7	7	6.1	+0.9	0.81	5	4.05
7	8	6.1	+1.9	3.61	1	3.61
7	9	6.1	+2.9	8.41	1	8.41
8	5	6.9	−1.9	3.61	1	3.61
8	6	6.9	−0.9	0.81	4	3.24
8	7	6.9	+0.1	0.01	3	0.03
8	8	6.9	+1.1	1.21	2	2.42
8	10	6.9	+3.1	9.61	1	9.61

Column Number	Y_i	M_c	$(Y_i - M_c)$	$(Y_i - M_c)^2$	f_i	$f_i(Y_i - M_c)^2$
9	6	7.9	−1.9	3.61	1	3.61
9	7	7.9	−0.9	0.81	2	1.62
9	8	7.9	+0.1	0.01	4	0.04
9	9	7.9	+1.1	1.21	1	1.21
9	10	7.9	+2.1	4.41	1	4.41
10	8	9.0	−1.0	1.00	1	1.00
10	9	9.0	0	0	2	0
10	10	9.0	+1.0	1.00	1	1.00
11	9	9.5	−0.5	0.25	1	0.25
11	10	9.5	+0.5	0.25	1	0.25
						$\Sigma = 115.90$

Lesson 22

22-1 $r^2 = 0.16$; 16 per cent by between-columns variance. By within-columns variance, 84 per cent. 16 per cent.

22-2 Total variance $= 10$. $r^2 = 3.6/10 = 0.36$. $r = \pm.6$.

22-3 0.1369, or about 14 per cent. About 86 per cent. Standard error is 0.93; it is reduced about 7 per cent by the correlation.

22-4 To determine $\Sigma(M_c - \overline{Y})^2$, the table is as follows:

M_c	$(M_c - \overline{Y})$	$(M_c - \overline{Y})^2$	f_c	$f_c(M_c - \overline{Y})^2$
1.5	−4.07	16.5649	2	33.1298
2.0	−3.57	12.7449	4	50.9796
3.2	−2.37	5.6169	6	33.7014
3.4	−2.17	4.7089	7	32.9623
4.4	−1.17	1.3689	12	16.4268
5.6	0.03	0.0009	19	0.0171
6.1	0.53	0.2809	18	5.0562
6.9	1.33	1.7689	11	19.4579
7.9	2.33	5.4289	9	48.8601
9.0	3.43	11.7649	4	47.0596
9.5	3.93	15.4449	2	30.8898
				$\Sigma = 318.5406$

The three sums of squares are: $\Sigma(Y_i - M_c)^2 = 115.90$

$$\Sigma(M_c - \overline{Y})^2 = \underline{318.5406}$$

$$\Sigma(Y_i - \overline{Y})^2 = 434.4406$$

The sum of the two components is within the rounding error of the value 434.5150 obtained by working back from the value of s_Y. Total variance, 4.622; between-columns variance, 3.357; within-columns variance, 1.233 (sum, 4.590). r^2 is 0.73, r is $+.86$. The proportion of variance accounted for is 73 per cent. The standard error of estimate is 2.15(0.52), or 1.12.

COMPLETED TRIANGULAR TABLE

N	$(2)^N$	$(1/2)^N$
1	2	$1/2$
2	4	$1/4$
3	8	$1/8$
4	16	$1/16$
5	32	$1/32$
6	64	$1/64$
7	128	$1/128$
8	256	$1/256$
9	512	$1/512$
10	1024	$1/1024$

```
                              1 - 1
                           1 - 2 - 1
                        1 - 3 - 3 - 1
                     1 - 4 - 6 - 4 - 1
                  1 - 5 - 10 - 10 - 5 - 1
               1 - 6 - 15 - 20 - 15 - 6 - 1
            1 - 7 - 21 - 35 - 35 - 21 - 7 - 1
         1 - 8 - 28 - 56 - 70 - 56 - 28 - 8 - 1
      1 - 9 - 36 - 84 - 126 - 126 - 84 - 36 - 9 - 1
   1 - 10 - 45 - 120 - 210 - 252 - 210 - 120 - 45 - 10 - 1
```

Index

SPECIAL ANSWER SHEET FOR LESSON 4

N	$(2)^N$	$(1/2)^N$
1	☐	☐
2	☐	☐
3	☐	☐
4	☐	☐
5	☐	☐
6	☐	☐
7	☐	☐
8	☐	☐
9	☐	☐
10	☐	☐